The Strategic Role of Software Customization

Matthias Bertram

The Strategic Role of Software Customization

Managing Customization-Enabled Software Product Development

Foreword by Prof. Dr. Harald von Korflesch

 Springer Gabler

Matthias Bertram
Koblenz, Germany

Dissertation Universität Koblenz-Landau, 2016

ISBN 978-3-658-14857-7   ISBN 978-3-658-14858-4 (eBook)
DOI 10.1007/978-3-658-14858-4

Library of Congress Control Number: 2016945106

Springer Gabler
© Springer Fachmedien Wiesbaden 2016

This Springer Gabler imprint is published by Springer Nature
The registered company is Springer Fachmedien Wiesbaden GmbH

This thesis is dedicated to my father

Reinhold Bertram

(1952-2014)

Foreword

Over the past decade, the software industry has developed three types of business logic: (1) the software product business, (2) the software service business and (3) the hybrid business. On the one hand firms following software product business logic develop highly standardized software products that are sold to a mass of customers in the market with limited or even without additional services. On the other hand firms that follow a software service logic develop software in the form of projects for one specific customer, which is implemented for that customer's IT landscape. However, the distinction between the software product and service businesses is not exclusive. Many companies that develop professional software products for the business-to-business market usually apply a hybrid business logic. They develop a core product that encapsulates common functionalities for their customers' businesses and also offer additional customization services to adapt their product to customers' needs. These software companies are challenged with specific issues from the software product and software project business logic.

Due to its economical and technological relevance, software product development and its adaption to customer needs has been the focus of researchers and managers in recent years. Researchers from the fields of computer science and information systems alike have contributed on various topics, such as the software development process, characteristics of software products, customer-specific software implementation, adaption or maintenance, customer integration in software development and implementation. Although existing research contributes to explaining software development and customer-specific adaption mechanisms, it largely neglects to explain the influence of customer-specific adaption on software product development and how software vendor firms align their software product management and customization activities.

To address this question, two qualitative investigations first draw on the conceptual foundation of the resource-based view of the firm, such as resources and capabilities as well as the dynamic capabilities theory. The first qualitative investigation focuses on vendor and customer firms to develop an in-depth understanding of the value of software customization as well as the vendor resources and capabilities necessary to successfully provide customization services. This investigation can be regarded as a pilot study that aims to develop an in-depth understanding of software customization as provided by vendor firms. The second qualitative investigation builds on the results from the first investigation and focuses on the dynamic capabilities necessary to generate a temporary competitive advantage from customization processes. This investigation can be regarded as an elaborative study that centers on software customization as an important innovation driver for software product management.

With this book Matthias Bertram contributes to the understanding of software product management by focusing on a part that has not received much attention yet: the strategic role of software product customization for software product development.

This book is Matthias Bertram's doctoral thesis at University of Koblenz-Landau and depicts a starting point of a fruitful career. While wishing the readers the same interesting insights I had when reading Matthias' dissertation, I can recommend it to academics and practitioners alike.

Prof. Dr. Harald von Korflesch
Koblenz, Germany

Preface

I would like to thank my mother Gisela, my brothers Christian and Markus, and my sister Stephanie, for their support and encouragement over the years.

Furthermore, I would like to thank:

- my advisor Prof. Dr. Harald von Korflesch, for giving me the freedom to be creative within my thesis and supporting me with fruitful feedback where necessary,

- my co-advisor Prof. Dr. Susan Williams, for her support and helping me to become a better qualitative researcher,

- my good friend Prof. Dr. Mario Schaarschmidt, for his critical, but always constructive feedback on my work. But mostly for his friendship over the last 15 years,

- my fellow PhD students and colleagues, for our talks and discussions.

Matthias Bertram
Dernau, Germany

Contents

List of Figures

List of Tables

Chapter 1

Introduction: The neglected role of customization for software product management

1.1 The business of software

In recent decades, software has transformed the way in which organizations and businesses coordinate and work, even going so far as to transform people's everyday lives. Software is used in notebooks and mobile devices; it is embedded actively and passively to steer cars, organize households, and label and control groceries. Enterprises rely on software systems to organize their workforce, bill their customers, and manage innovations. Software is ever-present and has become an important part of our society.

Basically, software refers to a computer program or data that can be stored electronically and used to perform various tasks. One way to categorize software is to separate *system software, application software* and *utility software* (Steinmueller 1995). *System software* is used to manage and control interactions between the hardware system and other types of software; *application software* is designed to allow the user of a system to complete specific tasks, and *utility software* refers to the software that is used to maintain the computer system but that does not directly interact with the hardware.

According to Gartner (2013), the worldwide software revenue stood at $407.3 billion in 2013, registering a 4.8% increase over 2012, which saw $388.5 billion in revenue. Within the software industry, only a few big players exist. However, these firms share approximately 50% of the market. The rest is distributed among small- and medium-sized companies. The biggest player is Microsoft, who continues to be the market leader in the segment and holds a 16% market share, followed by Oracle at 7.3% and IBM at 7.1%. SAP AG, as the largest European software vendor, is in position four, with approximately 5% market share. Within the IT industry in 2014, the software industry was expected to be the fastest growing segment, with expected growth of 7.1%, followed by IT consulting and systems integration services at 6.6%.

Companies within the software industry follow one of three business logics: the *software product business,* the *software service business* or the *hybrid software business* (cf. Cusumano 2004; Hoch et al. 1999; Tyrväinen et al. 2008). The *software product business* has the typical characteristics of traditional firms operating in consumer goods industries. Software is highly standardized and productized and sold to consumers in the market without additional services. An example of a pure software product business in the software industry is the software component business, in which software components are standardized and sold as off-the-shelf software. From a managerial perspective, the software product business logic addresses issues including productizing, channel management, alliance building and branding. In the *software service business*, companies provide professional software services for which customer organizations are usually charged hourly rates. Software is developed specifically for each customer. This usually takes the form of a project that includes development, integration with other software systems, user training, and maintenance services. The key managerial area in this scenario is managing projects for a few close customer firms and recognizing the importance of key individuals.

However, between those poles, some companies also employ a *hybrid software business* model that includes both product and service business strategies. They sell a product to a relatively anonymous market and provide installation, adaption and maintenance services. The distinction between the software product and software service businesses is not exclusive. Figure 1.1 illustrates the three different types of business logic and their relationship.

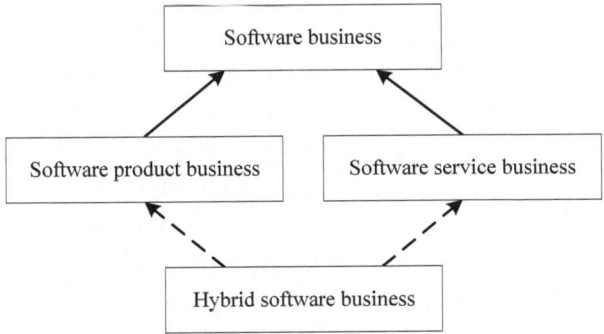

Figure 1.1: Types of software business logic

1.1.1   Tailor-made and software product development

According to Sawyer (2001), the concept of "make one, sell many" is common to all product software. He states that product software and tailor-made software can be distinguished by three major differences: *First*, whereas tailor-made software is oriented towards one customer, product software is market-oriented. *Second*, there are many more conditions for using a software product in terms of the hardware and software platform than there are for tailor-made software, which usually runs under one platform. *Third*, with software products, the vendor usually retains ownership of the software, while with tailor-made software, all of the corresponding artifacts (e.g., source code, documentation) are entirely sold to the customer. Taking a software engineering perspective, the academic literature and practice discuss the development process of tailor-made software and product software in four different areas. Table 1.1 summarizes those differences.

First, developing tailor-made software and developing product software are different from a *development life-cycle perspective*. While tailor-made software is complete and enters a maintenance state after a certain point in time, product software is continuously under development. Subsequent releases or bug fixes follow the initial implementation. Due to this, both types of software development can be based on different *life-cycle approaches*. For instance, Xu and Brinkkemper (2007) describe two major categories of software development life cycles: *sequential* and *incremental methods*. In a *sequential approach*, each phase of the development life cycle is performed and completed before the next phase starts. Sequential approaches are most suitable for software development projects with stable and clearly defined requirements. The typical development phases found in the literature are the Requirements, Design, Code, Test and Deployment phases. The core assumption behind a sequential life cycle model is that a problem can be completely described before a solution is designed. A specification that includes all aspects of a solution can be described before implementation, and all implementation can be completed before testing and deployment. Using an *incremental approach* means that the software is designed, implemented, and tested incrementally. This approach includes elements of both development and maintenance. The assumption behind the incremental development approach is that requirements will become clearer and will probably change during the implementation process. Therefore, the life cycle process consists of small iterations for each component of the software system, including collecting requirements, designing, coding, testing, and deploying. Xu and Brinkkemper (2007) argue that an incremental development approach is more suitable for the development of product software.

Second, major differences between tailor-made software and product software are the *origins of requirements and the management of releases*. For tailor-made software, there is a clear source of requirements - the customer - but this is not the case for product software development. Requirements management is a key success factor for product software and includes capturing market trends, analyzing requirements, and releasing the software at the right time. Mapping new market trends to product software design is one of the central elements of new product development (Garvin 1998; Hauser and Clausing 1988). However, capturing customer feedback is also important for enhancing the satisfaction of existing customers. Another aspect of product software requirement management is that product development firms look for new features that can help them enter new markets and change their product-market combination (Rao and Klein 1994).

Third, there is no standard for evaluating the influence of *product software's architecture on the development processes*. However, there are some architectural issues that are more important for product software than for tailor-made software. First, the different components of the product software architecture should only be weakly coupled and should be as independent as possible. The product's architecture must be able to adapt easily to new requirements from the always-changing environment and to new markets and customers. If it is sold to different market segments, such as different user groups (standalone, multi-user or enterprise) or different operating systems (Windows, Linux, or Mac), the product architecture must be able to support different versions, platforms or devices. Finally, if product software is part of a series of products, the architecture should form some type of structural commonality so that high-level design decisions do not need to be re-invented, re-validated, and re-described for each product. Architecture is important for tailor-made software as well; a future-proof architecture is crucial when developing product software. To support long-term uses, the architecture must be composed of clear distinguishable components.

Finally, in tailor-made software development, the software system is installed at a limited number of customer sites. The specificities and costs of implementation and delivery are accounted for within the initial contract. For product software, the developing firm must consider a higher number of unknown customers with an even larger number of unknown platform and operating system configurations. Manual installation is often used with

Table 1.1: Tailor-made vs. product software (see Xu and Brinkkemper 2007)

Development aspect	Tailor-made software		Software product	
	Contractual tailor-made software	In-house tailor-made software	Business-to-business software product	Business-to-consumer software product
Development life cycle & methods	Could follow "requirement-design-code-test-deploy" life cycle; Sequential or iterative methods and sequential model could provide benefits.	Could follow "requirement-design-code-test-deploy" life cycle; Sequential or iterative methods and sequential model could provide benefits.	Various development life cycles; Iterative methods.	Various development life cycles; Iterative methods.
Requirements & release management	One known consumer; Release date is fixed, with possible penalties for late delivery.	Limited number of end-users; Release decision can have certain flexibility.	Market determines requirements; Release decisions are critical to customer's business.	Market determines requirements; Release decisions are important for vendor and should also consider buying seasons.
Architecture	Is not as critical; Is selected by the developers.	Is not as critical; Is selected by internal IT department of the organization, which could have possible conflicting interests.	Is critical for the vendor; Requires a future-proof architecture.	Is critical for the vendor; Requires a future proof architecture.
Delivery and implementation	Penalties for late delivery; Possible to deliver and implement final system on site.	Possible to deliver and implement final system on site.	Delivery is critical for the vendor; Implementation is critical for the customer's business.	Delivery is critical for the vendor.

tailor-made software but is not possible in this scenario. Therefore, *delivery and implementation* for an unknown market is an important consideration for product software. This section emphasizes two different types of engineering approaches for software development. Additionally, work in software product management practice and theory has led to a framework that encapsulates the body of knowledge for managing software product development.

1.1.2 The role of software customization in the software business

Various scholars argue that the software business has transformed itself from a product business into a service or hybrid business and that today, most of the companies that develop professional software products for the business-to-business market apply a hybrid business logic (e.g., Cusumano 2008). Usually, these firms develop a core product that encapsulates common functionalities for their customers' business and also offer additional customization services to adapt their product to the customers' needs. These software companies are challenged with specific issues from the software product and software service business logic: they must provide standard software products that include standard maintenance and support services, and additionally, they must provide customization mechanisms that allow these software products to be adapted according to specific customer needs.

In recent years, providing this mechanism to customize software products to individual customer's needs has become a core business for the software industry (Cusumano 2004). Although it was initially a pure product-oriented business with license fees as the primary revenue source, the software business has evolved into a full service business obtaining additional revenues from maintenance, consulting, and customization. For instance, in 2007, IBM generated more than 50% of its total revenue through its consulting services, including product implementation and support (Spohrer and Maglio 2008).

Generally, the customization of software to customers' requirements is provided by either the software vendor or by third party IT consultancies. During customization projects, customer requirements are identified and transformed into an IT solution based on an existing software product. From a knowledge perspective, this is an interactive process during which customer and customizing company integrate their knowledge to arrive at a solution that fulfills the customer's demands (Ko et al. 2005). At the beginning of a customization project, the customer primarily possesses knowledge pertaining to what is needed, knowledge that might evolve to include the vendor's business knowledge, whereas the vendor primarily possesses technical knowledge, that is, knowledge pertaining to how to technically address upcoming demands. During the customization process, both types of knowledge must be integrated and embodied in the final IT solution. Because business knowledge is a form of market knowledge, which positively affects a firm's innovative performance (De Luca and Atuahene-Gima 2007), customer knowledge obtained through the delivery of customization services might lead to software product innovation.

Not surprisingly, customization appears to be a central topic in IS research. Predominantly, researchers focus on how software is delivered to customers in relation to distribution economics (cf. Brocke et al. 2010; van Fenema et al. 2007; Weinmann et al. 2011). Packaged software, as one incarnation of product software, represents one way to address the challenges of customization in many articles. For example, van Fenema et al. (2007) described packaged software as a "ready-made mass product offering users a solution based design process aimed at generic customer groups in a variety of industries and geographical areas." A more general focus is offered by Chiasson and Green's (2007) definition of packaged software. They argue that an important question in packaged software design and consumption is determining what the software can and will do to support, change, and inhibit desired organizational practices. To date, a considerable stream of research addresses the distribution (i.e., packaging) of product software and regards customization in an "after-production" sense.

Another stream of research in the IS literature addresses the development side of software in general as well as customer integration during the development processes in particular. For example, Piller et al. (2004) state that "within mass customization, customers are integrated into value creation by defining, configuring, designing, matching, or modifying their individual solution out of a list of options and pre-defined components". In a similar vein, Xin and Levina (2008) argue that clients not only customize the software to their needs but also change organizational practices to fit the software product. Additionally, research has focused on tailoring software development methods. For instance, Fitzgerald et al. (2006) argue that factors such as organizational issues, distributed teams, and the existence of legacy systems require different or changed development methods. In a similar vein, Slaughter et al. (2006) describe the strategy and process fit as being important for the development process. From their point of view, process customization or tailoring is important to meet the needs of specific organizations or projects. This involves adapting, particularizing, or selecting certain software processes. In summary, a considerable stream of research addresses customization as a form of co-creating value.

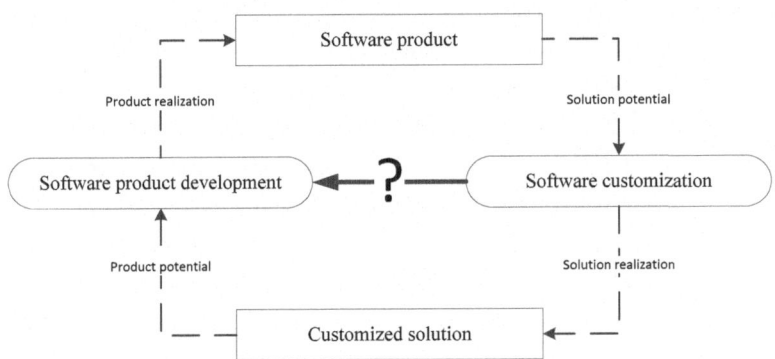

Figure 1.2: The role of software customization for software product development

The section above illustrates the reciprocal nature of customization in the field of IS. However, despite the existing body of knowledge on software customization, the question of how those customization-driven innovation impulses are addressed in vendors' software product development processes remains open in the IS literature. Figure 1.2 illustrates this identified lack of literature. The following sections review the IS literature with a strong engineering focus to double check if the identified gap also exists in this stream of research. In particular, this section describes perspectives on software development approaches and presents existing concepts of software product management.

1.1.3   Managing software product development

Over the last decade, the academic literature has provided several conceptual and empirical contributions to the topic of software product management. In particular, efforts have been made to develop a deeper understanding of software product management tasks and to delineate it from traditional software engineering. Central contributions have been made by van de Weerd et al. (2006), who present a reference framework for software product management that integrates not only its key process areas, namely portfolio management, product roadmapping, release planning and requirements management, but also the stakeholders and their relations. Additionally, in an empirical study, Ebert (2007) highlights the role of software product management. They found that with an empowered product management role, the success rate of projects improves in terms of schedule predictability, quality and project duration. Kittlaus and Clough (2009) elaborate on the importance of software product management and pricing as key success factors for any organization providing software to generate long-term success. However, software product management is not only a topic of scholarly interest. The *Software Product Management Body of Knowledge (SPMBoK)* of the *International Software Product Management Association (ISPMA)* describes a consensus of academic and industrial experts (International Software Product Management

Association 2014). The following section provides a short introduction to the academic and practical perspectives on software product management and future challenges.

1.1.3.1 Terms and definitions

Generally speaking, a product is *anything that can be offered to a market for attention, acquisition, use, or consumption that might satisfy a want or need* (Kotler and Armstrong 2011). Therefore, any physical objects, services, people, places, organizations, ideas, or mixtures of these can be regarded as products. The idea behind this definition is that people or organizations – or more generally, *the market* – provide some form of compensation to satisfy a specific (and comparable) need. In a similar vein, software products *are developed not for one specific customer but for an entire market* (Vlaanderen et al. 2010). A software product is a *product whose primary component is software* (Kittlaus and Clough 2009). However, there is one characteristic that distinguishes a software product from traditional goods: *software is an information good that manifests human know-how in bits and bytes* (Fricker 2012). It can become whatever function or application it addresses, and the distribution of extra copies does not require extra costs for the company (Cusumano 2004).

There exist several definitions of software products. Kittlaus and Clough (2009) uses the following product definition to define software products:

> *A product is a combination of (material and/or intangible) goods and services, which one party (called a vendor) combines in support of their commercial interests to transfer defined rights to a second party (called a consumer).*

They define a software product as "a product whose primary component is software" and further distinguish between *embedded software*

Embedded software is a piece of software that is not sold as a stand-alone software product, but is integrated in a non-software product.

and *OEM software*

OEM software product is a software product of software vendor A that is used by company B as a component under the covers of one of B's products (Kittlaus and Clough 2009).

Ebert (2009) provides a broader definition of a software product and includes additional material and services. According to his definition, a software product

is a deliverable that has a value and provides an experience to its users. It can be a combination of systems, solutions, materials, and services delivered.

Xu and Brinkkemper (2007) discuss different types of software products, including open source software and software-based services.

1. *Standard software* is software that is routinely installed by the vendor and/or IT staff on most computers within certain organizations. Standard software includes business applications such as Microsoft Office or LibreOffice and operating systems such as Microsoft Windows, MacOSX or Linux.

2. *Commercial software* is purchased through the retail market and must be licensed by a customer before usage. Without explicit permission from the software's author, the user is not allowed to make copies of commercial software.

3. *Packaged software* is commercial software that can be readily obtained from software vendors and that usually requires little modification or customization. The term is typically used in B2B scenarios and in the context of large enterprise software systems, such as enterprise resource planning (ERP) or customer relationship management (CRM) systems. Setting up *large packaged software* for specific customer needs might take weeks or months of deployment and customization work and might also include organizational changes in the customer's business environment (Light 2001; Light and Papazafeiropoulou 2004; Light 2005).

4. *COTS software (commercial off-the-shelf software)* refers to software that is developed for an entire market instead of individual customers. Usually, COTS software is used as is. However, it also might offer moderate personalization within the bounds of the application's ability. For instance, by allowing the appearance of COTS software to be modified, it can be altered without changing its original functionality.

5. *Shrink-wrapped software* is used for software sold on media that are boxed, shrink-wrapped and sold in retail stores. In the internet age, the term 'shrink-wrapped software' is also used for software that can be bought online and downloaded from the web. Shrink-wrapped software implies a widely supported standard platform.

6. The idea behind *open source software* is that if the source code is available to a community, the software can be enhanced, bug fixed and tested more quickly than proprietary software. Therefore, most open source software uses a type of license agreement that covers rights to modify, redistribute, and/or use for commercial purposes. However, *open source software* is not necessarily free. Open source software companies can earn profits by redistributing or offering additional services for their products such as implementation support, maintenance and training.

7. *Software as a service (SaaS)* describes an additional delivery and license model in which software is centrally hosted and licensed on a subscription basis. SaaS essentially extends the idea of the application service provider (ASP) model introduced during the early 1990s. While ASP was focused on hosting and managing third-party client-server software running on a customer's infrastructure or mandated separate instances, SaaS vendors typically develop and deploy their own software using internet-based multi-tenant software architectures.

Given these different terms for product software, it is important to standardize views and establish a single common definition. For this thesis, I rely on Xu and Brinkkemper's (2007) definition of a software product as follows:

a packaged configuration of software components or a software-based service, with auxiliary materials, which is released for and traded in a specific market.

1.1.3.2   The role of the product manager

The software product manager is the "mini CEO" responsible for the development of new software products and the management of innovations and further development of existing software products (cf. Gorchels 2006; Ebert 2007). He defines and implements strategies for these products and aligns them with market needs and corporate strategy and vision. In particular, the software product manager has the following responsibilities (cf. Kittlaus and Clough 2009; Fricker 2012):

- Assumes leadership for new product ideas and participates in their innovation.

- Is responsible for developing a product strategy that aims at sustainable economic success in line with the overall corporate strategy.

- Plans product scope and monitors its evolution in conjunction with development, which also includes planning the marketing mix and monitoring the product success.

- Represents the product inside and outside of the company and coordinates product operations with other business units.

To fulfill these responsibilities, the software product manager needs a specific set of personal skills. First, he/she should have a Master's in Informatics or Business Administration and should have developed a broad knowledge of relevant technologies and markets. Second, he should have the proven ability to communicate and negotiate with different types of stakeholders inside and outside of the company. Finally, he should have good self-management skills that allow him to work on many different tasks with changing priorities.

Ebert (2007) distinguishes three important roles in the area of software product management: (1) the *software project manager*, who is responsible for the successful delivery of one defined project; (2) the *software product manager*, who is responsible for many software projects and the resulting products over a much longer period of time; and (3) the *marketing manager*, who is educated in creating needs and a market for software products. As shown in Figure 1.3, the *software product manager* is involved in all life-cycle phases from strategy to concept definition, market entry, development and evolution. In contrast, *marketing* and *project managers* have limited and precisely defined project scopes, for instance, in research, development and service projects.

The *software product manager* is responsible for leading and managing several software products from inception to phase-out with the goal of maximizing business value. The software product manager has business responsibility beyond a single software project and works with numerous internal and external stakeholders to make a product a business success. In addition, the software product manager is responsible for the success of the entire product portfolio and determines what to make and how to make it. In this role, he approves roadmaps and content and determines what and how to innovate in new product development as well as managing the maintenance of existing products. Summing up, the software product manager is responsible for the entire value chain of a product along the life cycle and asks *What do we keep, what do we evolve, and what do we eliminate?*

The *marketing manager's* task is to determine how to sell a product or service, and he or she is therefore accountable for market and customer success. The marketing manager has a profound understanding of specific customer needs, potential market trends, sales perspectives and competitors. His task is to communicate the software product's value proposition to customers and sales. He executes the sales plan and asks *What markets will we address?*.

In contrast to the software product manager, the *project manager* has limited and more clearly defined responsibilities for business and customer success within a contract project. This includes the management and execution of the project plan. To do so, he determines how to best execute a project or contract (Royce 2010) and ensures that the project is executed as defined. He asks *How do we get all this done?*.

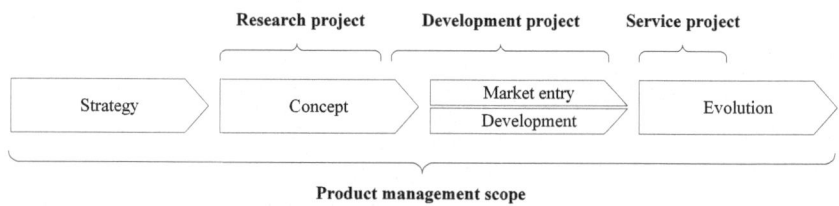

Figure 1.3: Software product management spans the entire product life cycle (see Ebert 2009)

1.1.3.3 Software product management artifacts, stakeholders and core competences

Figure 1.4 summarizes the core competences in software product management and the related internal and external stakeholders. Four main business functions are defined in the model: *portfolio management, product planning, release planning*, and *requirements management*. Each of these functions consists of a group of capabilities that are necessary to provide the business function. The arrows between the business functions and the internal and external stakeholders indicate the interaction between them. Respectively, business functions have interactions that are indicated by the arrows between them. Although the arrows between adjacent business functions indicate the main flow of the SPM process, there is also room for interaction between focus areas that are not directly connected. Figure 1.4 summarizes the aspects that will be described in more detail in the following section.

Professional product management is essentially a matter of the well-organized processing of issues related to products, requirements, and releases (cf. van de Weerd et al. 2006). The *product portfolio* represents the complete set of the company's products. While small, young or specialized software companies may only have a portfolio consisting of one product, larger or more mature and generalized companies may have several products in their *portfolio* generated by acquisition or product derivation. *Product line management* is a popular technique used in the telecommunications industry to efficiently organize products with a common set of features (see De Man and Ebert 2003). However, during the last decade, this technique has received increasing attention from the software industry as well. It has become an important competence for managing a set of software-intense systems sharing a common, managed set of features that satisfy the specific needs of a particular market segment or mission and that are developed from a common set of core assets in a prescribed way (Clements and Northrop 2001). Market analysis gathers the information needed by the organization to make decisions about its product portfolio (van de Weerd et al. 2006). Market analysis includes market trend identification, market strategy, customer win/loss analysis, competitor analysis, custom market analysis, and custom market trend identification (Bekkers et al. 2010). *Product lifecycle management* gathers information and is responsible for making decisions about the products in a portfolio according to their specific stage in the product life-

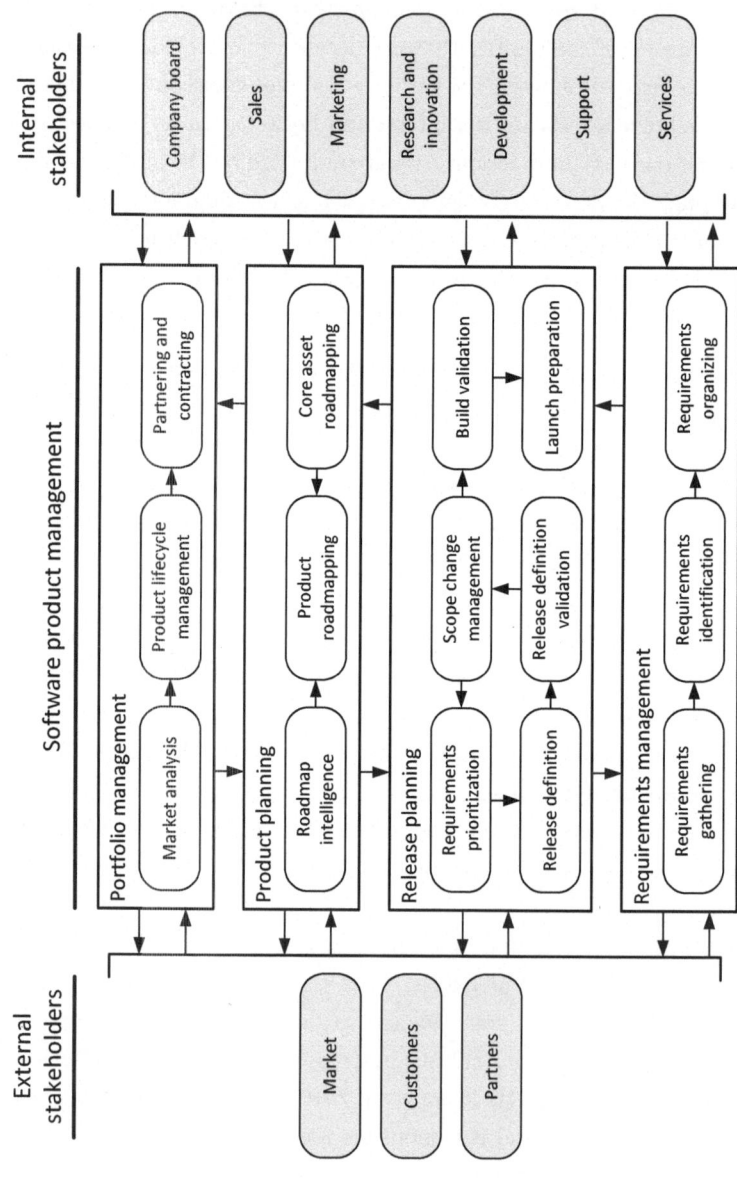

Figure 1.4: Core competences of SPM (see van de Weerd et al. 2006; Bekkers et al. 2010)

cycle. *Partnering and contracting* focuses on establishing partnerships and determining pricing and distribution.

Within the portfolio, each *product* has a release sequence of past, current and future releases. Thus, *product planning* is focused on gathering information and creating a roadmap for a product or product line and its core assets (Bekkers et al. 2010). Core assets, in this context, are components that are shared by multiple products. The roadmap consists of three competences: *roadmap intelligence*, which is the collection of information important for the creation of a roadmap; (2) *product roadmapping*, which addresses the actual creation of a roadmap; and (3) *core asset roadmapping*, which is concerned with planning the design and implementation of core assets.

Releases are numbered according to major, minor or bug fix releases (Kittlaus and Clough 2009). However, for marketing reasons, release numbers do not have to be sequential and may consist of the release year. Thus, many internal versions of a software product exist in a development company. Furthermore, several versions are delivered to customers, which leads to multiple external versions of a software product.

During *release planning*, the software product manager must address issues ranging from communication to documentation, training, and preparing for the implementation of the release itself. Release planning consists of several competences necessary to successfully create and launch a product release: (1) Requirements prioritization, where requirements are organized and prioritized; (2) release definition, where requirements for the next release are selected based on the prioritization; (3) release definition validation, where internal parties validate the release definition before its implementation during development, (4) scope change management, which handles changes in the scope of a release during its development; (5) build validation, which is performed after the development of a release to ensure validity; and finally (6) launch preparation, where internal and external stakeholders are prepared for the launch of the software release.

On the lowest level of the hierarchy, each release consists of a set of *requirements*, implementing additional technical or functional features. However, software also consists of non-functional requirements such as performance, security or access needs. *Requirements engineering* in software product management involves continuously gathering, identifying, and organizing potential requirements outside of release cycles. Requirement gathering refers to the acquisition of requirements from internal and external stakeholders. Requirements identification further describes the gathered requirements. Market requirements are rewritten as clear product requirements, and requirements with similar functionality are connected. Finally, requirements are organized and structured based on their shared aspects and depending on their stage in the life cycle. Furthermore, requirements organization describes the relationships between product requirements.

Software product managers are confronted with a large number of requirements originating from many different stakeholders. Those stakeholders may be located inside or outside of the company. Examples of internal stakeholders are the company board, research and innovation departments, service, development, support, or sales and distribution:

- The *company board* is responsible for defining the company's vision and mission and for communicating the product development strategy. It is also responsible for the management and supervision of different departments inside the company.

- *Research and innovation* is responsible for innovating existing products and developing concepts for new products.

- *Service* is responsible for implementation on the customer side. They also must be aware of new features developed for recent releases as well as new requirements originating with customers.

- *Development* is responsible for the execution of the release plan and the design of technical and functional requirements. A major challenge is that new requirements might arise during development if requirements are more complex than anticipated.

- Literature and practice distinguishes three types of *support*: first, second and third level support. First level support is responsible for answering customer questions. Second level support repairs small defects identified during first level support. Third level support repairs large defects. Third level support is usually handled by software developers.

- *Sales and marketing* represent the first contact for potential customers. New requirements are usually initially gathered here. They also must communicate new or upcoming features to customers or partners.

External stakeholders include the market, partners or customers. In contrast to their internal equivalents, who must act in accordance with corporate strategy, external stakeholders are harder to influence.

- The *market* is represented by actual and potential customers, competitors and analysts. It is the source of numerous market trends, which could either be explicitly communicated by market players or implicitly through product management.

- Software companies may have networks including numerous *partners*. Those partners might be implementation partners, development partners or distribution partners. However, partnerships might also include strategic alliances that combine products from different firms to empower both partner companies in a specific market.

- *Customers* are often the source of new feature requests. They might communicate those requests through sales, support, service or distribution to the product manager. The product manager might also be a channel for customer requests.

1.1.3.4   Software product management within the company

Software product management is not only a topic of scholarly interest. The *Software Product Management Body of Knowledge (SPMBoK)* of the *International Software Product Management Association (ISPMA)* describes the consensus of academic and industrial experts (International Software Product Management Association 2014). The SPMBoK builds on the previously mentioned frameworks but continuously evolves through discussion and adjustment by the ISPMA knowledge network. Figure 1.5 summarizes the functional areas described in the SPMBoK.

The focus of *strategic management* is understanding how a company achieves and sustains a competitive advantage (Barney 1991; Teece et al. 1997). In the SPMBoK, strategic management represents the interface between a company's higher-level management and software product management. The higher-level managers define the company's strategy by setting goals and constraints. This strategy represents the foundation for the portfolio of company offerings. The software product manager only participates in strategic management and does not assume leadership or responsibility. According to the SPMBoK, strategic management consists of six practices including (1) corporate strategy, (2) portfolio management, (3) innovation management, (4) resource management, (5) market analysis, and (6) product analysis (Fricker 2012).

Product strategy and *product planning* are the pillars of software product management. They describe what the software product will be and how it will be developed and used. The software product manager describes the goals of a software product and constrains its evolution. He is a business enabler and obtains support and commitment from the internal and external stakeholders. Furthermore, in these core activities, the software product manager takes leadership and is therefore responsible for decisions.

To realize the software product roadmap, the product manager relies on several company functions. *Development* implements the software, *marketing* identifies and wins customers, *sales and distribution* generate revenue,

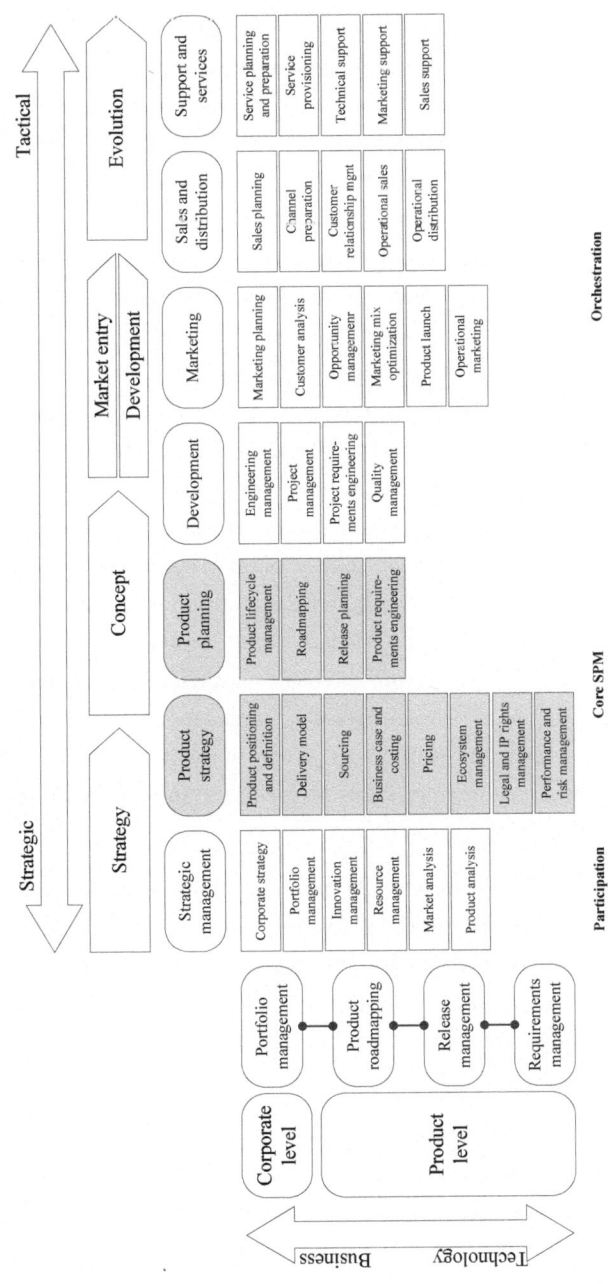

Figure 1.5: The software product management body of knowledge (SPMBoK) (see International Software Product Management Association 2014)

and *service and support* facilitate product use. In particular, with respect to development, software product management integrates *engineering management, project management, project requirements management,* and *quality management* to orchestrate development activities by jointly planning and steering the software specification and implementation and by evaluating and accepting the achieved results. Additionally, the interface between software product management and the company 'marketing' function consists of six practices: marketing planning, customer analysis, opportunity management, marketing mix optimization, product launch, and operational marketing. Software product management uses these activities to orchestrate marketing by jointly analyzing the market, customers and opportunities, launching products and winning new customers. With regards to 'sales and distribution', software product management uses the activities *sales planning, customer relationship management* and *operational product distribution* to orchestrate sales and distribution by jointly planning sales, preparing sales channels and supporting sales and product distribution operations. Finally, the interface with 'service and support' is realized by five practices: *service planning and preparation, service provisioning, technical support, marketing support* and *sales support.* Software product management uses these activities to orchestrate service and support by jointly supporting customer users, marketing, sales, and customer projects to facilitate the product's use and its business operations.

In total, the SPMBoK structures 38 practices along seven functional areas. According to this structure, the software product manager participates in strategic management and is directly responsible for product strategy, planning, development, marketing, sales and distribution and service and support. For a detailed description of each functional area, please see Appendix A of this thesis.

To date, scholars from the information systems discipline have contributed to the topic of software product management and customer integration as a source for innovation. For example, literature on the deployment of product software (e.g., enterprise resource planning software) emphasizes the need for a structured requirements engineering process in implementation projects (e.g., Daneva 2004; Light 2005). Additionally, the requirements engineering literature emphasizes the challenges in transforming customer needs into technical specifications (e.g., Alves et al. 2010; Castro et al. 2002; Saiedian and Dale 2000). With respect to the development side of software customization, the role of customer knowledge in the successful co-creation of value has been emphasized by multiple streams of research, such as information systems (e.g., Ko et al. 2005) and innovation management (e.g., Perks et al. 2012).

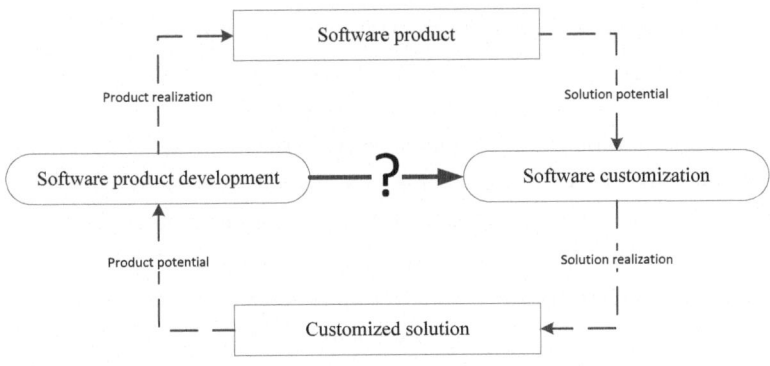

Figure 1.6: The role of software product development for software customization

The section above introduced the topic of software product management for this thesis and described the role of the software product manager as well as the existing conceptual framework for the management of software product development. This section shows that although the customer, along with other internal and external stakeholders, has been identified as a valuable resource for software product management, the topic of software customization as the source of the most intense interaction between these stakeholders has largely been neglected. Figure 1.6 illustrates this identified gap in the literature. Thus, in a similar vein as the software product customization literature, the literature on software products does not answer how customization-driven innovation impulses are addressed in the vendor's software product development process and how vendor firms address these impulses. Based on these identified gaps, the following section introduce the research questions and the related research objectives of this thesis.

1.2 Research relevance, research aim, and research questions

Due to its economical and technological relevance, product software development and its adaption to customer needs has been the focus of researchers and managers in recent years. Researchers from the fields of computer science and information systems alike have contributed on various topics, such as the software development process, characteristics of software products, customer-specific software implementation, adaption or maintenance, customer integration in software development and implementation. However, the strategic role of software customization in software product development has been neglected. Only recently has research started to establish the field of software productization to address the standardization potential of software and related services (cf. Artz et al. 2010).

This thesis aims to close this gap by developing a deeper understanding of software customization and its strategic role for software product development; further, it identifies the prerequisites that software vendor firms must fulfill to integrate both functions. Although the articles noted above contribute to explaining software development and customer-specific adaption mechanisms, they largely neglect to explain the influence of customer-specific adaption on software product development and how product development companies can benefit from customization activities.

Thus, the main objective of this dissertation is to expand and deepen research in the software product management domain and, more specifically, to explore the influence of customization activities on the development of product software to provide recommendations that help vendor companies to manage knowledge transfer between functions and to benefit from this transfer. Therefore, the primary research question of this dissertation is as follows:

MRQ: *How do software vendor firms align their software product management and customization activities?*

To address this question, the studies in this thesis draw on the conceptual foundation of the resource-based view of the firm (RBV), such as resources and capabilities as well as the dynamic capabilities (DC) theory. The RBV is a dominant perspective in strategic management. At its core, the RBV states that the resources or bundles of resources possessed by a company are the basis for superior firm performance (cv. Barney 1986, 1991; Conner 1991; Peteraf 1993; Wernerfelt 1984). According to the RBV literature, a firm's resources are the stock of available factors owned or controlled by the firm. They are converted into products and services by using a wide range of firm assets and bonding mechanisms; capabilities are defined as the firm's capacity to deploy resources (Amit and Schoemaker 1993). Dynamic capabilities (Teece et al. 1997) have attracted increasing attention within the management literature as an extension to the more static RBV. This construct was developed to address the question of how firms can successfully be managed in high-velocity environments. Because the achievement of long-term competitive advantage is harder in such a context, dynamic capabilities aim at building successive advantages by effectively responding to environmental shocks (D'Aveni 1994; Eisenhardt and Martin 2000).

Building upon this conceptual background, several research objectives need to be achieved to answer the main question. Although existing IS research has studied the knowledge characteristics of software products and services (Winkler et al. 2009) as well as software development and software business resources and capabilities (Väyrynen 2010), it still lacks consideration of the types of customization resources and capabilities a software vendor within the hybrid software business must develop and maintain to effectively deliver customization services. Therefore, the first objective of this thesis is to identify the knowledge resources and distinctive capabilities underlying successful customization activities as well as their value impact for vendor and customer firms. The sub-research questions are formulated as follows:

> **SRQ 1**: *Which resources and capabilities do software vendor firms need to offer valuable software systems to their customers?*
>
> **SRQ 2:** *What value does software customization provide for vendor and customer companies?*

Additionally, the thesis aims to explain how software companies strategically manage their development activities to benefit from innovation impulses from customization activities. As emphasized earlier, the academic literature introduced the term 'productization' to describe standard product development activities within the software business. Although this field is considered to be important for the delineation of software product management, research is still at the very early stages. Thus, to close this gap, the third sub-research question is formulated as follows:

> **SRQ 3:** *Which specific dynamic capabilities do software vendor firms develop to manage innovation impulses from software customization in their productization activities?*

1.3   Anchoring in the philosophy of science

Positioning oneself in both philosophy of science and the targeted academic discipline is the foundation for every serious scientific discussion. To do so, one must be aware of existing conceptions and schools of thought in philosophy of science as well as the characteristics of the targeted academic discipline. Before starting to present a research design, I would like to provide a short discussion of existing conceptions of truth and paradigms of inquiry to anchor my research in the philosophy of science and to position it in the field of information systems research.

The creation of scientific knowledge is strongly affiliated with the claim for truth. To be able to decide whether propositions are true, one needs a concept or a theory of truth. With respect to asking what the proper basis is for determining how words, symbols, ideas and beliefs can properly be considered to be true, whether by a single person or an entire society, philosophers have differentiated several theories of truth (c.f. Kirk 2002; Frank 2006). According to *the correspondence theory of truth*, a true statement or proposition corresponds to the part of reality it describes. However, because the perception of reality varies on an inter-personal and even on an intra-personal level, "the correspondence theory can hardly be used for testing "the truth" of a proposition" (Frank 2006, p. 14). In *the coherence theory*, truth requires that the propositions fit with an existing and accepted body of scientific knowledge. Therefore, this theory of truth suggests testing new propositions against accepted wisdom: "Only if they make sense in the light of existing knowledge, they are considered as possibly true." (Frank 2006, p. 14). From that perspective, the coherent theory would not allow new improved knowledge that is not compliant with existing tenets. Finally, according to the *consensus theory of truth*, consensual judgment based on human discussion can be considered to be the key to an acceptable notion of truth. For instance, if a group of scientists "after thoroughly considering and discussing a proposition comes to the joint conclusion that it is true, the proposition is regarded as true" (Frank 2006, p. 14). However, this theory of truth identifies neither the requirements for being considered qualified to judge nor what happens if two groups reach contradictory conclusions.

Struggling with the incompleteness of these concepts of truth, philosophy of science has created several "schools" (Frank 2006, c.f.) or inquiry paradigms (Denzin and Lincoln 1994, c.f.), which provide guidelines for scientific research. According to (Denzin and Lincoln 1994), *a paradigm*, in general, may be viewed as a basic belief system addressing ultimates or first principles. Furthermore, by defining the nature of the "world", the individual's place in it and the range of possible relationships, a paradigm represents a worldview for its holder. From the belief holder's point of view, the beliefs are basic in the sense that they must be accepted on faith. Inquiry paradigms, in particular, address what beliefs are about and what falls within the limits of legitimate inquiry. Denzin and Lincoln (1994) argue that the basic belief that underlies an inquiry paradigm can be summarized by the answers to three fundamental interconnected questions:

- *The ontological question:* What is the form and nature of reality and, therefore, what is there that can be known about it?

- *The epistemological question:* What is the nature of the relationship between the knower or would-be knower and what can be known?

- *The methodological question:* How can the inquirer (would-be knower) go about finding whatever he or she believes can be known?

Corresponding to these three questions, Denzin and Lincoln (1994) discuss four existing inquiry paradigms : Positivism, postpositivism, critical theory et al. and constructivism. Table 1.2 provides an overview of that discussion.

Positivism. Positivism's *ontological* base is *realism* (or *naive realism*). An apprehendable reality is assumed to exist, driven by immutable natural laws and mechanisms. From an *epistemological* perspective, investigator and investigated object are independent, and the investigator is capable of studying the object without influencing or being influenced by it (*dualism/objectivism*). Replicable findings are "true". *Methodologically* positivist research is *experimental/manipulative*; hypotheses are stated in propositional form and empirically tested for verification.

Postpositivism. Postpositivism's *ontological* base is critical realism. Reality is assumed to exist but to be only imperfectly apprehendable. The reasons for this difficulty are flawed human intellectual mechanisms and the fundamentally intractable nature of phenomena. *Epistemologically,* dualism remains the regulatory ideal but is abandoned, as it is not possible to maintain (*modified dualism/objectivism*). Replicated findings are *probably* true. From a methodological perspective, postpositivism research is *modified experimental/manipulative.* Hypotheses are falsified (rather than verified) by using *critical multiplism.* In general, inquiry is conducted in a more natural setting and discovery (e.g., by using qualitative techniques) is an accepted element in inquiry.

Critical Theory et al. The *ontological* base of critical theory et al. is historical realism. A (virtual or historical) reality is assumed to be apprehendable. Over time, social, cultural, economic, ethnic, and gender factors shaped a once plastic reality and reified it into a series of structures that are now taken as "real" for all practical purposes. The *epistemological* perspective is transactional and subjectist; investigator and investigated objects are interlinked in that the investigator's value system inevitably influences the inquiry. The *methodological* perspective of critical theory et al. is *dialogic and dialectical.* The transactional nature of inquiry requires a dialogue between investigator and investigated object, which must be dialectical in nature "to transform ignorance [...] and misapprehensions into more informed consciousness" (Denzin and Lincoln 1994, p. 110).

Constructivism. The *ontological* base for constructivism is relativism. Realities are formed as multiple, intangible constructions and are apprehendable. Although elements of these constructions are often shared among many individuals or cultures, their form and content is dependent on individuals or groups. Therefore, constructions are not more or less "true" but are simply more or less informed or sophisticated. As with critical theory, the *epistemological* perspective is *transactional and subjectivist*; investigator and investigated object are interactively linked and "findings" are literally created during the investigation process. *Methodologically,* constructivism takes a hermeneutical and dialectical perspective. Existing constructions are interpreted using hermeneutical techniques and contrasted through a di-

Table 1.2: Inquiry paradigms

Item	Positivism	Postpositivism	Critical Theory et al.	Constructivism
Ontology	Naive realism - "real" reality but apprehendable	Critical realism - "real" reality but only imperfectly and probabilistically apprehendable	Historical realism - virtual reality shaped by social, political, cultural, economic, ethnic, and gender values; crystallized over time	Relativism - local and specific constructed realities
Epistemology	Dualist/ objectivist; findings true	Modified dualist/ objectivist; critical tradition/ community; findings probably true	Transactional/ subjectivist; value-mediated findings	Hermeneutical/ dialectical
Methodology	Experimental/ manipulative, verification of hypotheses; chiefly quantitative methods	Modified experimental/ manipulative; critical multiplism; falsification of hypotheses; may include qualitative methods	Dialogic/ dialectical	Hermeneutical/ dialectical

alectical interchange to distill a more informed or sophisticated consensus construction.

Anchorage in philosophy of science. In line with the discussion above, the inquiry paradigm underlying this dissertation is postpositivism. The research is exploratory and partly explanatory in nature, with the goal of exploring and understanding a contemporary phenomenon within a real-life context; namely the strategic effects of customization knowledge on software product development. Regarding specific research methods, a qualitative and multi-case-study design (Eisenhardt 1989; Yin 2009) has been identified as the most advantageous research method. To ensure accuracy and consider alternative explanations Stake (1995), the qualitative research design considers at least two of the four triangulation types (data source, investigator, theory, and methodological triangulation) described by Denzin (2009) and Feagin et al. (1991), namely data source and methodological triangulation.

1.4 Research design and dissertation outline

1.4.1 Research design

The overall research design for this study was adapted from the method presented by Auerbach and Silverstein (2003). Instead of a traditional hypothesis-confirming approach, their qualitative approach aims for hypothesis generation. They argue that qualitative research should consist of several sequential studies. In particular, their approach consists of an initial exploratory approach that enables data-based theory development and an elaborative approach that builds upon the results from the first study and further develops these with respect to the initial research concern.

To answer the research questions, this thesis' research design first includes a qualitative investigation within vendor and customer firms to develop an in-depth understanding of the value of customization as well as the vendor resources and capabilities necessary to successfully provide customization services. This investigation can be regarded as a pilot study that aims to develop an in-depth understanding of software customization as provided by vendor firms. Thus, the first analysis addresses research questions one and two, in particular, with respect to the inside-out perspective on software customization.

The second qualitative investigation builds on the results from the first investigation and focuses on the dynamic capabilities necessary to generate a temporary competitive advantage from customization processes. Thus, this investigation can be regarded as an elaborative study that focuses on software customization as an important innovation driver for software product management. Thus, this study addresses research questions two and three, in particular, with respect to the outside-in perspective on software customization.

Each study includes Miles et al. (2013) phases of qualitative inquiry: data collection, data condensation, data display, and conclusion drawing and verification. Furthermore, to ensure research quality, each study reflects on (1) objectivity and confirmability; (2) reliability, dependability, and audibility; (3) internal validity, credibility, and authenticity; (4) external validity, transferability, and fit; as well as (5) utilization, application, and action orientation. The next section will describe how these phases and criteria were used to conduct the first exploratory investigation. Figure 1.7 illustrates the overall design of the investigation.

1.4.2   Dissertation outline

Table 1.3 summarizes the individual steps and the outline of the dissertation. Starting from the main research question, three sub-questions have been identified that will be addressed from a modified objectivist epistemological perspective and, thus, a postpositivistic theoretical perspective. Methodologically, the dissertation will employ two qualitative empirical investigations with respect to the relationship between customization and product develop-

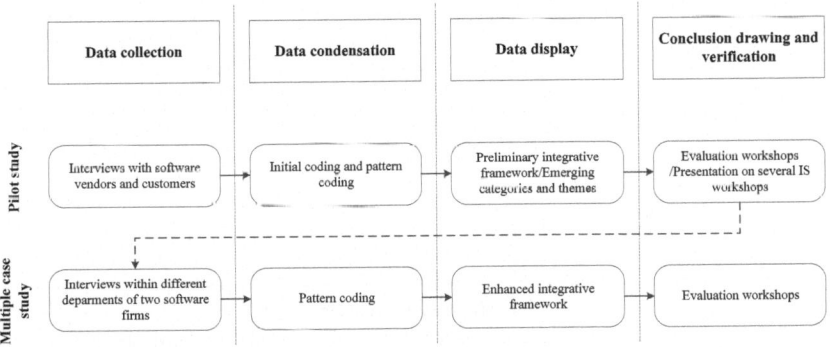

Figure 1.7: Overview of research design

ment in the hybrid software business. Each chapter is outlined further after the table.

The first chapter, *Introduction: The neglected role of customization in software product development*, provides an overview of the software business and explains the thesis' research concerns and relevance. In particular, it introduces the existing business logic in the software industry and highlights the neglected role of software customization as an innovation engine for software product development. Subsequently, the chapter formulates the thesis' research aim, objectives and questions and its anchorage in the philosophy of science. Finally, the chapter describes the overall research design and the structure of the thesis.

The second chapter, *Literature review: Software customization in the information systems literature*, briefly describes the existing body of knowledge on customization in general and software product customization in particular. The subsection *Concepts of customization* introduce the conceptualization of customization existing in the strategic management literature. In strategic management, customization is discussed under the term 'mass customization' and refers to the ability to provide customized products or services through flexible processes in high volumes and at relatively low costs. Following this general introduction, the larger part of the chapter describes an extensive

Table 1.3: Summary of research objectives and scope

Main research question
How can product software development companies strategically benefit from software customization.

Research objectives	Research questions
The *first objective* is to explore which resources are needed for companies to offer software product customization and which capabilities must be developed to leverage these resources.	Which resources and capabilities do vendor companies need to offer valuable software systems to their customers?
The *second objective* is to explore the nature of the value created by software customization for vendor and customer companies.	What value does software customization provide for vendor and customer companies?
The *final objective* is to explain how software development companies can benefit strategically from product software customization.	Which specific dynamic capabilities do software vendor firms develop to manage innovation impulses from software customization in their productization activities?

Scope and context			
Epistemology	Theoretical perspective	Methodology	Unit of analysis
Modified objectivism	Postpositivism	Qualitative research	Customization and development interaction

Table 1.4: Summary of research objectives and scope (continued)

Data collection and analysis
Conceptual literature: Product software development and customization **Theoretical literature:** (Knowledge) resources, capabilities and dynamic capabilities **Source:** Academic literature **Data reduction and analysis:** Systematic analysis of existing concepts
Pilot interview field study: A vendor and customer perspective on software customization resources, capabilities, and value **Source:** Key informants on the customer and vendor side **Technique:** Semi-structured interviews, digitally recorded and transcribed **Data reduction and analysis:** Initial and pattern coding approaches
Elaborative multi case study: Within two software development and solution provision companies **Source:** Key informants from marketing, development and customization departments **Technique:** Semi-structured interviews, digitally recorded and transcribed **Data reduction and analysis:** Initial and elaborative coding

Developing key outcomes and discussion
Response to findings regarding the association between current theory and current practice. Consolidation and further interpretation of outcomes addressing the supporting research questions. Address overall research question and ensure that the research problem has been addressed.

Summary, conclusion and outlook
Summarization of research objectives and contributions. Draw conclusions on presented findings and discussion. Present avenues for further research and highlight managerial implications.

analysis of the concept of customization in information systems literature. The results of this study revealed that in the information systems literature, customization is used in two streams of research: (1) from an outside-in perspective as a form of product delivery and (2) from an inside-out perspective as a form of co-creation of value. The study of information systems literature further confirmed the identified research gap.

The third chapter, *Theoretical foundation: The resource-based view (RBV) of the firm*, introduces the theoretical concepts of resources, capabilities, dynamic capabilities, and value. Starting with an overview of the existing theories of the firm, the resource-based view and related theoretical perspectives are described in more detail. Due to the knowledge-intensive perspective of this thesis, the chapter also introduces the knowledge-based view of the firm and absorptive capacity.

The fourth and fifth chapters of the dissertation *describe the qualitative investigations: (1) Exploring software customization from the vendors' and the customers' perspective* and *(2) Elaborating the strategic role of customization for software product development. These chapters* aim at an empirical investigation of all sub research questions. They include an interview study taking the vendor and customer perspective of software product customization and a comparative case study on the strategic importance of customization-driven innovations for software product development. The first empirical study described in this chapter investigates the vendor and customer perspective of customization. Based on the premise of the resource-based view of the firm as well as in-depth results from a qualitative interview study, the preliminary research framework is further developed and enhanced. The second study presents a comparative case study on the strategic role of software customization in software product management. Based on the theoretical concept of dynamic capabilities, in-depth interviews have been conducted and analyzed.

The last chapter, *Conclusion: Summary, implications, limitations and further research*, concludes the thesis with a short summary of the research concerns, methodology and contributions. It further describes implications for managerial practice as well as theory. Finally, the chapter describes methodological limitations and depicts avenues for further research.

Chapter 2

Literature review: Software customization in the information systems literature

2.1 Introduction

Companies increasingly need to understand their customers' wants and needs in order to strengthen their competitive position. Thus, in recent years, companies have started not only to discover customer needs by means of market research but also to integrate customers into the innovation process (Prahalad and Ramaswamy 2000; Von Hippel 2005). Concurrently, since the late 1970s, the co-creation of value has become a field of intense research in marketing and service science. Researchers have analyzed many different aspects of co-creation, for example, productivity gains through customer self-service (Czepiel 1990; Kelley et al. 1990), customer satisfaction, quality, employee performance and emotional responses (Bendapudi and Leone 2003), and the opportunity to differentiate products and services (Song and Adams 1993).

---

[1]Parts of the results reported in this chapter were presented at the IFIP 8.2 Workshop, 2012 in Tampa, FL, USA (Bertram et al. 2012)

Thereby, customization has emerged as a concept to provide customers with tailor-made products and services.

With respect to customization, researchers have further concluded that customers should not be recognized as passive receivers but should be seen as active and knowledgeable participants in common innovation or co-creation processes (Nambisan 2002). For example, (Firat et al. 1995) introduced the concept of customerization, which enables consumers to serve as co-producers of the product and service offering. Relatedly, (Ghosh et al. 2006), who investigated the role of control in complex product customization, stated that the success of customization is a function of the customer's knowledge. Thus, co-creation researchers assume an outside-in perspective of customization in that they focus on the integration of external resources into the innovation process.

Another stream of research pertaining to the concept of customization stems from economics and marketing. Here, researchers obtain an inside-out perspective in that they refer to customization as a way to tailor and deliver products and services according to customers' needs (Franke et al. 2009). They further highlight the role of mass customization, which enables customer-specific production with near mass production efficiency and the realization of economies of scale (Kotler 1989; Tseng and Jiao 2001).

However, the majority of articles in both areas have been written in a business-to-consumer (B2C) context, with an emphasis on the role of consumers and individual customers (Etgar 2008; Franke and Schreier 2007). Within business-to-business (B2B) contexts, such as in the market for business software (e.g., enterprise resource planning (ERP) software), concepts such as mass customization are comparatively rare because (1) buyers' markets usually consist of only a few firms and (2) products are generally more complex than in B2C scenarios (Ghosh et al. 2006).

2.2   Concepts of customization

2.2.1   Existing concepts of customization

The term customization refers to the adaption of a product or service according to specific customer needs (see Kotler and Armstrong 2011). The general assumption in the literature is that products or services create higher benefits for customers because they deliver a closer fit to preferences (Franke et al. 2009). Based on this assumption, customization has become of strategic value for firms (Ghosh et al. 2006). It allows them to better match their offerings with customer needs, fosters customer satisfaction and loyalty, and potentially leads to increased delivery performance and profit (Fornell et al. 1996; Perdue and Summers 1991). In recent years, researchers and practitioners have paid increasing attention to the concepts of customization. The academic literature discusses concepts of customization under the term 'mass customization' and adopts the service perspective.

The term 'mass customization' was first coined by Davis (1989). It relates to the ability to provide customized products or services through flexible processes in high volume and at relatively low cost (Pine II 1993). The literature provides two general definitions for mass customization (Da Silveira et al. 2001). The broad, visionary concept describes mass customization as the ability to provide individually designed products and services to every customer through highly agile, flexible and integrated processes (Pine II 1993; Eastwood 1996). Thus, mass customization reaches customers, as in the mass-market economy, but provides individuality for them, as in the pre-industrial economies (Davis 1989). In the narrower sense, mass customization is defined as a system that uses information technology, flexible processes, and organizational structures to deliver a wide range of products and services that meet the specific needs of individual customers at near mass production costs (Hart 1995a; Kotha 1995; Ross 1996; Joneja and Lee 1998). Thus, the idea of mass customization involves all aspects of product or service – sales, development, production and delivery – from the customer's options to delivering the finished product or service (Kay 1993; Jiao et al. 1998).

According to Da Silveira et al. (2001); Fogliatto et al. (2012), the concept of mass customization is the natural evolution of many ideas that have emerged over the past three decades such as just-in-time, lean production and agile manufacturing. The foundation of mass customization is based on three ideas: (1) new manufacturing and information technologies enable firms to deliver higher product or service variety at lower cost; (2) there is an increasing need for product customization (Kotler 1989); and (3) shorter product life cycles and expanded industrial competition increase the need to focus production strategies on individual customers (Kotha 1995; Pine II 1993). In contrast to conventional flexible systems where customer needs are anticipated by delivering wide variety (Åhlström and Westbrook 1999), mass customization aims at delivering products and services that best translate to the actual choices of individual customers (Da Silveira et al. 2001). Thus, successful mass customization may bring major competitive strategy and performance enhancements by producing items that are more meaningful and valuable to the customer than competitors' offerings (Hart 1995a, 1996).

Determining the level of individualization for mass customized products has been a major debate (Da Silveira et al. 2001). Purists argue that MC must include all requirements made by an individual customer. More pragmatic approaches argue that mass customization must follow customer needs, independent of the number of options actually offered.

Based on empirical observation, Gilmore and Pine II (1997) identify four levels of customization: *collaborative customization*, in which the designer is in dialogue with the customer; *adaptive customization*, in which customers can alter standard products during their usage; *cosmetic customization*, in which standard products are packaged individually for each customer; and *transparent customization*, in which standard products are adapted to individual needs.

Lampel and Mintzberg (1996) suggest five customization strategies, describing different configurations of standardized or customized processes, commodity or unique products, and generic or personalized customer transactions.

Pine II (1993) distinguishes five stages of modular production: *customized services*, in which standard products are tailored by marketing before being delivered to the customer; *embedded customization*, in which standard products are altered by customers during usage; *point-of-delivery customization*, in which additional customization work is done at the point of sale; *providing quick response*, which refers to the quick delivery of products; and *modular production*, in which standard components can be configured in a variety of products and services.

In a similar vein, Spira (1993) develops a framework that includes four types of customization: (1) *customized packaging*, (2) *customized services*, (3) *additional custom work*, and (4) *modular assembly*.

Based on this foundation, Da Silveira et al. (2001) proposed a framework that describes mass customization along the value chain from pure customization (individually designed products) to pure standardization. *Design* refers to collaborative projects, manufacturing, and the delivery of products according to customer needs. *Fabrication* refers to the manufacturing of tailor-made products following a pre-defined design. *Assembly* refers to the arrangement of modular components into different customer-specific product configurations. Levels 5 and 4 add *additional custom work* and *additional services* to standard products, often at the point-of-delivery. *Package and distribution* targets market segments by providing similar products in, for instance, different boxes or sizes. In *usage*, customization occurs only after delivery, through products or services that can be adapted to different functions of situations. Finally, *standardization* refers to no customization at all. Table 2.1 summarizes Da Silveira et al.'s (2001) generic levels of mass customization.

Table 2.1: Generic levels of mass customization, based on Da Silveira et al. (2001)

Generic levels	Gilmore and Pine II (1997)	Lampel and Mintzberg (1996)	Pine II (1993)	Spira (1993)
Design	Collaborative; Transparent	Pure customization		
Fabrication		Tailored customization		
Assembly		Customized standardization	Modular production	Assembling standard components into unique configurations
Additional custom work			Point of delivery customization	Performing additional custom work
Additional services			Customized services; Providing quick response	Providing additional services
Package and distribution	Cosmetic	Segmented Standardization		Customized packaging
Usage	Adaptive		Embedded customization	
Standardization		Pure standardization		

Mass customization involves major aspects of operations and is not the best strategy for every company. According to Da Silveira et al. (2001) and Fogliatto et al. (2012), the success of a mass customization strategy depends on a series of six external and internal factors. Factors 1 and 2 are market related, and factors 3 - 6 are organization based.

1. *Customer demand for variety and customization must exist.* Mass customization success depends on increasing customer demand for innovative and customized products. (Pine II 1993; Hart 1996)

2. *Market conditions must be appropriate.* Mass customization success depends on the timing of its implementation and on whether the company is regarded as innovative and customer driven (Kotha 1995).

3. *Value chain should be ready.* As a value chain-based concept, mass customization depends on the willingness of suppliers, distributors, and retailers to attend to the system's demands (Feitzinger and Lee 1997).

4. *Technology must be available.* The implementation of advanced manufacturing technologies is fundamental for mass customization success (Lau 1995; Pine II 1993).

5. *Product should be customizable.* Modularity enables simpler and lower-cost manufacturing and is a core concept of mass customization. To produce in short life cycles, mass customization processes also need rapid product development and innovation capabilities (Kotha 1995, 1996).

6. *Knowledge must be shared.* As a dynamic strategy, mass customization depends on the ability to translate customer demands into new products and services. To achieve this, companies must pursue a culture that emphasizes knowledge creation and distribution across the value chain (Pine II 1993; Kotha 1995, 1996).

This section has provided a brief overview of customization concepts and discussion in the academic and practical literature. It introduced the importance of customization by discussing the standardization versus individualization approaches. It has provided a definition of customization and general assumptions related to the understanding of mass customization as "customization with nearly production efficiency" (Tseng and Jiao 2001). Finally, I discussed the application of those concepts in the marketing, engineering and distribution literature. Based on this foundation, the following section will describe the research approach for my literature analysis in the information systems literature.

2.2.2 Software customization - a working definition

In the early days of software development, when software and hardware were still closely bundled, the prices for these systems were extremely high because the market for software products was nonexistent. These systems were generally solely developed for individual companies according to their individual needs and requirements. In the late 1960s, computer manufacturers started to unbundle hardware and software systems as the result of an IBM initiative (Xu and Brinkkemper 2007). As a consequence, an independent software market for business-to-business (B2B) was built, and during the 1980s, a new class of software vendors started to pre-build and offer software for a range of business functions that could be delivered separately on a large scale.

However, to address each customer's wants and needs, software was designed in such a way that each customer could adapt certain parts without changing the source code of the software (e.g., changing a desktop background, hiding navigation, etc.). Today, global enterprise software companies such as SAP, Oracle and Microsoft generally develop product software for wider, more anonymous (B2B) markets or industries. In these cases, requirements usually are not fully specified and are worked out in implementation projects with customers. Therefore, customization in information systems can be understood as a special type of co-creation of value and late product differentiation. The economic importance of these customization projects is very high. For example, IBM's total revenue in 2007 was \$99B, with more than 50% (\$54B) resulting from consulting services including customization (Spohrer and Maglio 2008).

As discussed, the service of customizing complex product software has become a business itself. Crucial to the existence of this service industry is that complex business software requires changes at the source code level to be adapted to a user firm's needs. In addition, as shown by Ghosh et al. (2006) for mechanical industries, within software customization projects, project success is a function of the customer's knowledge. In particular, compared to mass customization in B2C scenarios, in which customers can choose colors or materials for the desired product (Reichwald and Piller 2003), due to the complexity of business software, the customer is usually unable to communicate its needs in an appropriate format. In addition, the professional customer's needs change due to environmental turbulence and market dynamics. Consequently, the process of adapting a software product to the professional customer's needs can drag on and demand several iterations. Thus, instead of communicating needs just once, as in the case of mass customization in B2C contexts, customizing complex product software requires an iterative approach and is dependent on the customer's knowledge as well as his ability to communicate needs.

Based on these preliminary insights, the following working definition of customization is provided for the literature analysis, recognizing that customization in general and mass customization in particular need to be distinguished more specifically in the context of software products:

Customization is the process of configuring, parameterizing, or generally adapting an IS artifact to a customer's needs.

2.3   Systematic literature analysis

According to authors such as Huff (2009) or Creswell (2009), one of the
most well established methods for integrating research findings and assessing
the cumulative knowledge within a domain is a qualitative literature review.
This method allows researchers to analyze and evaluate both qualitative and
quantitative literature within a research domain to draw conclusions about
the state of a field. Because this method is well established, researchers have
performed literature reviews and adapted this method to their needs and
thereby developed several approaches to reviewing literature. For example,
Huff (2009) differentiates between at least four types of literature reviews:
(1) a survey to identify key issues and trends, (2) a critical review to identify
arguments, standards and the potential for new contributions, (3) a systematic review to expose quantitative and qualitative results across several areas
of interest and (4) a supportive review to generate new ideas and to resolve
specific problems from existing literature. These four differ, for example, in
purpose and in their primary and secondary sources of literature. Figure 2.1
illustrates the four types of literature analysis over time.

The research aim of this section is to draw a coherent picture of customization ideas and concepts in the current IS literature and thereby to
help categorize the existing ideas and concepts and furthermore identify the
potential for future contributions to that field. Hence, according to Huff's
(2009) systematic literature review approach, this paper uses a critical review
approach.

Journal and conference publications are both highly accepted channels for
communicating research findings to the IS research community. Therefore,
major IS journals and conferences were chosen as primary sources for the
review Webster and Watson (2002). The implemented research design is
divided into two sequential phases: *literature selection* and *literature analysis.*
The aim during the first phase - literature selection - was to identify relevant
papers in major IS journals and conferences. During the second phase -

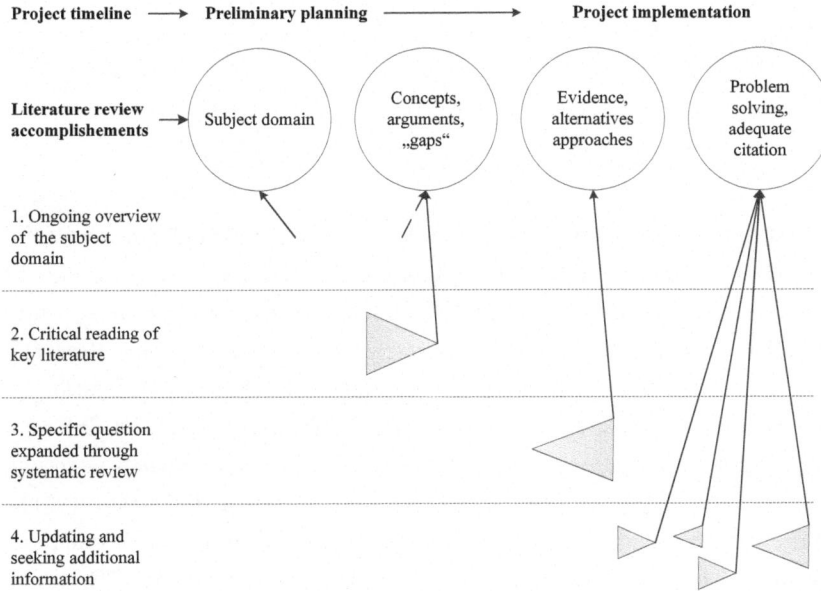

Figure 2.1: Types of literature review based on (Huff 2009)

literature analysis - an in-depth analysis of the selected papers was conducted. Figure 2.2 illustrates the research process.

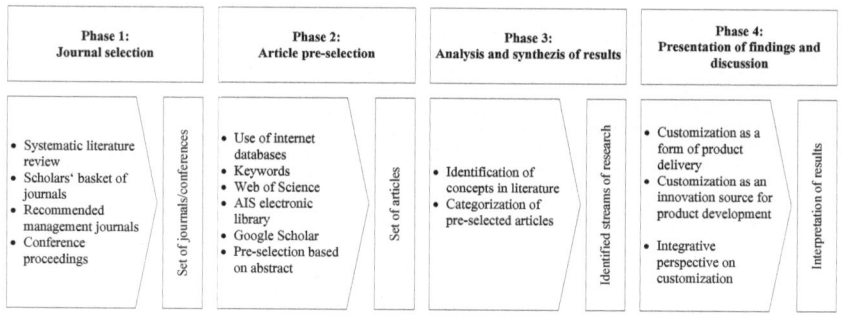

Figure 2.2: Phases of initial literature analysis

During the selection phase, the pool of journals and conference proceedings relevant to my study was first determined. With respect to journals, the research was concentrated on the senior scholars' basket of journals, which includes six journals (i.e., MIS Quarterly, Information Systems Research, Journal of Management Information Systems, Journal of the Association for Information Systems, European Journal of Information Systems, Information Systems Journal), as well as on general management journals as recommended by Fisher et al. (2007), Jourdan et al. (2008), and Mustafee (2011). With respect to conferences, the proceedings of the International Conference on Information Systems (ICIS) and the European Conference on Information Systems (ECIS) were included. Additionally, the proceedings of the Wirtschaftsinformatik conference was included because this conference (1) is the major German-speaking conference for IS research and (2) receives a higher share of design-oriented papers Österle et al. (2011), which was considered to be important given the aim of providing a coherent picture of customization.

As resources for potential articles, the ISI Web of Knowledge and the electronic library of the Association of Information Systems (AISel) were used for the review. In each database, titles and abstracts of the research articles

Table 2.2: Selected journals and number of articles in the initial review

#	Journal	Acronym	# Articles	# Preselect
1	MIS Quarterly	MISQ	8	4
2	Information Systems Research	ISR	7	3
3	Communication of the ACM	CACM	3	2
4	Journal of Management Information Systems	JMIS	5	5
5	Management Science	MS	16	15
6	Journal of the ACM	JACM	0	0
7	European Journal of Information Systems	EJIS	9	9
8	IEEE Transactions on Software Engineering	IEEETSE	8	4
9	Information Management	I&M	4	1
10	Harvard Business Review	HBR	20	8
11	Wirtschaftsinformatik	WI	4	3
	Total Journals		84	54

#	Proceedings	Acronym	# Articles	# Preselect
1	European Conference on Information Systems	ECIS	12	6
2	International Conference on Information Systems	ICIS	5	3
3	Wirtschaftsinformatik	WIP	6	2
	Total Proceedings		23	11
	Total		107	65

were searched using the phrases "customizing", "customization", "customising", and "customisation". While the search engine and interface in the case of the ISI Web of Knowledge was very user friendly, a little more manual effort was needed in the case of the AISel to restrict the search to the designated conferences. Finally, the research was limited such that only papers with a publication date after 2001 were considered. This resulted in a superset of 84 journal articles and 23 conference proceedings.

As a final step in the research selection phase, the abstracts of those 84 articles were analyzed to preselect relevant articles for further analysis. As a categorization code, a very simple A, B and C scheme was used, where A meant that the article fit our topics well (i.e., customization in IS and B2B), C meant that it did not fit at all and B meant that the article fell somewhere in between A and C. All articles within categories A and B were considered to be relevant for the research aim. Ultimately, a set of 54 journal papers and 11 conference papers was identified for the literature analysis. Table 1 summarizes the results of the selection phase.

After the pre-selection process, the in-depth analysis and synthesis of the identified articles was organized as follows. For each paper, the underlying research approach and definitions for customization concepts were identified. During the analysis, two streams of research in the field of software customization emerged: software customization as a form of product delivery and software customization as a form of co-creation. The following section presents those streams and discusses the associated papers.

2.4 The duality of software customization in IS research

2.4.1 Customization as a form of product delivery

As expected, customization appears to be a central topic in IS research. Predominantly, researchers focus on how software is delivered to customers in relation to distribution economics (Brocke et al. 2010; van Fenema et al. 2007; Weinmann et al. 2011). Packaged software, as one incarnation of product software, is presented as one way to address the challenges of customization in many articles within my review. For example, van Fenema et al. (2007) described packaged software as a "ready-made mass product offering users a solution based design process aimed at generic customer groups in a variety of industries and geographical areas." A more general focus is delivered by Chiasson's and Green's (2007) definition of packaged software; they argue that an important question in packaged software design and consumption is determining what the software can and will do to support, change, and inhibit desired organizational practices.

In a similar vein, Sia and Soh (2007) describe the package-organizational fit as the central point of interest for package customization. Regarding uncertainty in customization projects, Safadi and Faraj (2010) describe workarounds as a valid way to address unanticipated requirements during the development or implementation of a software package. They define this post-implementation phenomenon as non-compliant user behavior vis-à-vis the intended system design. Although in extreme cases, formal systems are entirely bypassed, workarounds are widespread among organizations. From an architectural point of view, (Czarnecki et al. 2006) describe software product lines as a tool "to improve productivity, time-to-market, and quality of application development by leveraging the commonalities of systems within an application domain while managing their variations" to address some of the above-described challenges.

Table 2.3: Customization definitions and concepts

Author	Definition/Concept	Paper Type
Customization as a form of distribution		
Safadi and Faraj (2010)	Computer workarounds are a post-implementation phenomenon that is widespread in organizations. They are commonly defined as non-compliant user behaviors vis-à-vis the intended system design, and they may go so far as to bypass the formal systems entirely.	Case study
Brocke et al. (2010)	Although known primarily as a production principle [...], mass customization has also been applied to intangible products [...] with a focus on distributive and marketing aspects when mass customizing offerings and deals.	Conceptual paper
Chiasson and Green (2007)	One important question in packaged software design and consumption is determining what the software can and will do to support, change, and inhibit desired organizational practices.	Case study (Participation)
Dewan et al. (2003)	Improvement in manufacturing flexibility allows the mass customization of consumer products without significantly compromising cost efficiency. Not surprisingly, mass customization has begun to erode the domain of mass-produced standard items.	Game theory

Table 2.4: Customization definitions and concepts (continued)

Author	Definition/Concept	Paper Type
Customization as a form of distribution		
Keßler and Alpar (2008)	Both [OS and COTS software] need to be customized to fit the requirements of the adopting organization. Configuration and parameterization are the approaches of choice in this case. If they are not sufficient, customization of the SW code is necessary.	Action research
Swaminathan and Tayur (2003)	The internet has increased customers' expectations for complete customization at a nominal charge. Even before the advent of e-business, firms faced the challenge of mass customization and high product variety, but this has increased immensely over recent years.	Conceptual paper
van Fenema et al. (2007)	Packaged enterprise software is a ready-made mass product offering users a solution-based design process aimed at generic customer groups in a variety of industries and geographical areas. Packaged software can be contrasted with custom-built approaches based on the organization of the development and delivery processes.	Conceptual paper (Qualitative interviews)
Weinmann et al. (2011)	Product configuration systems are useful instruments for individualization in the field of mass customization.	Experiment

To date, a considerable stream of research has addressed the means of distribution (i.e., packaging) of product software and regards customization in an "after-production" sense. Because this perspective developed from a logic in which a product is first produced and then distributed, it corresponds with the inside-out perspective of customization in IS introduced earlier.

2.4.2 Customization as a form of co-creation of value

Another stream of research in the IS literature addresses the development side of software as well as customer integration during the development processes in particular. For example, Piller et al. (2004) state that "within mass customization, customers are integrated into value creation by defining, configuring, designing, matching, or modifying their individual solution out of a list of options and pre-defined components". In a similar vein, Xin and Levina (2008) argue that clients not only customize the software to their needs, but also change organizational practices to fit the software product.

Additionally, research has focused on the tailoring of software methods to development contexts. Fitzgerald et al. (2006) argue that factors such as organizational issues, distributed teams, and the existence of legacy systems require different or changed development methods. In a similar vein, Slaughter et al. (2006) describe strategy and process fit as being important for the development process. From their point of view, process customization or tailoring is important to fit the needs of specific organizations or projects. This involves adapting, particularizing, or selecting certain software processes.

2.5 The reciprocal nature of software customization

While there is a common understanding of customization as the adaption of software products or more general IT artifacts to specific customer needs,

Table 2.5: Customization definitions and concepts (continued)

Author	Definition/Concept	Paper Type
Customization as co-creation		
Piller et al. (2004)	Within mass customization, customers are integrated into value creation by defining, configuring, designing, matching, or modifying their individual solution from a list of options and pre-defined components.	Conceptual paper
Xin and Levina (2008)	In such cases, clients can either change their organizational practices to fit the software or customize the software application and incur some cost to fit their needs.	Hypotheses development
Czarnecki et al. (2006)	The goal of SPLs is to improve productivity, time-to-market, and the quality of application development by leveraging the commonalities of systems within an application domain while managing their variations. SPLs package these commonalities in domain-specific platforms, which may be customized through configuration settings or code extensions.	Conceptual paper
Fitzgerald et al. (2006)	A related stream of research has focused on the tailoring of software methods to the actual needs of the development context. Factors such as organizational issues [...], distributed teams [...], or the existence of legacy systems [...] often require the use of a different method or at least changes to the existing method.	Interviews
Slaughter et al. (2006)	Process customization or tailoring involves adapting, particularizing, or selecting certain (often standard or ?best practice?) software processes to fit the needs of specific organizations or projects.	Case study (Qualitative interviews)

the existing IS literature primarily uses concepts of customization from other disciplines. For example, the term 'mass customization' has almost always been defined in relation to industrial contexts without providing a sufficient definition in relation to the characteristics of IS artifacts. Furthermore, the literature differs to a great extent in describing the level of customization because the term is used for the configuration, parameterization, adaption or development of existing or new source code.

For customer- and vendor-related reasons, the intensity of interaction in customization projects can be very high. For instance, because of a high level of innovation, neither the customer nor the vendor is able to pre-estimate the effort required to implement desired functionalities (Chiasson and Green 2007; van Fenema et al. 2007). In these cases, customization requires the customer's support to understand and change his processes (e.g., by means of consulting services). On the vendor side, the software product's "manufacturing flexibility" or architectural agility may not be sufficient to implement the desired functionality in a standardized way, and for example, the source code might need to be changed (Keßler and Alpar 2008). Thus, customization (in general) can be defined as a highly iterative form of IS implementation or adaption, where vendor and customer interactions are so intensive that it is not possible to handle them in single iterations of knowledge transfer.

> *Customization is the process of configuring, parameterizing or, in general, adopting an IS artifact to a customer's need in more than one iteration. In this case, either the customer is NOT able to communicate his requirements in one step OR the vendor's manufacturing and distribution system is NOT capable of delivering the customized artifact in one additional step and a more intensive interaction between those two parties is necessary.*

In contrast, mass customization focuses on the efficiency aspect of customization. The term was initially introduced by Davis (1996) and later defined in the industrial engineering work of Tseng and Jiao (2001) as "producing goods and services to meet individual customer's needs with near mass production efficiency". Within IS, product configuration is an instrument for implementing mass customization (Weinmann et al. 2011). Due to the efficiency aspect of mass customization, the customer must have a sufficient understanding of his requirements, while the vendors' delivery system must be flexible (and standardized) enough to integrate these requirements into the existing product. Thus, at least one iteration of knowledge transfer occurs: the customer provides his knowledge on the requirements to the vendor, and the vendor reacts by delivering a customized product. With respect to IS research and regarding the efficiency aspect, mass customization is defined as follows:

Mass customization is the process of configuring, parameterizing or generally adapting an IS artifact to a customer's needs in one iteration. This happens only if the customer is able to communicate his requirements in one step and if the vendor's manufacturing and distribution system is capable of delivering the customized artifact in one additional step.

The review revealed that current studies differentiate customization by means of level (customization and mass customization) and intention (co-creation of value and product distribution). Although existing literature considers these aspects to a certain extent, it lacks research studies that integrate the accumulated body of research. For instance, while the literature differentiates the level of customization between customization in general and mass customization approaches, further studies are needed that investigate the influence of the underlying customization technique on these levels. To date, the existing literature describes product configuration as a tool for implementing mass customization functionality. Considering my definitions of customization and mass customization based on interaction efficiency, mass customization might also be implemented using other techniques such as parameterization or source code development. Additionally, further research studies are needed investigating how customization intention influences software product management and vice versa. For instance, from a vendor perspective, co-creation of value projects might be valuable for orienting the software product. From this point of view, such projects can be considered a crucial investment in software product management. Here, future research should focus on identifying the drivers and barriers of those customization activities and on understanding how vendors value and balance the co-creation of value and product distribution projects.

Second, as already mentioned, customization strongly depends on interaction and knowledge transfer between vendors and customers. Considering customization as a service, a reciprocal knowledge exchange from vendor to customer (inside-out) and from customer to vendor (outside-in) can be assumed. In this area, further research is needed to investigate the influence of the customization level and intention on the characteristics and transfer of exchanged knowledge. Regarding the level of customization, I assume that due to interaction intensity with respect to tangible and intangible knowledge, customization (in general) is a richer medium of knowledge transfer than mass customization. However, within mass customization, the vendor's manufacturing system must be close to the customers' requirements to provide efficient customization functionality. In this case, I assume that the vendor already has a certain knowledge base about the topic of interest, which facilitates the exploration and assimilation of new knowledge. Here, I state that future research in the context of customization should place more emphasis on knowledge characteristics and on the knowledge exploration, assimilation and exploitation processes.

As expected, the IS literature has paid attention to both customization as a form for realizing economies of scale by using "make one, sell many"-approaches (inside-out) and as a way of integrating customers into the innovation process (outside-in). Surprisingly, the combination of both perspectives has been somewhat neglected by IS research. Regarding customization as understood in practice, that is, the customization of large business software in B2B contexts, the customer provides his knowledge in his area of expertise as well as his requirements in multiple iterations. Thus, the customer complements the vendor's knowledge at a technological and a market level not only at a distinct point in time, as with mass customization, but also continuously. Because frequently receiving formulated requirements is demanding, vendors in a customization scenario must develop a particular type of absorptive capacity (Lichtenthaler 2009) to sufficiently benefit from external knowledge. However, as the review shows, reciprocal knowledge flows pertaining to customization and customizing are largely neglected within the IS literature.

In summary, from the observation, it can be posited that the existing literature is limited to regarding knowledge transfer between vendor and customer in multiple iterations, which drives us to delineate future research areas. To clarify these assumptions, Figure 2.3 shows the reciprocal "inside-out" and "outside-in" relationship between the vendor and the customer. For reasons of simplicity, intermediates such as consultants and professional services are left out and subsumed under the term 'vendor'. Although the research results highlight the differences in the definition and application of customization concepts in the IS literature, further research in this area is needed, especially with regard to the interaction of software product management and software customization.

2.6 Summary

The objective of this section was to explore and summarize the existing concepts of software product customization. Although research has contributed to understanding (mass) customization, it has only begun to explore both fields in the context of the software business. In this section, I provided a systematic review of the concepts behind software product customization in the IS literature.

Recent research has contributed the field of software product management in three different fields. It has found definitions and provided several categorizations for software products. Furthermore, it has provided conceptual models for the strategic and operational perspective of software product

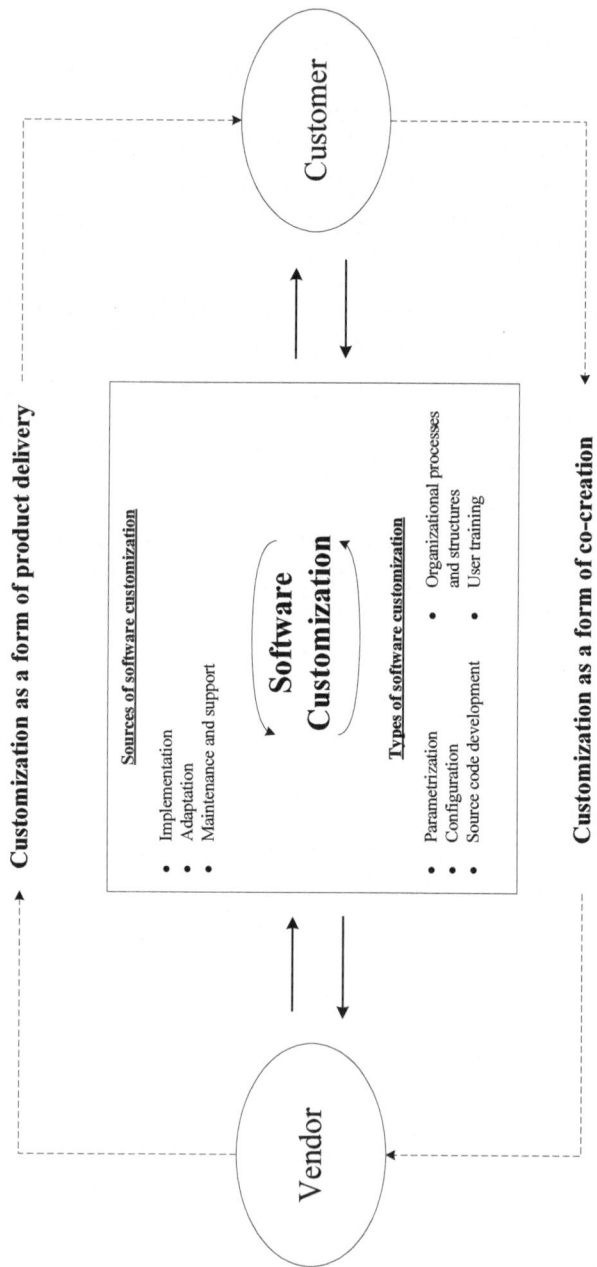

Figure 2.3: The concept of customization in the IS literature

management. However, to date, the distinction between software product management and classical or traditional software engineering is not clear. Many overlapping areas still must be analyzed and systematized. Software product lines might be a good option as a starting point for the integration of both streams of research.

In contrast to software product management, research on software customization still lacks integrated conceptual models. Existing research can be categorized in two different streams: customization as a form of product delivery and customization as a form of co-creating value. Finally, there is virtually no research on the reciprocal nature of software customization. Although existing research has covered customer integration and the knowledge transfer from vendors to customers during customization projects, it still lacks an integrated conceptualization of software customization. This supports the validity of the initial research question and the analysis of the interaction between product management and customization as a research objective for this thesis.

Chapter 3

Theoretical foundation: The resource-based view (RBV) of the firm

Regarding resources and products as two sides of the same coin (Wernerfelt 1984), the resource-based view (RBV) of the firm is one of the dominant perspectives in strategic management (Newbert 2007). At its core, the RBV states that the resources or the bundles of resources a company possesses are the basis for achieving competitive advantage (cf. Barney 1986, 1991; Conner 1991; Peteraf 1993; Wernerfelt 1984). Since its introduction, the RBV has become one of the most widely accepted theoretical perspectives in the strategic management field as a framework for explaining the conditions under which a firm may gain a sustained competitive advantage (Armstrong and Shimizu 2007). Management scholars have debated the relative importance of internal firm resources and capabilities (cf. Prahalad and Hamel 1990) versus environmental factors (cf. Porter 1979) to sustaining competitive advantage. Evidence suggests that both internal and external factors are crucial to competitive success (cf. Hart 1995b).

The purpose of this chapter is to introduce and to discuss the RBV as a theoretical lens for the subsequent studies in this thesis. Therefore, the first section describes the complementary contribution of the early RBV to the (market-oriented) theory of the firm and compares key characteristics of the RBV and transaction costs economics (TCE). The second section outlines seminal contributions in the development of the RBV towards a theory, examining the introduction, growth and maturity stages of this development. The third section describes the concept of dynamic capabilities as an important extension of the traditional RBV. The fourth section takes a critical perspective and discusses limitations and weaknesses of the RBV as discussed in the literature. Finally, the chapter concludes with an illustrative summary of the theoretical lens provided by the RBV and a preview of the following chapter.

3.1   Origins and development of the RBV

Thirty years after its introduction, the academic literature indicates that the RBV of the firm has reached maturity as a theory. Barney et al. (2011) see four reasons for this. First, scholars have increasingly referred to the term *resource-based theory* instead of *resource-based view*. Second, the RBV has given rise to other "spin-off perspectives", such as the knowledge-based view (Grant 1996b), the natural-resource-based view (Hart 1995b) and dynamic capabilities (Teece et al. 1997). Third, insights generated based on the RBV have been integrated with those of other perspectives, for instance, institutional theory (Oliver 1997) and organizational economics (Combs and Ketchen 1999). Finally, the RBV has reached a point where retrospective assessments have been warranted, such as empirical evidence related to RBV core elements (Crook et al. 2008), a critical examination of the methodologies used to apply the RBV (Armstrong and Shimizu 2007), and a review of critiques (Kraaijenbrink et al. 2010). Collectively, these developments support Barney's (2011) suggestion that the RBV has reached maturity as a theory.

The following paragraphs describe the development of the RBV from its first mention in the early 1980s up to today. During this time, three phases of development can be distinguished: introduction, growth and maturity. The introduction stage took place from the 1980s to 1991, the growth stage between the years 1992 and 1999 and the maturity stage between 2000 and today.

3.1.1 Introduction stage: Conceptual foundation of the RBV

The introduction phase is characterized by mostly conceptual contributions to the core ideas of the RBV. The initial roots of the RBV lie in Penrose's (1959) seminal work on the growth of the firm and the importance of organizational resources. However, the RBV only began to take shape in the 1980s as a complement to the market-oriented frameworks (e.g., Porter's (1980) five-forces model) dominating at that time. Lippman and Rumelt (1982) started by describing the concepts of imitability and causal ambiguity, which subsequently became core elements of the RBV. The actual term *resource-based view* was first introduced by Wernerfelt (1984), who theorized about the value of focusing on a firm's resources rather than its products. Two years later, Barney (1986) was the first to describe how organizational culture can be regarded as a source for sustained competitive advantage. At the end of the 1980s, Dierickx and Cool (1989) emphasized the usefulness of resources if no effective substitutes are available.

The largest impact on the distribution of the RBV during its introduction phase can surely be related to the 1990 *Strategic Management Journal* special issue on this new theoretical perspective. This special issue includes Barney's (1991) article, which presented a detailed definition of resources and a full set of characteristics that make them a potential source of sustained competitive advantage: valuable, rare, inimitable, and non-substitutable (VRIN). Other articles in this special issue provided contributions to the role of resources and their synergy in contexts of diversification (Harrison et al. 1991), CEOs

and their idiosyncrasies as a valuable resource of the firm (Castanias and
Helfat 1991), organizational identity as a core competency leading to competitive advantage (Fiol 1991), and a comparison of the RBV with industrial-
organization economics (Conner 1991). Figure 3.1 illustrates some of the
core contributions during the introduction stage of the RBV.

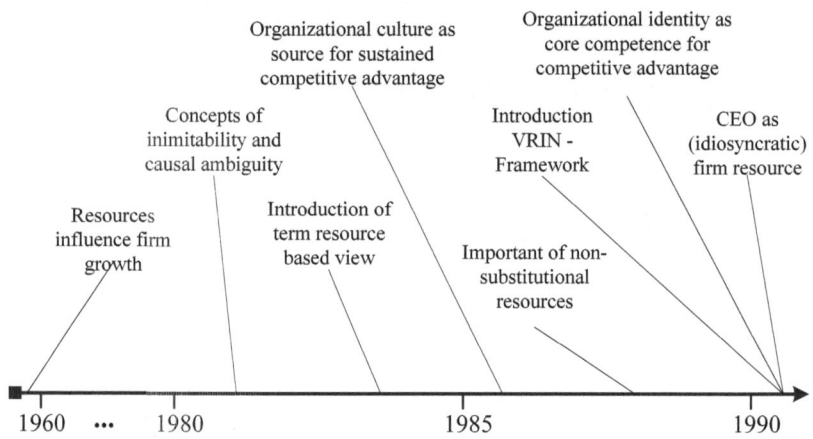

Figure 3.1: Conceptual contributions during the introduction stage

The following paragraphs briefly describe some of the key contributions
to the introduction of the RBV. Penrose's (1959) *The Theory of the Growth
of the Firm* is one of the earliest contributions to today's RBV of the firm.
Although her early work was considered to be one of the most influential theories in decades (Marris 1961), her *Theory of Growth of the Firm* 'turned out
to be no more than a footnote in the history of the neoclassical theory of firm'
(Pitelis 2009). However, today her work is one of the most cited articles in the
field of strategic management and thereby has become the *canonical reference* for resource-, knowledge- and capabilities-based approaches to business
strategy (Pitelis 2009).

According to her work in the 1950s, the economic theory of the firm had
no firms in it. Instead, for mainstream economic theorists at that time, *the
firm* was primarily a set of supply and demand functions. Penrose (1959)

concluded that such a theory of the firm could not be easily adapted to "the analysis of the expansion of the innovating, multi-product, flesh and blood organization that businessmen call firms" (p. 13). Accordingly, she defined the firm as a collection of productive resources under administrative coordination and authoritative communication that produces goods and services for sale in the market for a profit (Penrose 1959, 1985, 1995). The essential difference between economic activity in the firm and that in the market "is that the former carried on within an administrative organization, while the latter is not" (Penrose 1959, p. 15). Thus, administrative coordination and authoritative communication define the boundaries that distinguish the firm from the market.

Building upon Penrose's work, Wernerfelt (1984) noted that for the firm, resources and products are two sides of the same coin. However, since Penrose's (1959) seminal work on the growth of the firm, relatively few academic studies had looked at a broader set of firm resources. Thus, he claimed that firms should be analyzed from a resource perspective on the level of the firm and not just from a product perspective on the level of the industry. By analyzing from a resource perspective, Wernerfelt (1984) saw the potential for addressing key issues in the formulation of strategy for diversified firms that were largely neglected at the time:

1. On which of the firm's current resources should diversification be based?

2. Which resources should be developed through diversification?

3. In what sequence and into what markets should diversification take place ?

4. What types of firms will it be desirable for this particular firm to acquire?

Although Wernerfelt's (1984) paper was meant to be only "a first cut at a huge can of worms" (p.180), his purely conceptual work can be regarded as one of the most influential contributions to the early RBV of the firm. By emphasizing the importance of a resource-based perspective in contrast to the prevalent product perspective of the firm, Wernerfelt threw a different light on strategic options. In particular, three contributions to the - at that time - emerging RBV can be identified. First, by introducing the concept of *resource position barriers* in an analogy to entry barriers, he highlighted the importance of resources to the strategic position of a firm. A holder of resources is able to maintain a relative position vis-à-vis other holders and third persons as long as these act rationally. In fact, if the firm already possesses a resource, it affects the costs and revenues of subsequent acquisitions adversely. Second, by introducing the *resource-product matrix*, he provided a visualization for the balance between the exploitation of existing and the development of new resources in an analogy to the growth-share matrix. In a resource-product matrix, the checked entries indicate the importance of a resource to a product and vice versa. Finally, by regarding *acquisitions as the purchase of a bundle of resources* in a highly imperfect market and concentrating on rare resources, firms can maximize that imperfection and the opportunities for cheap buys and good returns.

Subsequently, Barney (1991) positioned the RBV against the structure-conduct-performance (SCP) paradigm and developed a conceptual model based "on the impact of resource heterogeneity and immobility on sustained competitive advantage" (p. 103). Based on a brief analysis of strategic planning, information processing, and a firm's reputation among customers and suppliers, Barney (1991) stated that to become a source of sustained competitive advantage, a resource must have four attributes: (1) it must be valuable for implementing strategies to improve a firm's efficiency and effectiveness, (2) it must be rare in that other firms cannot similarly exploit that resource, (3) it must be imperfectly imitable so that firms that do not possess that resource cannot obtain it and finally, (4) it must be non-substitutable so that firms that do not possess it cannot substitute with another resource. He integrated these characteristics into a framework that describes the relationships between important strategic resources and sustained competitive advantage. This early framework – he correctly concluded – would have implications for strategic management theory and other business disciplines, such as the relations between sustained competitive advantage and social welfare, sustained competitive advantage and organization theory and behavior, and firm endowments and sustained competitive advantage.

Also in 1991, Conner (1991) investigated whether the RBV had the potential to become the kernel of a unifying paradigm for strategy research and thereby a theory of the firm. To address this question, she compared the RBV to five theories used in the IO view: the neoclassical theory's perfect competition model, Bain-type IO, the Schumpeterian and Chicago responses, and transaction cost theory (TCE). Based on that analysis – with special emphasis on transaction cost theory – she described how the RBV "explains the reasons for existence of the firm and what limits its size and scope" (p. 139). From her perspective, the fundamental difference between the resource-based theory and transaction cost theory is as follows:

"Transaction cost theory assumes that the same productive activity can be carried on either within the firm or by a collection of autonomous contractors: that is, except for problems of opportunism, the same inputs can be used equally productively in a firm or a market context. Resource-based theory, on the other hand, draws from the vision of the firm as a unique combination of inputs to question this assumption. In a RBV of the firm, team-specific assets within the firm will be more specific to other teams inside the firm than to teams outside the firm, and hence more productive." (p. 142)

Table 3.1 summarizes selected key contributions to the introduction of the RBV. The next section will provide a brief overview of the growth stage of the RBV in the period between 1992 and 2001.

Table 3.1: The introduction stage of resource-based theory: selected key papers, based on Barney et al. (2011)

Author(s)	Date Key Contribution
Penrose (1959)	Theorized about how a firm's resources influence its growth; in particular, growth is constrained when resources are inadequate
Lippman and Rumelt (1982)	Explained the concepts of inimitability and causal ambiguity; these concepts became core elements of the RBV
Wernerfelt (1984)	Emphasized the value of focusing on firms' resources rather than on their products; coined the term 'resource-based view'
Barney (1986)	Theorized about how organizational culture could be a source of sustained competitive advantage
Dierickx and Cool (1989)	Developed the notion that resources are especially useful when no effective substitutes are available
Barney (1991)	Presented and developed the core tenets of the RBV; presented a detailed definition of resources; articulated the full set of characteristics that make a resource a potential source of competitive advantage (i.e., valuable, rare, inimitable, and nonsubstitutable)
Harrison et al. (1991)	Highlighted the value of resources and synergy between resources in the context of diversification
Castanias and Helfat (1991)	Characterized CEOs as firm resources that possess varying (idiosyncratic) qualities and quantities of general, industry-specific, and firm-specific skills
Fiol (1991)	Proposed organizational identity as a core competency leading to competitive advantage
Conner (1991)	Juxtaposed the RBV with industrial-organizational economics in order to demonstrate that the RBV is developing as a new theory of the firm

3.1.2   Growth stage: Characteristics of resources and capabilities

The growth stage of the RBV was initiated by the 1991 special issue and took place during 1990. The growth stage was marked by a deeper discussion of the characteristics of resources, especially as concerns the separation of resources and capabilities (Amit and Schoemaker 1993), the importance of knowledge as a resource (Grant 1996b), and special forms of capabilities such as combinative capabilities (Kogut and Zander 1992) and dynamic capabilities (Teece et al. 1997).

Along with those mentioned above, several other studies contributed to the growth stage of the RBV Table 3.2 (see Barney et al. 2011). For instance, Kogut and Zander (1992) introduced the concept of combinative capabilities and emphasized the importance of knowledge as an organizational resource. Hart (1995b) introduced and developed a conceptual spin-off of the RBV called the natural-based view of the firm. In their paper, Grant (1996b) provided the foundation for a new theory of the firm and articulated the knowledge-based view as a spin-off of the RBV. In their award winning paper, Miller and Shamsie (1996) tested the resource-performance link while measuring resources directly. Comparing opportunism and knowledge perspectives, Conner and Prahalad (1996) identified situations where the application of opportunism-based arguments and knowledge-based arguments could lead to opposing predictions regarding the organization of economic activity. Combining two theoretical perspectives, Oliver (1997) theorized about how the RBV and institutional theory together could better explain sustained competitive advantage. Building on the core ideas of the RBV, Teece et al. (1997) introduced the concept of dynamic capabilities and particularly explained competitive advantage as arising from the confluence of assets, processes, and evolutionary paths. In an additional paper, Coff (1999) initiated the discussion of how the excess profits derived from resources might be appropriated by various stakeholders. Finally, Combs and Ketchen (1999) examined how to reconcile competing predictions from the

RBV and organizational economics about the choice of organizational form.
Figure 3.2 illustrates the core contributions to the RBV during its growth
stage.

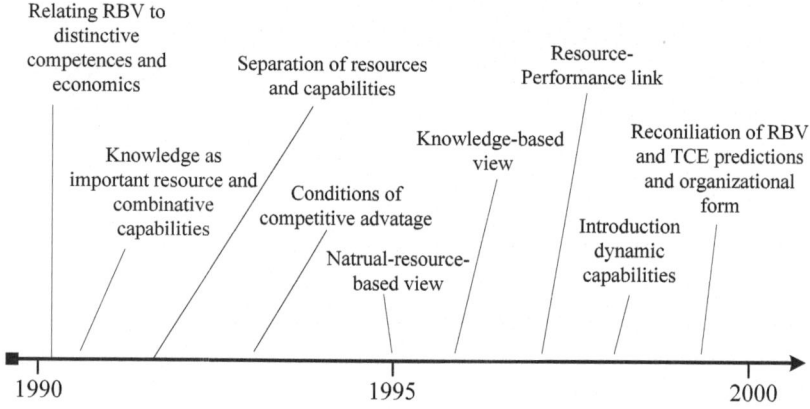

Figure 3.2: Conceptual contributions during the growth stage

The following paragraphs briefly describe some of the key contributions
to the growth phase of the RBV. Mahoney and Pandian (1992) emphasized
the RBV's theoretical foundation. They assumed that the RBV was not only
stimulating conversation within strategy research, organizational economics
and industrial organization research but that it was also providing a framework for increased discussion between these research perspectives. Therefore,
they posited that the RBV offered an opportunity for debate between scholars
from different research perspectives. In particular, their review of the RBV-
related literature at that time revealed three major research programs that
were intertwined in the resource-based framework. First, the RBV incorporated concepts from mainstream strategy research, such as distinctive com-
petencies of heterogeneous firms. Second, the RBV fit comfortably within
the conversation of organizational economics. Finally, the resource-based approach was complementary to industrial organization analysis. In particular,

it contains elements of both the Harvard and Chicago schools of industrial organization thought

In a very similar vein to Barney (1991), Peteraf (1993) developed a resource-based model of competitive advantage by linking firm resources and performance. To do so, she identified four theoretical conditions – or cornerstones – that underlie competitive advantage. First, along with Barney (1991), she argued that resources are heterogeneous across firms and that some resources are superior to others with respect to economical production or customer satisfaction. Such resources are seen as the source of Ricardian and monopoly rents. The second condition was that heterogeneity can be preserved, and therefore ex post limits to competition must exist. With this condition, Peteraf (1993) referred to Barney's (1991) imperfect imitability and non-substitutability. The third important condition was the imperfect mobility of resources. While perfect immobility represents resources that cannot be traded at all, resources that are imperfectly mobile can be traded but are more valuable within the firm that currently employs them than within other firms. Peteraf's (1993) last condition was the existence of ex ante limits to competition, which prevent ex ante costs for necessary resources from offsetting the expected rents.

Amit and Schoemaker (1993) further articulated the theoretical foundations for the RBV by replacing the strategy field's concept of key success factors with the notions of (1) strategic industry factors, which they defined as a set of resources and capabilities that have become the prime determinant of economic rents, and (2) strategic assets, which they defined as a firm-level construct, referring to the set of firm specific resources and capabilities developed by management as the basis for creating and protecting the firm's competitive advantage. According to them, resources are "stocks of available factors that are owned or controlled by the firm", and capabilities "refer to a firm's capacity to deploy Resources" (Amit and Schoemaker 1993, p. 4). In particular, they concluded that the rent-producing capacity of these strategic assets partly depends on their own unique characteristics as well as on the extent to which they overlap with the industry-determined strategic industry factors. Table 3.2 summarizes selected key contributions to the growth of the RBV.

Table 3.2: The growth stage of resource-based theory: selected key papers, based on Barney et al. (2011)

Author(s)	Date Key Contribution
Mahoney and Pandian (1992)	Further delineated the RBV by relating it to distinctive competencies, organizational economics, and theory on industrial organization
Kogut and Zander (1992)	Introduced the concept of combinative capabilities; emphasized the importance of knowledge as a resource
Amit and Schoemaker (1993)	Split the overall construct of resources into resources and capabilities
Peteraf (1993)	Outlined the conditions under which competitive advantage exists
Hart (1995b)	Introduced and developed a conceptual spin-off of the RBV called the natural-resource-based view of the firm
Grant (1996b)	Articulated the knowledge-based view of the firm as a spinoff of the RBV
Miller and Shamsie (1996)	Tested the resources-performance link while measuring resources directly; winner of Academy of Management Journal's annual best paper award
Conner and Prahalad (1996)	Identified situations where the application of opportunism-based arguments and knowledge-based arguments may lead to opposite predictions regarding the organization of economic activity
Oliver (1997)	Theorized about how the RBV and institutional theory together can better explain sustained competitive advantage
Teece et al. (1997)	Built on the RBV to introduce the concept of dynamic capabilities; in particular, explained competitive advantage as arising from the confluence of assets, processes, and evolutionary paths
Coff (1999)	Initiated discussion of how the excess profits derived from resources might be appropriated by various stakeholders
Combs and Ketchen (1999)	Examined how to reconcile competing predictions from the RBV and organizational economics about the choice of organizational form

3.1.3 Maturity stage: From a view to a theory of the firm

According to Barney et al. (2011), the academic literature indicates that the RBV has reached the maturity stage. The reasons for this - for instance, the transition from a RBV to a resource-based theory or the integration of the RBV with other theoretical perspectives - were described briefly at the beginning of this chapter. This maturity stage was initiated by Alvarez and Busenitz's (2001) paper on the contribution of the RBV to entrepreneurship research and their articulation of further avenues for RBV research. This research started at the turn of the millennium and is still ongoing today. Furthermore, Wright et al. (2001) explained the contributions of the RBV to human resource management research and called for further contributions in that area of investigation. Additionally, Makadok and Barney (2001) built theory about the information that firms should emphasize as they attempt to purchase scarce resources. Makadok (2001) synthesized the ideas on excess profits offered by the RBV and by theory on dynamic capabilities. Opening a new field of discussion, Lippman and Rumelt (2003) introduced micro-foundations of the RBV with respect to a payments perspective. In the field of entrepreneurship, Ireland et al. (2003) introduced strategic entrepreneurship, in which firms recognize the resources required to exploit growth opportunities to create and sustain competitive advantage. Complementing the work of Teece et al. (1997), Winter (2003) introduced and explained the concept of higher order capabilities. Fueling the research on micro-foundations, Gavetti (2005) built theory about the micro-foundations of dynamic capabilities by emphasizing the roles of cognition and hierarchy. Similarly, Teece (2007) specified the nature and micro-foundations of the capabilities necessary to sustain superior enterprise performance in an open economy with rapid innovation and globally dispersed sources of invention, innovation, and manufacturing capability. Explicating the RBV, Sirmon et al. (2007) built theory about the underexplored processes (which they called the "black box") that lie between resources on the one hand and superior profitability on the other. Finally, Armstrong and Shimizu (2007) reviewed and critiqued the research methods used in resource-based inquiry. However, although many authors have emphasized the importance of a RBV of the firm and contributed to its development and growth, the theory is not without critique (cf. Priem and Butler 2001a; Kraaijenbrink et al. 2010).

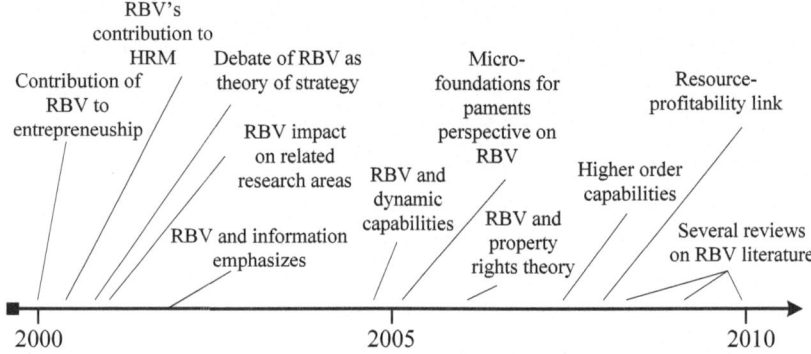

Figure 3.3: Conceptual contributions during the mature stage

The following paragraphs briefly describe some of the key contributions to the maturity phase of the RBV. Barney et al. (2001) organized a new special issue to assess contributions to the RBV. To analyze the impact of the RBV since Barney's (1991) initial contribution, they adopted a dual approach: (1) they asked contributors from the 1991 issue to revisit their earlier articles and to consider further developments to the RBV and (2) they analyzed new full-length papers contributing to specific subjects of the RBV. According to their analysis, the RBV has (1) substantially contributed to the emerging field of strategic human resource management; (2) substituted and complemented research in the field of economics and finance, especially in the field of corporate restructuring; (3) potential to influence research in the field of entrepreneurship, especially with respect to the entrepreneurial processes of cognition, discovery, understanding market opportunities, and coordinating knowledge; (4) only gained little attention in the field of marketing as a frame of reference for advancing marketing theory or for analyzing core challenges in marketing practice; and (5) enriched established research of multinational corporations and market entries in the field of international business. Fi-

nally, Barney et al. (2001) concluded that articles from the 1991 special issue
"have made giant contributions to the study of management"(p. 637). The
following description of articles in the section will further elaborate on the
establishment of the RBV in different research areas.

Foss and Foss (2005) complemented the work of Conner (1991) and Amit
and Schoemaker (1993) by further describing the relationship between resources and transaction costs and how property rights economics furthers
the RBV. In particular, the questions they address are as follows: How do
transaction costs influence value creation and appropriation? And which
new insights regarding opportunities for value creation and appropriation
have been provided by a transaction cost focus? Their conceptualization
provides insight into value creation and value appropriation. In particular,
the value that a resource owner can create or appropriate not only depends
on the use, scarcity and outside options of the resource but also on the costs
of trading and protecting the property rights to the attributes that com-
prise the resource. Thus, they state, transaction costs influence the value
of resources, along with conditions of scarcity, demand, imitability and sustainability. Finally, they conclude that property rights economics can significantly contribute to the RBV analysis of strategic opportunities.

Crook et al. (2008) addressed the critique of the RBV that possible intervening steps between strategic resources and performance remain largely
unexplored. Therefore, they applied a meta-analysis, a technique that sta-
tistically aggregates empirical findings to discern whether relationships exist
and to provide estimates of their size, to assess the extent to which strategic resources relate to performance. In sum, they analyzed 125 studies
from the RBV involving 127 samples. Their study makes three contributions: (1) they provide a rigorously derived estimate of how much resources
influence performance, (2) they examine how much stronger the strategic
resources-performance relationship is when studies investigate resources that
more closely meet Barney's (1991) criteria; and finally, (3) they offer preliminary evidence regarding how much the resources-performance link differs
when performance measures reflect or do not reflect potential appropriation.

Their results provide evidence for the notion that the RBV "has become one of the most influential perspectives guiding strategic management" (Crook et al. 2008, p. 1153). Thereby, their results contrast with Newbert (2007), who stated that the RBV "has only modest support overall" (p. 121). Table 3.2 summarizes selected key contributions to the growth of the RBV.

The maturity phase introduced and further developed the concept of dynamic capabilities. As this is a core concept for this thesis, the following section will more closely elaborate on that construct.

3.2 Theoretical extensions of the RBV

3.2.1 The knowledge-based view (KBV) of the firm

Over the last several years, knowledge has become an important component of strategic management research. The concept of knowledge has been used in a variety of topics within strategy (see Eisenhardt and Santos 2000) such as strategic alliances (see Mowery et al. 1996; Simonin 1999), capability transfer (see Zander and Kogut 1995; Szulanski 1996), mergers and acquisitions (see Singh and Zollo 1999) and product development (see Hansen 1999; Hargadon 2002). The knowledge-based view (KBV) of the firm is a perspective that considers knowledge to be the most important and significant strategic resource of the firm (Grant 1996b). In line with the RBV, proponents of the KBV argue that heterogeneous knowledge bases and capabilities between firms are the main sources of sustained competitive advantage and superior firm performance. In this thesis, the KBV is viewed as an important theoretical extension providing the conceptual language and tools for analyzing knowledge as a firm resource. The following paragraphs will briefly describe the KBV's origins and development, core contributions and some examples of empirical research using the KBV as a theoretical underpinning. The section concludes with a discussion of critiques and limitations of the KBV.

Table 3.3: The maturity stage of resource-based theory: selected key papers, based on Barney et al. (2011)

Author(s)	Date Key Contribution
Alvarez and Busenitz (2001)	Explained the contributions of the RBV to entrepreneurship research and articulated further contributions that could be made
Priem and Butler (2001a,b); Barney (2001)	Debated the usefulness of the RBV as a theory of strategy and organization
Wright et al. (2001)	Explained the contributions of resource-based view (RBV) to human resource management research and articulated further contributions that could be made
Barney et al. (2001)	Identified the impact of the RBV on related subject areas
Makadok and Barney (2001)	Built theory about the information firms should emphasize when they attempt to purchase scarce resources
Makadok (2001)	Synthesized the ideas offered by the RBV on excess profits and theory on dynamic capabilities
Lippman and Rumelt (2003)	Initiated discussion of the micro-foundations of the RBV by introducing a payments perspective
Ireland et al. (2003)	Introduced strategic entrepreneurship as recognizing the resources required to exploit growth opportunities to create and sustain competitive advantage
Winter (2003)	Introduced and explained the concept of higher order capabilities
Gavetti (2005)	Built theory about the micro-foundations of dynamic capabilities by emphasizing the roles of cognition and hierarchy
Foss and Foss (2005)	Built conceptual bridges between RBV and property rights theory
Teece (2007)	Specified the nature and micro-foundations of the capabilities necessary to sustain superior enterprise performance in an open economy with rapid innovation and globally dispersed sources of invention, innovation, and manufacturing capability
Sirmon et al. (2007)	Built theory about the underexplored processes (i.e., the "black box") that lie between resources on the one hand and superior profitability on the other
Armstrong and Shimizu (2007)	Reviewed and critiqued the research methods used in resource-based inquiry
Crook et al. (2008)	Used a meta-analysis to establish that strategic resources explain a significant portion of variance in performance across extant evidence
Kraaijenbrink et al. (2010)	Considered the merits of prominent critiques of RBV

In the field of strategic management, the concept of knowledge is usually applied from a Western epistemology (Eisenhardt and Santos 2000). Within strategic management, knowledge is considered to be "justified true belief" and modeled as an "unambiguous, reducible and easily transferable construct, while knowing is associated with processing information" (Eisenhardt and Santos 2000, p. 3). This perspective put the focus of theories on the explicit nature of knowledge and considers organizations to be machine-like knowledge keepers and information processors. However, in contrast with this traditional conception, a newer view of knowledge based on Polanyi's 1962 distinction between explicit and tacit knowledge has emerged.

Table 3.4: Selected core contributions to the KBV

Author	Contributions and definitions
Dierickx and Cool (1989)	Conceptualized the knowledge of firms in terms of stocks and flows
Kogut and Zander (1992)	Emphasized knowledge as an important source of competitive advantage and that firms are better at creating and transferring knowledge within the organization
Nonaka and Takeuchi (1995)	Provided a framework for understanding the integration of individual and organizational knowledge
Grant (1996b,a)	Further articulated the theoretical foundation for a knowledge-based theory of the firm as a theory of organization (Grant 1996b) and as a theory of strategy (Grant 1996a)

Dierickx and Cool (1989) conceptualized the knowledge of firms in terms of stocks and flows. According to their definition, stocks of knowledge are accumulated knowledge assets, while flows describe knowledge streams within and between organizations. In line with the RBV, they argue that superior stocks and flows are sources of sustained competitive advantage and superior performance. In a very similar vein, Kogut and Zander (1992) also emphasized knowledge as an important source of competitive advantage. By positing that firms are better at creating and transferring knowledge within the organization, they provided the foundation for a knowledge-based theory of the firm. They concluded that firms are able to grow and deter competitive imitation only by continuously recombining their knowledge and applying it to new market opportunities (Eisenhardt and Santos 2000). Thus, in a competitive environment, sustained superior performance can only be reached through continuous innovation.

Building on and complementing Kogut and Zander's (1992) work, Nonaka and Takeuchi (1995) provided a framework for understanding the integration of individual and organizational knowledge. The framework contains individual knowledge creation and organizational crystallization processes that constitute a highly iterative knowledge spiral. This spiral continuously shifts between tacit and explicit knowledge at the individual and organizational levels. Their framework proposes that the knowledge creating process depends on several enabling conditions, namely the existence of redundancy, requisite variety and creative chaos (Eisenhardt and Santos 2000).

Starting with his contribution in the 1996 Strategic Management Journal special issue, Grant further articulated the theoretical foundation for a theory of the firm (Grant 1996b,a). Both contributions - as a theory of organization (Grant 1996a) and as a theory of strategy (Grant 1996b) - have been widely applied in the field of strategic management (Eisenhardt and Santos 2000). In particular, tacit knowledge is seen as the source of sustained competitive advantage. However, because production activities usually require the combination of specialized and individual knowledge, organizational capabilities are crucial for achieving an advantage. According to (Grant 1996b), the ability to integrate this individual knowledge and apply it to new products or services is the essence of the firm. Based on this understanding, Grant (1996a) proposed a knowledge-based theory of the firm in which sustained competitive advantage is determined by non-proprietary knowledge in the form of tacit individual knowledge. Because this tacit individual knowledge is both unique and immobile, the firm's ability to integrate it becomes a critical element for sustained competitive advantage. Finally, Grant (1996a) described three characteristics of knowledge integration that increase strategic value: (1) the efficiency of integration as a function of common knowledge and the frequency and variability of tasks; (2) the scope of that integration, as it facilitates the creation and preservation of competitive advantage; and (3) the flexibility of that integration to include new knowledge (Eisenhardt and Santos 2000).

Eisenhardt and Santos (2000) conclude that given the current theoretical perspective on knowledge, the KBV cannot be regarded as a full theory of strategy that goes beyond the RBV of the firm and the related dynamic capabilities approach. If knowledge is conceptualized as a resource, the KBV simply becomes a special form of the RBV. However, they admit that the KBV as a theoretical extension provides useful insights:

> *So, what is the KBV? Our view is that KBV offers enormously useful theoretical insights, well grounded in empirical findings that address the multi-level social processes through which knowledge is sourced, transferred and integrated within and across organizations. Although KBV is not fully developed, there is already a surprisingly consistent body of empirical results that is capable of informing theory-building and managerial practice. These findings point to a knowledge-based theory that is consistent with a pluralistic understanding of knowledge, and a view of organizations as complex adaptive systems, where meaning is socially constructed through ongoing activities of semi-autonomous groups. The implications for strategy remain more distant.* (Eisenhardt and Santos 2000, p. 46)

3.2.2 High-velocity environments and dynamic capabilities

Dynamic capabilities (Teece et al. 1997) have attracted increasing attention within the management literature in recent years. Introduced as an extension to the more static RBV, the dynamic capabilities construct was developed to address the question of how firms can successfully be managed in *hyper-*

competitive (D'Aveni 1994) or *high-velocity environments* (Eisenhardt and Martin 2000). Because in such a context, the achievement of long-term competitive advantage is harder, dynamic capabilities aim at building successive advantages by effectively responding to environmental shocks (D'Aveni 1994; Eisenhardt and Martin 2000).

Barreto (2010) argues that the rapidly expanding dynamic capability literature has resulted in three challenges: (1) it has provided successive and distinct definitions of the construct that might lead to confusion among researchers; (2) it has led to a rich but complex and somewhat disconnected body of research pointing in disparate directions; and finally, (3) despite the substantial body of work, dynamic capabilities have been subject to some important criticisms. The following section will provide a brief overview of the introduction of the construct by Teece et al. (1997) as well as its further development by Eisenhardt and Martin (2000) and others. Table 3.5 illustrates definitions and key contributions to the concept since it was introduced in 1997 (see Barreto 2010).

In 1994, Teece and Pisano (1994) first defined the subset of competences and capabilities that allow the firm to create new products and processes and to respond to changing market circumstances. However, it was not until 1997 that Teece et al. (1997) proposed a framework of dynamic capabilities to overcome the limitations of the classical RBV, namely its static nature and its inability to explain firms' competitive advantage in changing environments (Priem and Butler 2001a). Therefore, they define dynamic capabilities as "the firm's ability to integrate, build, and reconfigure internal and external competences to address rapidly changing environments" (Teece et al. 1997, p. 516).

In 2000, Eisenhardt and Martin (2000) attempted to clarify the RBV's logic of dynamic capabilities, resources, and competitive advantage. Therefore, they defined dynamic capabilities as the "firm's processes that use resources to match and create market change; dynamic capabilities thus are the organizational and strategic routines by which firms achieve new resource

Table 3.5: Enhancing the RBV: Dynamic capabilities (see Barreto 2010)

Author	Contributions and definitions
Teece and Pisano (1994)	The subset of competences and capabilities that allow the firm to create new products and processes and respond to changing market circumstances
Teece et al. (1997)	The firm's ability to integrate, build, and reconfigure internal and external competences to address rapidly changing environments
Eisenhardt and Martin (2000)	The firm's processes that use resources to adapt to and create market change; dynamic capabilities are thus the organizational and strategic routines by which firms achieve new resource configurations as markets emerge, collide, split, evolve, and die
Teece (2000)	The ability to sense and seize opportunities quickly and proficiently
Zollo and Winter (2002)	A dynamic capability is a learned and stable pattern of collective activity through which the organization systematically generates and modifies its operating routines in pursuit of improved effectiveness
Winter (2003)	Dynamic capabilities operate to extend, modify, or create ordinary capabilities
Zahra et al. (2006)	The abilities to reconfigure a firm's resources and routines as envisioned and deemed appropriate by its principal decision maker(s)
Teece (2007)	Dynamic capabilities can be disaggregated into the capacity (a) to seize and shape opportunities and threats, (b) to seize opportunities, and (c) to maintain competitiveness through enhancing, combining, protecting, and, when necessary, reconfiguring the business enterprise's intangible and tangible assets
Helfat et al. (2009)	The capacity of an organization to purposefully create, extend, or modify its resource base

configurations as markets emerge, collide, split, evolve, and die" (p. 1107). Following Teece and Pisano (1994); Teece et al. (1997) and Eisenhardt and Martin (2000), several alternative conceptualizations of dynamic capabilities were subsequently offered. Table 3.5 illustrates some of the main "follow-up" definitions.

According to Barreto (2010), some of these "follow-up" definitions are closer to the classical RBV while others focus more on the evolutionary aspects of economics. Therefore, and because of the initially described rapid expansion of the literature, these definitions vary significantly in terms of "nature, specific role, relevant context, creation and evolution mechanism, types of outcome, heterogeneity assumptions, and purpose of dynamic capabilities" (Barreto 2010, p. 259). For instance, (Teece 2000) defined dynamic capabilities as the ability to sense and seize opportunities quickly and proficiently. For (Zollo and Winter 2002), a dynamic capability is a learned and stable pattern of collective activity through which the organization systematically generates and modifies its operating routines in pursuit of improved effectiveness. Similarly, (Winter 2003) argues that dynamic capabilities operate to extend, modify, or create ordinary capabilities. From a top-management perspective, (Zahra et al. 2006) define dynamic capabilities as the ability to reconfigure a firm's resources and routines as envisioned and deemed appropriate by its principal decision maker(s). In their most recent work, (Teece 2007) argues that dynamic capabilities can be disaggregated into the capacity (a) to seize and shape opportunities and threats, (b) to seize opportunities, and (c) to maintain competitiveness by enhancing, combining, protecting, and when necessary, reconfiguring the business enterprise's intangible and tangible assets. For (Helfat et al. 2009), a dynamic capability is the capacity of an organization to purposefully create, extend, or modify its resource base.

Based on his analysis of the dynamic capability literature and past research, Barreto (2010) suggested his own definition of dynamic capabilities that "accommodates old and new suggestions within the field and also attempts to overcome some of their limitations" (p. 271):

A dynamic capability is the firm's potential to systematically solve problems, formed by its propensity to sense opportunities and threats, to make timely and market-oriented decisions, and to change its resource base. (Barreto 2010, p. 271)

According to Barreto (2010), this definition has several advantages over earlier definitions "relating to the nature of the construct, in terms of either form or substance" (p. 272): (1) it is an encompassing but coherent definition that captures the richness and the essence of a large body of work; (2) by considering dynamic capability as the potential to systematically solve problems, it attempts to clarify the nature of the construct; (3) the noun 'potential' fulfills two roles: (a) it highlights that dynamic capabilities are not viewed as a synonym to success and (b) it avoids framing the concept in a dichotomous way, instead allowing different firms to have different levels of dynamic capabilities.

The following section will provide a brief overview of the importance of knowledge as an organizational resource and of the KBV of the firm.

3.2.3   Firm-level value creation and capture

As already mentioned during the introduction to the RBV, strategic management scholars have used the term 'value' to define resource capability outputs. However, more recently, they have started to reconsider the concept of value and, more precisely, the distinction between value capture and value creation. In strategic management, the concept of value has typically been viewed from the producer's perspective rather than from a consumer perspective. Priem (2007) sees two reasons for this:

1. a major objective in strategic management is to create value for stakeholders, which leads to the question of which resources explain differences in firm performance and an internal firm perspective on value, and

2. industrialization has increasingly separated production and consumption decisions, which leads to a separation in production decisions on resources and consumption decisions on alternatives.

Following this rationale in this thesis, I focus on the producer perspective of value while remaining aware of the entire body of work on the consumer-oriented value perspective in the service and marketing literature (cf. Grönroos and Ravald 2011).

In their early discussion on the nature of value, Bowman and Ambrosini (2000) provide a conceptual discussion of value creation and value capture. To overcome the definitional problem that arose from using the term 'value' to refer to different phenomena, they distinguished two types of value: use value and exchange value. They define use value as the

> "perceived used value that is subjectively assessed by the customer who uses consumer surplus as the criterion in making a purchase decision". Exchange value, they define as "the price paid for the use value created, which is realized when the sales takes place" (p. 4).

Based on the conceptual separation, they were able to describe and explain value creation and capture processes more clearly. According to their work, value creation refers to a process of use value transformations between certain organizations and the realization of exchange value through it. In the example below, Organization A produces use value and offers it to Organization B. Thus, by exchanging use value, an exchange value for Organization A is created. Organization B, however, transforms the use value by adding labor or other (production) factors and creates a new use value for an Organization C. This process repeats for Organization B and C. Figure 3.4 illustrates the transition of use and exchange value among multiple firms.

Value capture describes the concept of capturing value from transformation processes. Value capture is determined by the bargaining relationships

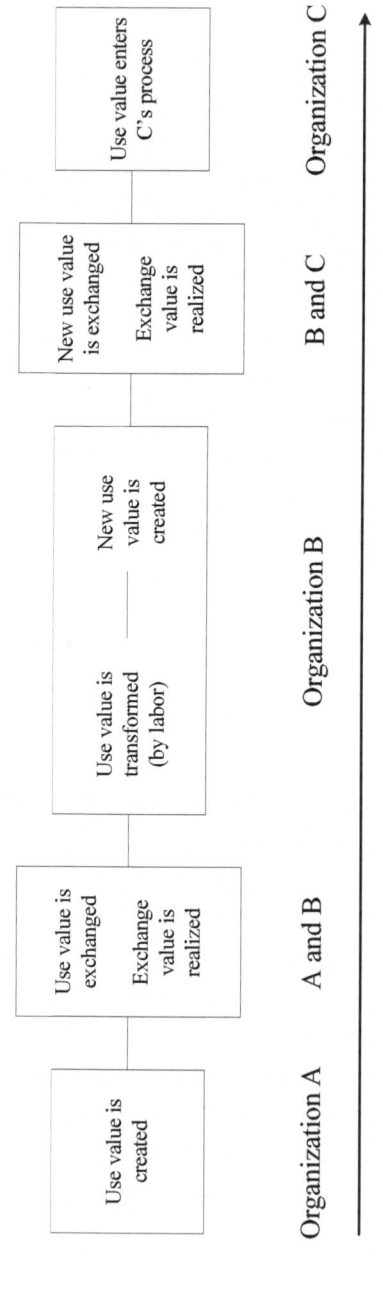

Figure 3.4: Transition of use and exchange value based on Bowman and Ambrosini (2000)

between the firm and the customer and between the resource provider and the firm. Profits are determined through exchanges between the firm and resource sellers or customers. Thus, the RBV perspective on internal idiosyncrasies in the resource bundles processed by the firm and the market-oriented perspective on the external relationships of the firm with suppliers and buyers each explain one half of the story. According to Bowman and Ambrosini's work on business processes, the organization that creates value does not necessarily have to be the one that captures the exchange value. Thus, the capture of value is not only determined by the organization that produces value but also by bargaining relationships.

Lepak et al. (2007) broaden Bowman and Amborsini's definition of use and exchange value. They argue that for a analytical discussion of value, value creation and value capture, it is important to not only include an organizational perspective but also to include multiple levels of analysis. Thus, they define the concepts of use and exchange value on the individual, organizational and social levels.

Thus, they define use value as "the specific quality of a new job, task, product, or service as perceived by users in relation to their needs". In a similar vein, they broaden the initial definition of exchange value: "either the monetary amount realized at a certain point in time, when the exchange of a new task, good, service, or product takes place, or the amount paid by the user to the seller for the use value of the focal task, job, product, or service."

Additionally, Lepak et al. (2007) broaden the concept of value creation by discussing it on three levels of analysis: the individual, the organization, and society. First, individuals create value through creative actions with the goal of making their job/service more novel and appropriate in the eyes of their employer or of a potential end user in a specific context. Second, different stakeholders have different, and perhaps competing, opinions and viewpoints of what they consider to be valuable. Thus, organizations must recognize and reconcile these differences in targets and in producers of value of among stakeholders. Finally, the creation of value on a societal level is greatly distinguished from the individual or organizational level: on a societal level, actors intentionally or unintentionally create value for society and value for themselves at the same time. This discussion shows that value creation is a very unique issue depending on the level of analysis.

To understand the concept of value capture at multiple levels of analysis, Lepak et al. (2007) introduce the concept of value slippage. Value slippage refers to a situation where the party that creates new use value does not retain the newly created value. This occurs if, for instance, the use value is high, while the exchange value is low. They argue that, similar to the value creation process, the value capture process differs depending on the level of analysis and that each level applies different competition and isolating mechanisms to explain value slippage. Completion will lead to the decline of exchange value as other suppliers will seek to replicate a new value. In a similar vein, isolation mechanisms are barriers that may prevent replication of the value creation task or process. Thus, they enable the source of value creation to capture most of the value created.

Figure 3.5 illustrates the components of value creation and capture on the firm level according to (Lepak et al. 2007).

3.3 The RBV as a complement to the theory of the firm

The following paragraphs will elaborate on the key characteristics of transaction cost economics - as one example of a "theory of environmental factors" - and compare them to those of the RBV. The term "transaction cost" was coined by Ronald Coase, who introduced it in his theoretical framework for predicting whether certain economic tasks would be performed *in firms* or *in the market* (Coase 1937). Transaction cost reasoning became widely known as part of Oliver E. Williamson's (1975) Transaction Cost

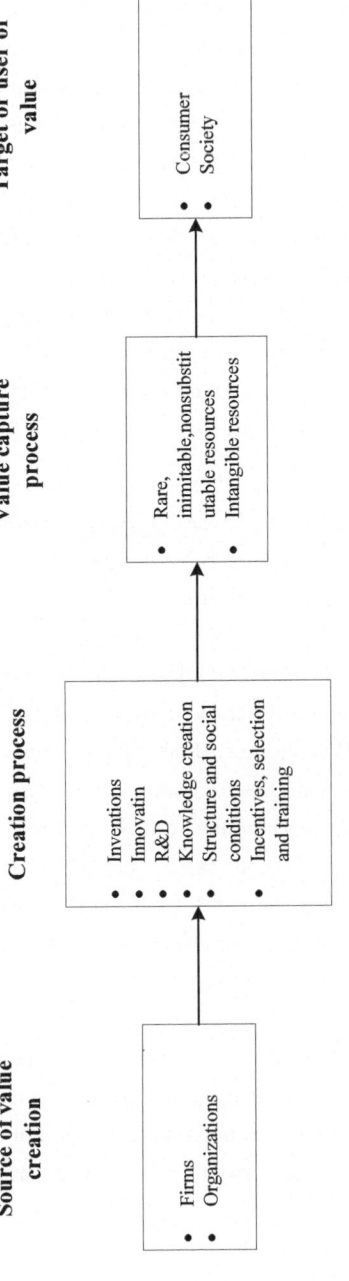

Figure 3.5: Firm-level value creation and capture based on Lepak et al. (2007)

Economics, for which he was awarded the Nobel Memorial Prize in Economics in 2009. Williamson's (1975; 1985) major contribution was to build a predictive theory by micro-analytically approaching the firm as a governance structure and by identifying the particular transaction characteristics that play an important role in comparative institutional assessments (Madhok 2002). According to Williamson, the determinants of transaction costs are *frequency, specificity, uncertainty, limited rationality, and opportunistic behavior* (Williamson 1975). Today, transaction cost economics is used to explain not only the obvious cases of buying and selling but also vertical and lateral integration, transfer pricing, corporate finance, marketing, the organization of work, long-term commercial contracting, franchising, regulation, and many others (cf. Shelanski and Klein 1995).

According to Madhok (2002), there are numerous reasons why the supporters of the two theories –TCE and RBV – have avoided a dialog; see (Table 3.6). First, in contrast to the TCE perspective on the theory of the firm, the RBV is *a theory of a (particular) firm*. Thus it is not a surprise that both theories basically address two different questions: TCE tries to answer (broadly) *why firms exist,* while the RBV asks *why they differ* (or why there are performance differences across firms). Thus, their domain of interest is correspondingly different: TCE searches for a efficient governance structure, while the RBV searches for competitive advantage or superior performance. Because both theories focus on two different aspects of economic activity, exchange and production, their focus of analysis differs: it lies on the transaction for the TCE and on a firms' resources/capabilities for the RBV. Accordingly, one analyzes transaction attributes (e.g., specificity of assets, measurement difficulty), while the other analyzes resource attributes (e.g., value, imitability, stickiness). Given their paradigmatic differences and the fact that the TCE primarily focuses on costs while the RBV emphasizes resources/capabilities, "it is not altogether unexpected that their respective approaches to understanding firm behavior and economic organization differ and that they have paid inadequate attention to understanding how the two aspects of production and exchange relate to one another" (Madhok 2002, p. 540).

Table 3.6: Transaction cost and resource-based theories of the firm: a comparison based on Madhok (2002, p. 540)

	Transaction cost theory	Resource-based theory
Broad theoretical arena	Theory of *the* firm	Theory of *a* firm
Primary theoretical question	Why do firms exist?	Why do firms differ?
Primary driver	Search for an efficient governance structure	Search for a competitive advantage
Primary domain of interest	Exchange and the transaction	Production and firm resources/capabilities
Primary focus of analysis	Transaction attributes (e.g., asset specificity)	Resource attributes (e.g., value, stickiness)
Primary emphasis	(Transaction) Costs	Firm resources, skills, knowledge, routines

Despite their different perspectives and paradigms, there are several elements that link the two theories (Madhok 2002). First, a firm can be seen as both a collectivity of transactions as well as a bundle of resources. Additionally, governance skills, both within and across firm boundaries, can result in performance differences and competitive advantage. If firms are superior to markets for reasons of efficiency, this may well be not just because of reduced transaction costs but also due to productivity-increasing factors tied to superior capabilities and resources. Second, scholars have documented support for both kinds of costs, and interestingly, Madhok (2002) states that a large part of the make-or-buy decision can be explained by variations in internal organizational costs, most of these stemming from a dissimilarity of skills with respect to the relevant task.

In sum, the tendency to focus on transaction costs in the strategic literature is not always sufficient and reflects a lack of scholarly dialogue. Rather, as a result of the commonalities and interdependencies, the challenge and the opportunity of both perspectives "lies in uncovering the interrelationships between these two sets of costs and, correspondingly, between hierarchical (production) and market (exchange) relations. Such a theoretical schema would considerably improve our insight into economic organization" Madhok (2002, p. 540).

3.4   Challenges of applying the RBV

As already highlighted, the RBV has become one of the dominant theories in strategic management. Given its elegant simplicity and its immediate face validity, the RBV's core message is appealing, easily grasped, and easily taught (Kraaijenbrink et al. 2010). Scholars have extensively criticized and discussed the RBV for many weaknesses Priem and Butler (see 2001a,b); Barney et al. (see 2001). However, critiques are valuable for advancing understanding, and an explicit and lively discussion of limitations reveals areas for potentially improving the RBV. Along these lines, Kraaijenbrink et al. (2010) categorizes and assesses eight categories of critiques, adding comments about their severity and impact. The following paragraphs will briefly summarize those critiques and their implications.

The first critique Kraaijenbrink et al. (2010) describe is that the RBV has no managerial implications or operational validity (see Priem and Butler 2001a). The RBV proposes to develop and obtain VRIN resources and capabilities but does not provide explanations for how this should be done. Furthermore, it suffers from tension between descriptive and prescriptive theorizing (Lado et al. 2006) as well as from trivializing property rights issues and exaggerating the extent to which resources can be controlled or future value can be predicted. (McGuinness and Morgan 2000). As a second critique, Kraaijenbrink et al. (2010) formulate that the RBV entails an infinite regress (Priem and Butler 2001a, see). The point of this critique is that identifying higher-order capabilities can be extended ad infinitum and can lead firms into an endless search for these types of capabilities. Third, Kraaijenbrink et al. (2010) describe the RBV's applicability as being limited

Table 3.7: Summary and assessment of critiques of the Resource-Based View (RBV) (see Kraaijenbrink et al. 2010)

Critique	Assessment
1. The RBV has no managerial implications	Not all theories should have direct managerial implications. Through its wide dissemination, the RBV has evident impact.
2. The RBV implies infinite regress	Applies only to abstract mathematical theories. In an applied theory such as the regress RBV, levels are qualitatively different. It may be fruitful to focus on the interactions between levels rather than to consider higher levels as a source of SCA.
3. The RBV's applicability is too limited	Generalizing about uniqueness is not impossible by definition. The RBV applies to small firms and startups as well, as long as they strive for a SCA. Path dependency is not problematic when not taken to the extreme. The RBV applies only to firms in predictable environments.
4. SCA is not achievable	By including dynamic capabilities, the RBV is not purely static, although it only explains ex post, not ex ante, the sources of SCA. Although no CA can last forever, a focus on SCA remains useful.

Note: SCA = sustained competitive advantage; TCE = transaction cost economics; VRIN/O = valuable, rare, inimitable, and nonsubstitutable resources and capabilities plus organization.

because (1) the notion of resource uniqueness denies the RBV the potential for generalization (Gibbert 2006a,b), (2) the RBV only applies to large firms (Connor 2002), and (3) referring to the "sustainability-attainability" discussion, only firms that posses VIRN resources can acquire and apply additional resources (Miller 2003). (4) Kraaijenbrink et al. (2010) argue that sustainable competitive advantage (SCA) is not achievable. Instead, skills and resources constantly change, which leads to the creation of continuously changing temporary advantage (cf. Eisenhardt and Martin 2000).

Table 3.8: Summary and assessment of critiques of the RBV (continued)

Critique	Assessment
5. The RBV is not a theory of the firm	The RBV does not sufficiently explain why firms exist. Rather than requiring this explanation, the RBV should be further developed as a theory of SCA and leave additional explanations of firm existence to TCE.
6. VRIN/O is neither necessary nor sufficient for SCA	The VRIN/O criteria are not always necessary and not always sufficient to explain a firm's SCA. The RBV does not sufficiently consider the synergy within resource bundles as a source of SCA. The RBV does not sufficiently recognize the role that judgment and mental models of individuals play in value assessment and creation.
7. The value of a resource is too indeterminate to provide for useful theory	The current conceptualization of value turns the RBV into a trivial heuristic, an incomplete theory, or a tautology. A more subjective and creative notion of value is needed.
8. The definition of resource is unworkable	Definitions of resources are all inclusive. The RBV does not recognize differences between resources as inputs and resources that enable the organization of such inputs. There is no recognition of how different types of resources may contribute to SCA in a different manner.

Note: SCA = sustained competitive advantage; TCE = transaction cost economics; VRIN/O = valuable, rare, inimitable, and nonsubstitutable resources and capabilities plus organization.

Fifth, it is argued that the RBV is not a theory of the firm. The RBV explains differences between firms and explains why firms exist. However, to explain why firms exist and why they are better than markets at rent creation, specific references especially to asset ownership and opportunism are required (see Foss 1996a,b). Sixth, Kraaijenbrink et al. (2010) state that the VIRN/O characteristic is neither necessary nor sufficient for SCA. For instance, Armstrong and Shimizu (2007); Newbert (2007) argue that there is a lack of empirical support for the notion that VRIN/O lead to SCA. Furthermore, it has been noted that the possession of resources is not sufficient, and the organization needs to be able to deploy them to attain SCA (cf. Peteraf and Barney 2003). Seventh, another critique that has been widely discussed is that the value of a resource is too indeterminate to provide for useful theory (Kraaijenbrink et al. 2010). Instead, the claim is that the RBV is a tautology that fails to fulfill the criteria for a true theory (Priem and Butler 2001a,b). Finally, the RBV is criticized because its definitions of a resource are inclusive and unworkable (Kraaijenbrink et al. 2010). These inclusive definitions are problematic because (1) they do not distinguish between resources and capabilities and (2) the RBV does not address how different resources contribute in a different manner to a firm's SCA.

Table 3.7 summarizes the eight critiques as well as the Kraaijenbrink et al. (2010) answer to each of them. According to them, the current RBV can withstand the first five critiques (Critiques 1–5), especially when the RBV's variables, boundaries and applicability are more clearly specified. However, they also claim that the last three critiques (Critiques 6–8) address essential concepts - resource and value - of the RBV and threaten its status as a core theory. Therefore, they suggest three avenues for further research and theorizing: (1) demarcating and defining resources, (2) more investigation and development of a subjective firm-specific notion of resource value and (3) positioning the RBV as a theory of sustained competitive advantage. This thesis tries to address those limitations, starting with summarizing the theoretical RBV framework as a foundation for the following analysis.

3.5 Summary and theoretical lens

This chapter briefly introduced the origins and development of the RBV as a theory of the firm. It provided an overview of the three developmental phases of the RBV, provided a closer look at dynamic capabilities as a theoretical extension of the core concepts and finally illustrated different types of value as strategic outputs of resources and capabilities. The next chapter covers the methodological foundation of this study and presents its overall research framework. Figure 3.6 summarizes and illustrates the important contributions to the RBV and provides the foundational theoretical lens for the rest of this thesis.

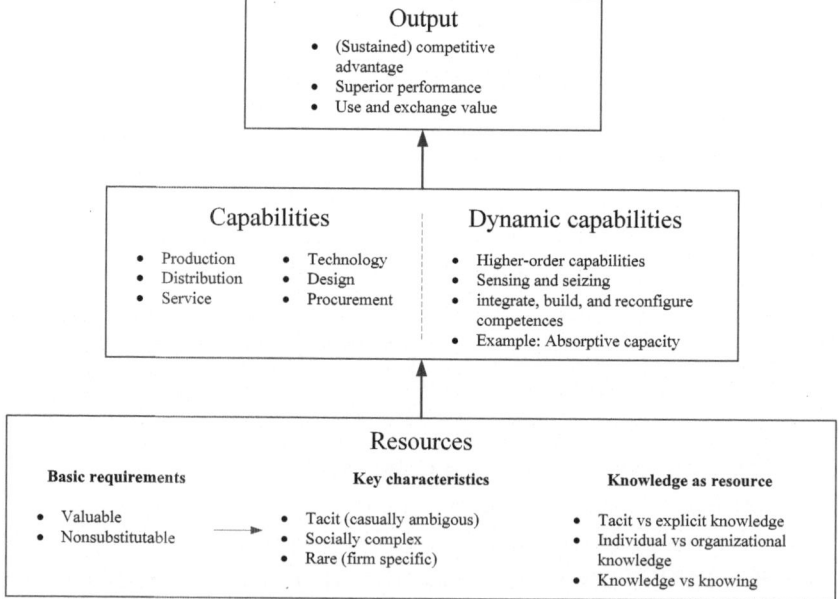

Figure 3.6: Overview of the RBV and the theoretical lens

Chapter 4

Qualitative investigation I: Exploring software customization from the vendors' and customers' perspectives

The study in this chapter builds upon the existing body of knowledge on software customization and the concepts of resources, capabilities and value from the RBV as presented in the last two chapters. It aims to provide a deeper understanding of software customization activities from a software vendor firm's perspective. Thus, the study presented in this chapter can be regarded a pilot study to address the thesis' main research question:

> **MRQ:** *How do software vendor firms align their software product management and customization activities?*

To answer this question, several research objectives need to be achieved. This first study's objective is to identify the knowledge resources and distinctive capabilities underlying successful customization activities as well as their value impact for vendor and customer firms. Thus, it specifically addresses the following sub-research questions:

SRQ 1: *Which resources and capabilities do software vendor firms need to offer valuable software systems to their customers?*

SRQ 2: *What value does software customization provide for vendor and customer companies?*

To answer these questions, this chapter employs a qualitative interview study design involving multiple customer and vendor firms on the topic of software customization and investigates the resources and capabilities necessary to provide customer oriented use value as well as vendor-oriented exchange value through customization activities. Figure 4.1 illustrates the data collection, consolidation, and display steps employed in this study were evaluated through presentation in practical and theoretically oriented workshops.

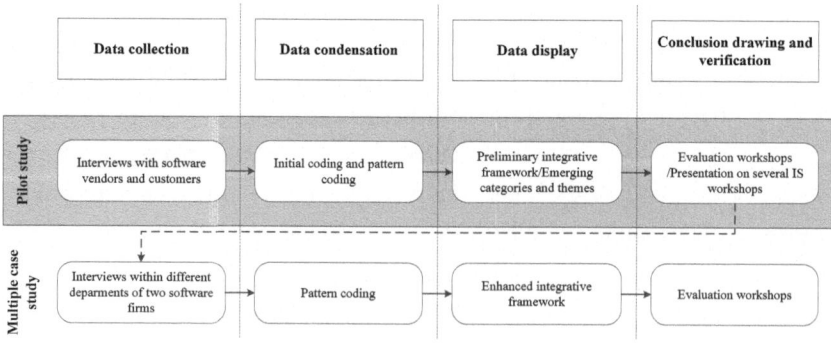

Figure 4.1: The integration of qualitative investigation I in the overall research design

4.1   Empirical setting and data collection

This study was designed following the procedure used by Ulaga and Reinartz (2011). Based on insights from the analysis of the software customization literature and the recommendations presented in the methodological foundation of this thesis, I crafted a semi-structured interview guide that aimed to identify the key characteristics of software customization as well as the resources and capabilities necessary to provide efficient and effective software customization activities. It also aimed to identify the value provided by customization activities from both a vendor and a customer perspective.

The interview guide was pre-tested with two experienced participants from software development companies; this allowed me to familiarize myself with the topic of customization and to craft the interview guide for subsequent interviews. The participants were a senior developer from a company that develops software for the telecommunication business and a senior consultant from a company that develops innovation management software. Both companies later became part of this study in the elaboration phase. Data from these interviews were transcribed and reviewed several times to identify themes and specific issues raised by the interview participants.

Throughout the initial analysis of the two interview transcripts, it became clear that customization activities are a multi perspective topic and that many stakeholders are involved in this process. Recurring examples of stakeholders from a vendor perspective, for instance, were the support and service department, the product development department and the marketing and sales department. It also became very clear that customization strongly depends on the customer's integration into the process. Accordingly, I adapted the interview guide in that form, so that it addresses the participants' opportunities to benefit from customization activities and their participation in and control of customization tasks.

---

[2]Some of the results reported in this chapter were presented at the SIG SVC pre-ICIS Workshop 2013 in Milan, Italy (Bertram et al. 2013)

Ultimately, data for the study were collected through twenty-two semi-structured interviews with key informants of vendor and customer organizations operating in the business-to-business software development and implementation industry. Specifically, I conducted thirteen interviews at software vendor firms and nine interviews at customer firms (see Table 4.1 and Table 4.2).

4.1.1   Sample characteristics

The interviews aimed to gather an in-depth understanding of customization experiences from both the vendor and the customer perspectives. Informants on both sides were people with several years of experience in customization projects, such as CEOs, CTOs, Senior Developers/Consultants and Department Heads; they were identified via a snowball method.

The key characteristics in Table 4.1 show that respondents from the vendor side represent industrial companies operating in various product markets including health care, mechanical engineering, social platform applications, software for service firms, monitoring and work-flow systems, email marketing and document management as well as consultancies and business intelligence. With one exception, the sample ranged from small- to mid-sized software companies employing up to 110 people. The exception is from the health care business and is a holding company that employs 8000 people in total. The interviewed managers in the firm were key decision makers such as senior developers or consultants, including also several executive board members.

As illustrated in Table 4.2, the respondents from the customer side represent industrial companies operating in various service or product markets including utilities, financial services, telecommunication services, IT services in the aviation industry and consulting services. Again with one exception, the sample ranges from small- to mid-sized software companies. The exception is from the aviation industry, where several department managers and

Table 4.1: Interview participants on the software provider side

Code	Name	Position	Age	Tenure	Firm Size	Revenue	Product/service offered
IV01	Bernd	CEO	47	23	8600**	€400m**	Software for health care administration
IV02	Greg	SM	37	3	80	€15m	Software for health care administration
IV03	Peter	CTO	41	11	N.A.	N.A.	Information management
IV04	Kurt	CEO	39	5	110	€18m	Software individualization/Mechanical engineering
IV05	Silvio	CTO	31	3	15	N.A.	Social platform applications
IV06	Georg	CEO	54	16	30	N.A.	Software for service firms (leasing)
IV07	Jörg	MD	33	8	50	€6m	Software for service firms (car retailer)
IV08a	Sven	CEO	50*	7	>80	€10m	Monitoring and workflow systems
IV08b	Harald	CTO	40*	12	>80	€10m	Monitoring and workflow systems
IV09	Armin	CEO	49	8	30	€4.5m	E-mail marketing
IV10	Timo	MD	37*	11	25	N.A.	Document management and system integration software
IV11	Stefan	CEO /CTO	40	6	40	N.A.	Third-party service provider BI
IV12	Werner	Entre-preneur	42	25	1	N.A.	Software development consultant

CEO-Chief executive officer; CMO-Chief marketing officer; CTO-Chief technology officer;
MD-Managing director; SM-Senior manager; DM-Department manager
*Estimated; **Figures pertain to holdings

senior project managers were interviewed. Again, the interviewed managers were key decision makers such as senior project managers and department managers, including also several executive board members.

Table 4.2: Interview participants on the software customer side

Code	Name	Position	Age	Firm Size	Revenue	Product/service offered
IC01	Sascha	CTO	51	400	€320m	Utility company
IC02	Gerd	PM	37	>100.000	€33bn	Financial services / banking
IC03	Bernd	PM	35	70	€450m**	Telecommunication services
IC04	Ahmed	MD	55	N.A.	N.A.	Book retailer
IC05	Roland	MD Maintenance	39	26500	€4bn	IT service provider aviation industry
IC07	Carsten	MD Support	37	26500	€4bn	IT service provider aviation industry
IC08	Klaus	PM	42	26500	€4bn	IT service provider aviation industry
IC09	Ingo	PM	40	26500	€4bn	IT service provider aviation industry
IC10	Dieter	PM	52	26500	€4bn	IT service provider aviation industry
IC11	Kai	DEV/PM	38	N.A.	N.A.	Consulting company

CEO-Chief executive officer; CMO-Chief marketing officer; CTO-Chief technology officer; MD-Managing director; SM-Senior manager; DM-Department manager
*Age estimated; **Figures pertain to holding

In developing the sample, I aimed to maximize diversity among the participating firms so that I could uncover critical customization resources and capabilities. However, the study participants and firms also needed to share some characteristics to allow for comparability. With respect to the vendor side, I only conducted interviews in firms that develop and customize their own software product or that provide software customization based on third-party products with a substantial amount of development and standardization activities.

Regarding the customer side, I aimed for firms where the software solutions used represent an important part of the company's business functional-

ity. In a similar vein, I sought diversity in the functions and hierarchical levels
represented by the participants. With the desired focus on key informants,
I needed participants that were empowered to make influential decisions for
their representative firms. Therefore, I invited only senior-level managers to
participate. The respondents' ages ranged from 31 to 55 years. Finally, the
qualitative sample consisted of key decision makers in 22 vendor or customer
firms. Regarding the exploratory nature of the study, the sample size is consistent with the sample sizes recommended for such research as described by
McCracken (1988).

4.1.2   Interview guide

The interviews were semi-structured to focus on the participants' experience
of customization activities and on customer integration and innovation topics
from both software vendor and customer perspectives. During the interviews,
informants were encouraged to talk freely about their real life experiences
with customization projects. The implementation of the interviews followed
the guidelines introduced by Myers and Newman (2007).

In the first part of the interviews, respondents were informed about the
topic and aims of the interview. Then, as an "ice-breaking" opening question,
they were asked about their position in the company and how long they
had been working for that company. This question was initially used as
an easy entry question to help the respondents relax at the start of the
interview and was not aimed to gather relevant data. However, it provided
interesting contextual and demographic data regarding the respondent and
their experience in their line of work. It also provided valuable information
to generally characterize each company's type of business.

In the second part, I asked the participant to talk about the products and/
or services that had been adapted to meet the customer's needs and how the
customer was involved and integrated in those customization activities. This
part of the interview aimed to generate examples of customization activities

and experiences and to develop an understanding of different types of software customization.

In the third part, I asked participants about their own experience with customization projects in their company. Examples of the types of questions asked are as follows: How are customization activities organized? Who leads customization activities? How is the customer integrated? How does customization regard future (strategic) developments, for instance, with respect to standardization or creating flexibility? In this section, I mainly attempted to understand how managers judged the efficiency and effectiveness of customization outcomes beyond revenues and margins.

In the closing section of the interview, respondents were asked to report their views of the customization activities needed to address customer solutions. I also asked for any potential topics that they felt had not been addressed in the interview but that might also be of interest in the domain of customization. Table 4.3 summarizes the interview guide for this study.

Due to the exploratory nature of the research design, the semi-structured interview guide was used for both customer and vendor interviews. However, I integrated template instructions for addressing questions differently in vendor versus customer interviews. To avoid the potential pitfalls of interview research (Myers and Newman 2007) such as "active listening" (McCracken 1988), I carefully phrased questions to elicit responses in an objective, non-directive manner. I also tried to let the interview participant choose the direction of the interview, only intervening when a topic shifted too far from my objectives. My main objective was to facilitate the emergence of key characteristics, capabilities and resources grounded in the manager's own language rather than to capture already specified variables.

Table 4.3: Interview guide template

I. Introduction

Introduction/purpose: My name is ... from University ... and we are performing research on the customizing process within [company name].

Selection process: You have been nominated to participate because ... .

Discussion: We are interested in having a discussion on how you go about your work and on your experiences.

Authorization: We want to ensure that we have your authorization for the interview and we ask your permission to record our discussion. We guarantee that you will be treated anonymously.

II. Opening question

What is your position in [company name]?

How long have you been working for [company name]?

What is your background [technical/managerial]?

III. Understanding Customization

What does customizing mean for [company name]? Distinction between customizing/maintenance? Different levels/types of customizing?

What economic influence does customizing have for [company name]?

What type of products do you customize? In-house products/third-party products?

What influence does customizing have on your product/service portfolio?

What are the typical challenges of customizing? Functional and/or technical knowledge?

How do you rate or calculate the cost/prices of customizing projects?

IV. Experience with customization projects

How is customer integration organized during the customizing process?

How are customization projects organized? How would you describe the knowledge transfer in customization processes/How is it organized?

Does the knowledge transfer influence the ongoing (future) customization project? If so, how?

How important is standardization/modularity with respect to customer integration?

V. Closing

Thank participant.

Transcription entirely confidential.

Ask for permission to contact again in case of unclear recording.

4.2   Data analysis and interpretation

The interviews lasted between 45 minutes and two hours. Each interview was audiotaped and transcribed verbatim. This resulted in approximately 400 pages of raw interview material for this first interview study. Regarding the exploratory nature of this study and my postpositivistic stance, I applied an analysis approach that can be characterized as hybrid top-down/bottom-up approach.

Top-down, I employed existing theoretical concepts, such as resources, capabilities, and value, as the theoretical lens for my analysis. Bottom-up, I used first and second-cycle coding mechanisms to identify instances of those concepts in the interview transcripts. This hybrid approach helped me to structure my analysis and simultaneously left me the freedom to develop finely granulated instances of theoretical concepts. The aim of the analysis was to detect variation and similarities in how informants experienced customization projects and their influence on the software vendor's competitive advantage. Figure 4.2 illustrates the hybrid research approach.

4.2.1   Analytical lens

The theoretical concepts for the top-down perspective were drawn from the RBV of the firm. As described in the theoretical foundation section of this thesis, the RBV regards firms as bundles of resources that they employ using specific capabilities. According to the literature, a firm's resources are the stock of available factors owned or controlled by the firm and converted into products and services using a wide range of firm assets and bonding mechanisms (Amit and Schoemaker 1993). This study focuses on which of these resources may be most critical and useful for deploying software product customization.

Capabilities are defined as the firm's capacity to deploy resources. They are usually used in combination based on organizational processes to affect

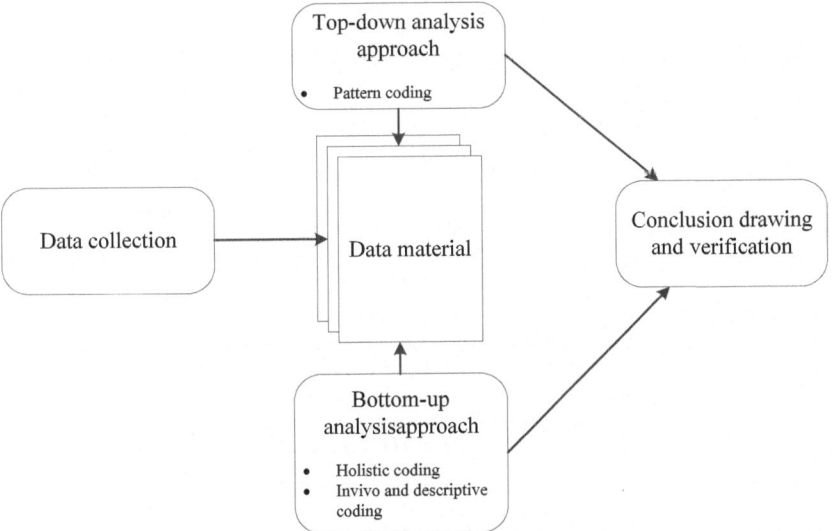

Figure 4.2: Top-down and bottom-up research approaches

the desired end. Therefore, they can be characterized as information-based, tangible and intangible processes that are firm specific and developed over time through complex interactions among the firm's resources (Amit and Schoemaker 1993). Furthermore, according to Day (1994), distinctive capabilities are those that must be superior if the business is to outperform the competition.

The theoretical lens included the concept of value as defined in the strategic management literature: use value and exchange value Lepak et al. (2007). *Use value* refers to the specific quality of a new task, product, or service as perceived by users in relation to their needs. However, these judgments are to high degree individual specific (Bowman and Ambrosini 2000) and include, for instance, the speed or quality of performance of a new task or the aesthetics or performance features of a new product or service. *Exchange value* refers to the amount paid by the buyer to the producer or the specific quality of customer knowledge assets, and it is realized when a product or service is sold. Table 4.4 illustrates the core components of the theoretical lens.

Table 4.4: RBV-related codes from the theoretical and analytical lens

Code structure	
Resources	The stock of available factors owned or controlled by the firm and converted into products and services using a wide range of firm assets and bonding mechanisms (Amit and Schoemaker 1993).
Capabilities	The firm's capacity to deploy resources. They are generally used in combination based on organizational processes to affect a desired end. Capabilities can be characterized as information-based tangible and intangible processes that are firm specific and developed over time through complex interactions among the firm's resources (Amit and Schoemaker 1993).
Values	Use value or exchange value: Use value refers to the specific quality of a new task, product, or service as perceived by users in relation to their needs. Exchange value refers to the amount paid by the buyer to the producer or the specific quality of customer knowledge assets, and it is realized when a product or service is sold (Bowman and Ambrosini 2000; Lepak et al. 2007).

4.2.2   Coding cycles

During the *first coding cycle*, I tried to grasp an overview of basic themes and issues in the text material. For this purpose, I employed a holistic coding approach that aimed to capture and represent the essence of text excerpts or passages (Dey 1993). Holistic coding is a very common coding technique with no preliminary restrictions. It is applicable to cases in which qualitative researchers already have a general idea of the data to be investigated and allows them to "chunk the text in broad topics, as a first step to seeing what is in there" (Bazeley 2003, p. 67). Because there is no restriction to the length of holistic codes, they can be as short as a word or as long as an entire study. In my case, the code length ranged from one to a few interview paragraphs. To focus my later analysis, I additionally weighted each holistic code as having high (H), medium (M), or low (L) relevance for my further research. However, I did not exclude any holistic codes from my further analysis.

In the *second coding cycle*, I used invivo and descriptive coding to further analyze the holistic codes (cf. Saldaña 2009; Miles et al. 2013). Both coding techniques are very simple but helpful for developing a more specific picture of the data material. Invivo codes are exact words or phrases directly from the data material, which the qualitative researcher uses as codes. Descriptive codes on the other hand are descriptive captions, which the qualitative researcher annotates to text passages. While invivo codes are useful to highlight interesting concepts directly in the data material, descriptive codes help summarize the data.

I coded each new transcript starting with the holistic codes most relevant to my research concerns. I compared the resulting codings with preliminary coding outcomes. Thereby, I developed a coding plan that included the identified resources, capabilities and values, that specified respective properties for each of these constructs and that delivered several examples to illustrate the construct's meaning and context.

To decide whether to include a specific resource, capability or value, I followed the advice of Tuli et al. (2007) and relied on three key criteria:

- Is the resource, capability, and/or value applicable beyond a very specific context?

- Did multiple participants mention the resource, capability, and/or value?

- Does the resource, capability, and/or value go beyond the obvious to provide interesting and useful conclusions?

I also included codes for demographic data and other topics that were not directly the focus of my research concern but that might help me to place ideas into the broader context, for instance, the participant's education or professional history.

The *third coding cycle* aimed at strategically reassembling data that were split during the initial coding process. These methods are "advanced ways of reorganizing and reanalyzing data coded through first cycle methods" (Saldaña 2009). As described by Morse (1994), these coding methods fit into categories to develop a coherent synthesis of the data corpus. Although several higher-cycle coding methods exist, the common goal of all them is "to develop a sense of categorical, thematic, conceptual, and/or theoretical organization" (Saldaña 2009) from an array of first or second cycle codes, resulting in a shorter list of broader categories, themes, or concepts.

With my research objectives and theoretical lens in mind, I used pattern coding for the third-cycle analysis. According to Miles and Huberman (1994), pattern codes are

> "explanatory or inferential codes, ones that identify an emergent theme, configuration or explanation. They pull together a lot of material into a more meaningful and parsimonious unit of analysis. They are sort of meta-code."

Accordingly, this method is appropriate for developing the major themes of the data, i.e., the search for rules, causes, and explanations along with the formation of theoretical constructs and processes. Thus, during this coding cycle, I did not look for specific words or statements but tried to relate invivo and descriptive codes and to specify the properties and dimensions of patterns in the data material.

4.2.3   Descriptive results

The results descriptively presented in the following section represent accounting of the codings found in the interview material. Although the results may suggest evidence for my initial research questions, the results presented here do not claim statistical generalizability.

4.2.3.1   First and second coding cycle

The first and second coding cycle resulted in a total of 1852 coding segments. Of these codings, 71% were found in vendor interviews and 29% resulted from customer interviews. Figure 4.3 illustrates an overall view of the study's codings from the first two cycles and their distribution across vendor and customer interviews.

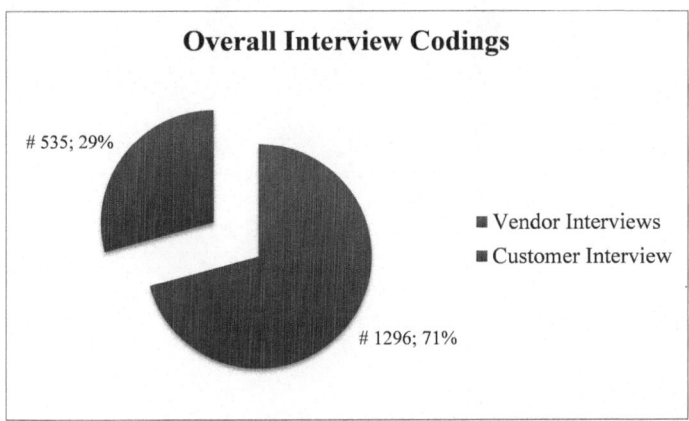

Figure 4.3: Codings in vendor and customer interviews

These 1852 codings could be further categorized according to the theoretical concepts as follows: 661 codings were assigned to the resource category, 816 (45%) were assigned to the capabilities category and 354 (19%) were assigned to the value category. Figure 4.4 illustrates an overall view of the study's codings in the first cycle and their distribution across vendor and customer interviews.

4.2.3.2   Third coding cycle

During the third coding cycle, the codes identified in the resource, capability and value categories were further analyzed using pattern coding. This coding

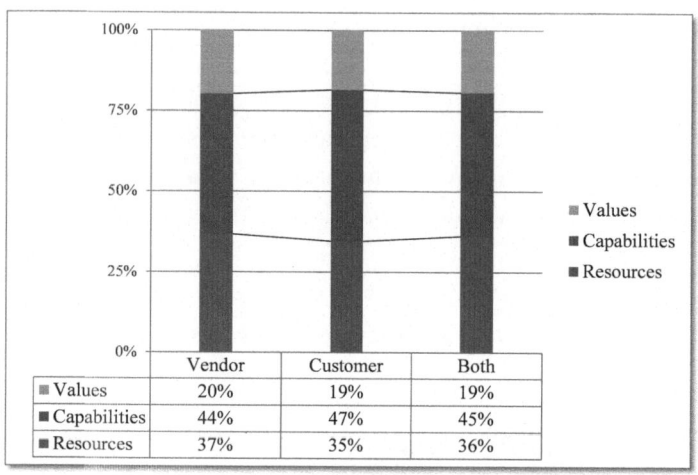

	Vendor	Customer	Both
■ Values	20%	19%	19%
■ Capabilities	44%	47%	45%
■ Resources	37%	35%	36%

Figure 4.4: Codings in theoretical concepts

cycle resulted in eight patterns of values, four patterns of resources, and six patterns of capabilities.

I was able to discover several codings for the two types of values: use value and exchange value. As Figure 4.5 shows, two-thirds of the interview quotes could be assigned to customer-oriented use value (*Value 2*) and only one third to vendor-oriented exchange value (*Value 1*). Interestingly, examining the vendor and customer interviews separately reveals that while the distribution of those relating to value is balanced on vendor side (56% to 44%), for the customer interviews, most quotes were with respect to use value (93%).

Four resources were named: *Resource 1 - Customer business and market knowledge, Resource 2 - Customization management knowledge and experience data, Resource 3 - Product functionality and flexibility,* and *Resource 4 - Product-related software development assets.* The overview of all interview codings shows that most coding examples were found for *Customization management knowledge and experience data* (42%), *Customer business and market knowledge* (25%), *Product functionality and flexibility* (17%), and *Product-related software development assets* (15%).

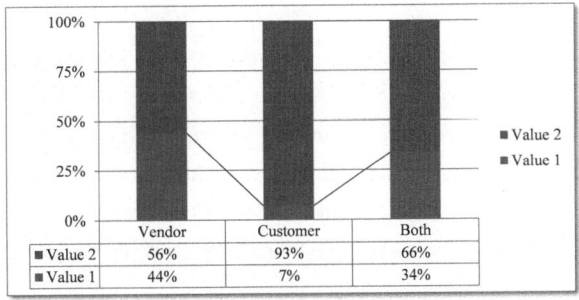

Figure 4.5: Second coding cycle: Values

As Figure 4.6 illustrates, the most coding examples were found for *Customization management knowledge and experience data* in both vendor interviews and customer interviews. However, the data also suggest that while vendor firms are more balanced in the valuation of resources, customer firms care less about vendor-oriented resources, such as *Product functionality and flexibility* (10%) and *Product related software development assets* (5%).

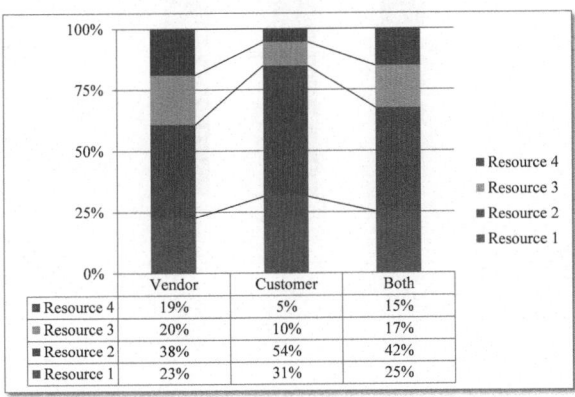

Figure 4.6: Second coding cycle: Resources

Similar to the identification of customization resources, a set of six distinctive customization capabilities was identified, including *Capability 1 - Business analysis and interpretation capability, Capability 2 - Customer integration and expectation management capability, Capability 3 - Requirements management and negotiation capability, Capability 4 - Future-proof solution design capability, Capability 5 - Solution deployment and initialization capability,* and finally *Capability 6 - Solution adjustment capability.* Figure 4.7 illustrates that *Customer integration and expectation management capability,* with approximately 25% of the codings, was the most frequently mentioned capability. *Solution deployment and initialization capability,* with approximately 10% of the codings, was mentioned the least in the interviews.

Taking a closer look at vendor and customer interviews separately reveals that during the customer interviews, more coding matched the first three capabilities. The last three capabilities were mentioned less frequently. Although this is also the case for the vendor interviews, a more "balanced" distribution of codings among interviewees can be seen for these.

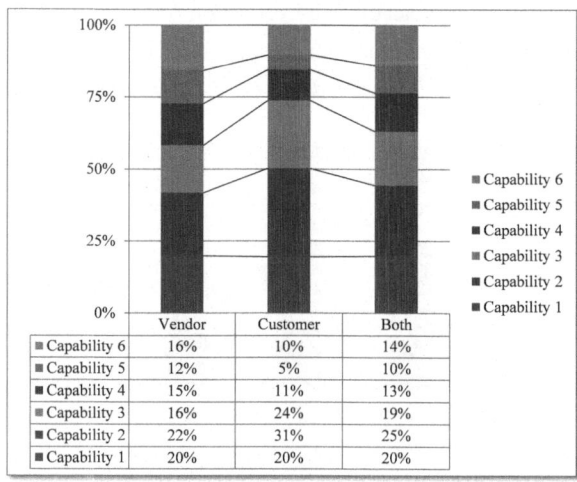

Figure 4.7: Second coding cycle: Capabilities

The above section presented some descriptive results from the three coding cycles. It illustrated the identified patterns and how many codes were identified for each of them. The next chapter will elaborate on these patterns by interpreting them, developing themes and clarifying the relationships be-

tween them. It will use interview examples to highlight the importance of
each theme for the different vendor and customer interview participants.

4.3   Findings and discussion

Following the described research design theory approach, this pilot study
identified four unique resources, six distinctive capabilities and two types of
value important in software customization. Figure 4.8 integrates the identified resources, distinctive capabilities, and value types into an overall research
framework.

4.3.1   Strategic resources for software customization

A firm's resources are the stock of available factors owned or controlled by
the firm and converted into products and services using a wide range of firm
assets and bonding mechanisms (Amit and Schoemaker 1993). This study
focuses on determining which of these resources could be the most critical
and useful for deploying software product customization. The interviews
revealed four unique resources: (1) *customer business and market knowledge,*
(2) *customization management and experience data,* (3) *product functionality
and flexibility,* and (4) *product related software development assets.* Table 4.5
summarizes those resources.

4.3.1.1   Customer business and market knowledge

Software customization is not just about installing a software product in a
customer's IT landscape; it includes the adjustment of technical and organizational processes on the customer side. Knowing both the customer and
the business that the customer operates in is crucial for software business
firms. The resulting knowledge of the customer's business characteristics as
well as market knowledge represent a unique asset for most software cus-

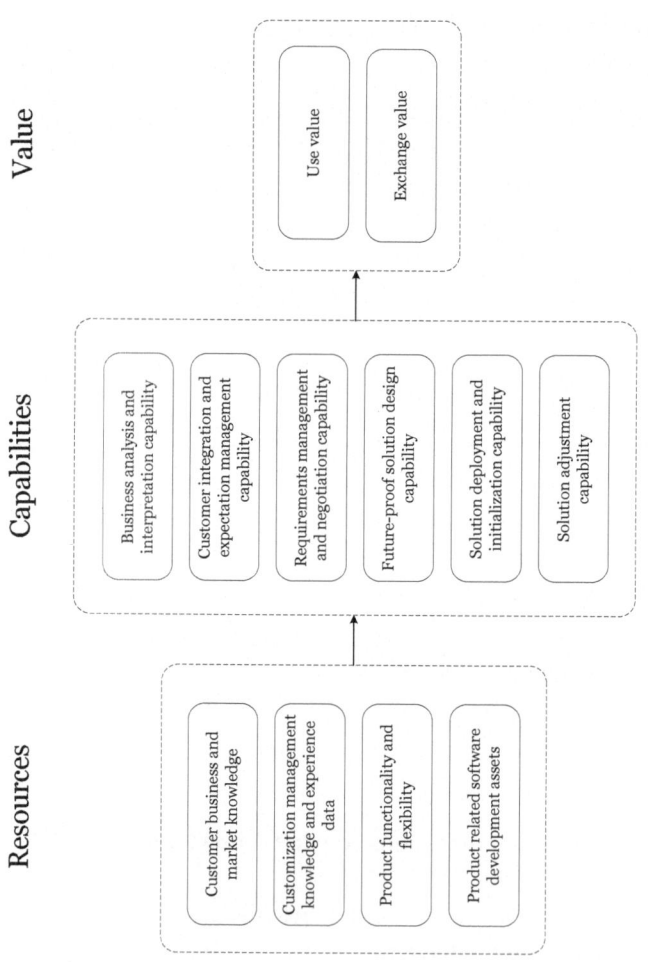

Figure 4.8: Resulting overall framework

Table 4.5: Summary of resource definitions and examples

Unique resource	Definition	Example
Customer business and market knowledge	The stock of resources invested in a firm's understanding of recent developments and needs in potential customers' businesses and provider markets.	Knowledge of competing and complementary products and legal requirements
Customization management knowledge and experience data	The stock of service data collected throughout a firm's history of completed or ongoing customization projects.	Service data from issue tracking or project management systems
Product functionality and flexibility	The stock of business functionalities already implemented within a software product and the flexibility supported by a solution provider.	Specific and general business functions and configuration mechanisms
Product-related software development assets	The stock of resources invested in a firm's software development infrastructure.	Software development infrastructure and employees with software development skills and experience

tomization vendors in my study. Therefore, I define *customer business and market knowledge* as the stock of resources invested in a firm's understanding of recent developments and needs in (potential) customers' businesses and markets.

Customer business knowledge, in particular, refers to the specific stock of resources invested in a firm's understanding of a certain customer's business implementation. It is a necessary prerequisite for identifying and defining customer value. It includes a profound knowledge of not only what a customer firm "thinks" it needs but also what it really needs. As one project engineer from a customer firm explained, the responsible department might not always know how processes and structures are organized, but it still wants software to support those processes:

> *The most important things are processes. The department sometimes does not even know how their process works, but wants a software to support it. The definition of processes, who works with what, when do they work with it, is there additional data need, and if where does it come from, are other departments involved? Many project engineers do not look what is going on in other departments. Filtering this is one of my tasks.* (Customer, IC05)

To perform successful customization projects, the vendor needs to know how a customer firm interprets its business and to identify potential for improvement. This includes knowledge of the customer's vision as well as its strategic and operational goals. From a software vendor perspective, *customer business knowledge* is one prerequisite for identifying customer value. For instance, the interview participant from the industrial machine industry highlighted the benefits of using their software solution for managing full service contracts and the expected return on investment:

> *It is this customer value that we can commercialize!* (Vendor, IV05)

The coding results suggest that identifying customer value includes knowledge of the customer's existing and potential core business such as existing business requirements and ongoing product and service innovations, vendor-customer relationships in the customer's business, or legal developments and regional differences in that area.

In contrast to customer business knowledge, *market knowledge* refers to the resources invested in a firm's understanding of developments in the software vendor's target market. This includes a broader perspective of customer business knowledge as an aggregate from multiple customer firms as well as an in-depth understanding of complementary products and services on the market and the strengths and weaknesses of competitor firms. In particular, it includes knowledge about developments of new or existing complementary and competitive products and services, innovations in software implementation methods and technologies, or innovations in hardware and software infrastructure.

Market knowledge is important for continuously providing state-of-the-art products and services and for identifying market opportunities for both the vendor firm and its customers. Customer firms expect the vendor company to not only provide them with a software product that fits their needs but also to enlighten their understanding of the "standard business". For instance, as the interview participant from the book retailing business revealed,

> *Elaborating the customer is important. I would call it customer consulting. There are cases where customers have wishes or ideas that are unsuitable, just because they are not thinking outside their own box. In this case, the vendor has to guide the customer. And of course, this generates costs.* (Customer, IC03)

From a vendor perspective, market knowledge is important because it helps them to position themselves in the best possible way. Therefore, vendor firms need to know how other products and services in the market complement their offering and vice versa. Market knowledge also enables vendors to react to the strengths and weaknesses of competitor products or to services already installed or planned in customer environments. The interview participant from the health care business explained that they address different market segments with different degrees of customization. For instance, in the segment of registered doctors, they maintain 60,000 installations of their software. Customization for this number of installations is not individual; it is closer to a standard installation. However, with respect to hospitals and their more complex installations, customization services become more important (Vendor, IV01).

4.3.1.2 Customization management knowledge and experience data

In customization projects, it is not just important to know what a certain customer needs or what a market has to offer; software vendor companies also need knowledge of how to manage customization projects and of how the previous customization projects with customer firms have performed. Multiple patterns from the analysis have revealed that customization management knowledge combined with experience information from earlier customization projects is a unique asset for software firms. Therefore, I define *customization management knowledge and experience* data as the stock of customization management resources and project data collected through a firm's history of completed and ongoing customization projects.

Customization management knowledge refers to standardized customization delivery processes, project templates and best practices, and different customization approaches. Combined with knowledge about the proposed type of customization project and its affiliated risks, these resources form a important asset that contributes to successfully managing customization projects.

The interviews revealed that some software vendors offer at least two types of customization approaches, following either a sequential waterfall-like process or a prototype-oriented agile project process. While the agile process is more flexible and less restrictive with respect to project communication and milestones, the sequential process is more suitable to minimizing the risks from multiple customer changes. Depending on the customers' previous experience with customization projects and their expectations, vendor firms tend toward using one or the other. In particular, the sequential process is used for standard customization projects and the more agile process is used for innovative customization projects. As the document management solution provider explained,

> *Projects are evaluated up front and categorized as standard or innovative projects. Standard projects are managed by professional services. In innovative projects, the software development department is involved because a higher degree of innovation is needed. Usually, those projects are accompanied by a market analysis. Those innovative projects are initiated by the customer asking for a pilot project or a prototype.* (Vendor, IV10)

Customization experience data refers to experience generated by customization projects for specific existing customers. It includes explicit service information stored in information systems such as ticket systems or project management software as well as implicit knowledge about customer employee behavior stored in the minds of team members. Both types of knowledge are important for successful software customization. Explicit knowledge, such as open or pending customer requests from former customization projects, is an important source of value. Customers expect the vendor to remember what they have already told him. As the interview participant from the software service industry explained,

> *We maintain a service portal to measure service quality. There are several types of service cases, such as change requests, support questions, or error messages. We use MIS technology to analyze the service cases. Thus, I am able to tell you the state of each service case. How long did it take to fix something and what were the reasons for this. Was it a functional problem or was*

our employee perhaps involved in to many projects. You can read
some things from analyzing service cases. (Vendor, IV06)

Vendor companies use this information to identify value potential for
the customer and for themselves. This knowledge of customer employees
is essential for managing customer expectations, which are an important
success factor for customization projects. This implies the alignment of sales
and customization activities. For instance, as the interview participant for
the book retailing business explained,

Sometimes during the sales phase, expectations are created which
cannot be fulfilled during the customization process. This is fatal
for the success of a customization project. (Customer, IC04)

Expectation management is especially important in markets where only
a few big customer firms exist (see quotes on exchange values: *vendor repu-*
tation: Vendor, IV01).

4.3.1.3   Product functionality and flexibility

Customization generally relies on a balance of standard functionality and
adaption flexibility. Research on mass customization, for instance, has revealed that vendors who offer customization services position themselves between pure product standardization and individual development or manufacturing. In the context of the software business, balancing standardization and
flexibilization is even more complex. Software is a product of the human mind
and therefore tacit and intangible. Understanding a software product's core
functionalities and flexibilization potential is therefore essential for successful customization projects. Thus, I define *software product functionality and*
flexibility as the stock of business functionalities already implemented within
the software product and the flexibility supported by the service provider.

This resource refers to the product's existing business and technical functionalities that support general and anonymous market needs as well as the

ability to change those functionalities according to the customer's specific requirements. While the product's existing functionality is important for realizing standard services, its flexibility enables it to react to customer-specific requirements or innovative customization projects. These aspects are contradictory but crucial for successful customization delivery. For software product customization, this is the existing product's functionality and flexibility.

The third unique resource aims to capture what several interview participants described as "the (product or solution) standard". For vendor firms, a profound knowledge of their product's functionality and flexibility is important to evaluate the potential and the risks of customization projects. Customization projects that can be managed using standard functionality are usually less innovative, and the risk of not fulfilling the customer's expectations is lower in these cases. Customization projects with a higher need for flexibility also mean a higher risk for the vendor and customer company.

Customer firms know this and try to find software solutions with standard functionalities to prevent consulting effort. As the interview participant from the utilities company explained,

For me, customization is adapting a standard software product to my actual needs. For instance, usually the software product has some kind of database with standard input fields. But it is also possible to add new fields that are important for my organization and which no one else needs. [...] The next level of customization is the adaption of business processes supported by the software product. However, in this case, consulting activities provided by the vendor become more and more important. (Customer, IC01)

Vendor companies use different levels of standard functionality and flexibilization to address different markets. As the interviewee participant from the email communication business described,

> *The bigger the firm, the bigger the need to customize.* (Vendor,
> IV09)

4.3.1.4 Product related software development assets

Software customization is all about bringing customer-specific functionality
into the customer firm and providing reliable adjustment mechanisms. Software development or source-code development represents the most flexible
but also the most complex customization mechanism. In B2B scenarios,
sometimes requirements cannot be implemented without additional development. Thus, software development techniques represent a unique and valuable asset for vendor companies. I therefore define *software product related
development assets* as the stock of resources invested in the firm's software
development infrastructure.

From a technical point of view, several techniques or types of customization activities exist. Customization can either be realized by configuring one
(often monolithic) application by setting database switches, changing configuration files, or parameterizing several software modules to build the desired
solution. Furthermore, customization can be realized by extension programming. Especially in complex and/or innovative customization projects, the
product's existing functionality is often not sufficient to fulfill the customer's
needs, and the software product provides rich development functionalities
and support. In these cases, solution providers need product-related software
development know-how and the associated assets to ensure support services
and product update security. For instance, as the interview participant from
the mechanical engineering industry explained,

> *Our industrial services are not products in the original sense. We
> develop customer-oriented, customer-specific individual software
> solutions. Our projects always include a solution-solving process.
> Our software products are pre-structured and pre-developed tools
> provided by Siemens, SPS Software or S7. Those are [third-party]*

standard products that we use as a basis for individual solutions.
(Vendor, IV04)

4.3.2 Distinctive capabilities for software customization

Capabilities are defined as the firm's capacity to deploy resources. They are generally used in combination based on organizational processes to affect a desired end. Therefore, they can be characterized as information-based tangible and intangible processes that are firm specific and developed over time through complex interactions among the firm's resources (Amit and Schoemaker 1993). Furthermore, according to Day (1994), distinctive capabilities are those that must be superior if the business is to outperform the competition. The interviews revealed six of those distinctive capabilities, which are summarized in Table 4.6.

4.3.2.1 Business analysis and interpretation capabilities

Business analysis and interpretation capabilities refer to the service provider's capacity to analyze a customer's business needs, interpret them based on existing customer business and market knowledge, and reflect those needs against supported business functionality and flexibility in the existing software product. For instance, as the interview participant from the mechanical engineering industry explained,

> *Our problem is not to provide software. Our problem is to understand the machines that have to be automated. How do they work? What are the technical processes behind that? Imagine a rolling line that produces filled chocolate: the sheath has to be casted, centrifuged, and cooled down. Finally the chocolate has to be filled in. Once we have understood how this works, we can start thinking about software. (Vendor, IV01)*

Table 4.6: Summary of capabilities definitions and primary resources

Distinctive capability	Definition	Primary resources
Business analysis and interpretation capability	Business analysis and interpretation capability refers to a service provider's ability to analyze a customer's business needs, interpret them based on existing customer business and market knowledge and reflect those needs against supported business functionality and flexibility in an existing software product.	Customer business and market knowledge; product functionality and flexibility
Customer integration and expectation management capability	Customer integration and expectation management capability refers to a provider's ability to integrate customers into the customization process and to manage customer expectations to successfully meet defined goals.	Customization management knowledge and experience data
Requirements management and negotiation capability	Requirements management and negotiation capability refers to a provider's ability to manage customer requirements during a customization project. This includes gathering, prioritizing and managing customer requirements along with negotiating conflicting requirements.	Product functionality and flexibility; customization management knowledge and experience data
Future-proof solution design capability	Future-proof solution design capability refers to a provider's capacity to design a future-proof software solution based on a product's functionalities and a specific customer's needs.	Customization management knowledge and experience data; product-related software development assets
Solution deployment and initialization capability	Solution deployment and initialization capability refers to a provider's ability to deploy a developed solution for a customer and to initiate that solution with respect to the existing IT landscape or formerly used (legacy) systems.	Product-related software development assets
Solution adjustment capability	Solution adjustment capability refers to a provider's ability to adjust a deployed software solution according to changed requirements during and after the initial implementation.	Product functionality and flexibility

According to my interview analysis, this capability includes capacities on the provider side such as (1) adapting to a customer's way of thinking, (2) anticipating future solution usage (and requirements), (3) identifying and communicating optimization potential when working on the customer side, and (4) actively presenting new product features to the customer. The underlying primary resources for this capability are customer business and market knowledge and product functionality and flexibility.

4.3.2.2   Customer integration and expectation management

Customer integration and expectation management reflects the provider's capacity to integrate the customer into the customization service and to manage customer expectations to successfully meet defined (and undefined) goals. One important aspect of customer integration is earning the customer's trust. As the CEO from the email marketing software provider explained,

> *Our consultants and project managers need to earn the customer's trust to be able to do their job. This is essential for customization services. If our consultants promise something, they have to keep it. (Vendor, IV4)*

Furthermore, this capability includes tasks such as (1) identifying key users and integrating them early and continuously in the process, (2) leading the customer through complex situations, (3) explicating customer expectations to reduce the risk of unsatisfying service outcomes, and finally, (5) managing the vendor's reputation when providing customization services to strengthen the chances of follow-up projects. While capabilities usually draw on a number of different resources, the underlying primary resource here is customization management knowledge and experience data.

4.3.2.3   Requirements management and negotiation capability

The provider's capacity to manage customer requirements during the customization project, including gathering, prioritizing and managing the state of customer requirements as well as negotiating conflicting requirements. I thus define requirements management and negotiation capabilities as the service provider's capacity to harvest requirements from partially incomplete, sketched customer business needs and to negotiate unexpected (and conflicting) requirements to provide the optimum customer solution based on the existing product's functionality. For instance, channeling customer input is one important aspect of requirements management. As the CEO from the email marketing software explained,

> *Some customers flood you with trivialities. Others are more professional. Depending on that, we organize interface structures for channeling customer input. (Vendor, IV04)*

As defined by my interviews, this capability includes (1) Anticipating future usage scenarios for the customer and for product development, (2) professionally handle unexpected customer requests, (3) foster customer commitment on requests, and (4) use IT systems to store and track customer requests. The underlying primary resources for this capability are product functionality, product flexibility, customization management knowledge and experience data.

4.3.2.4   Future-proof solution design

The provider's capacity to design a future-proof software solution based on the product's functionalities and a specific customer's needs. For instance, rebuilding interfaces of existing legacy systems might be one solution to ease the customer's transformation from one solution to another. As the CEO from the monitoring software company explained,

> *If our system has to replace a legacy system, we might start by*
> *rebuilding known interfaces or processes to provide a solid foun-*
> *dation for future developments (Vendor, IV09)*

According to my interview analysis, this capacity also includes activities such as (1) integrating the customer into the design phase, (2) respecting the customer's experience with legacy systems, (3) establishing a flexible design process that supports the non-sequential nature of customization services, and (4) managing non-technical aspects of product customization. Because existing templates from former projects can be considered to be best practices, the underlying resource for this capacity is customization management assets and customization experience data.

4.3.2.5   Solution deployment and initialization

The solution provider's capacity to deploy a designed solution to a customer and to initialize this solution by migrating data from existing sources to provide a useful system. As discovered in my interview results, this capability includes (1) providing the customer with all information (and competences) needed to use the deployed solution (e.g., training, support, documentation), (2) migrating data from different sources to initialize the solution, (3) the capacity to integrate the solution into an existing IT landscape, and (4) resolving potential conflicts with third party systems on the customer side (e.g., firewalls, drivers, virus scanner). Data migration is particularly mentioned as one important capacity. Service providers often develop their own tools to ease customer migration to their systems. As the SM from the health care industry explained,

> *We are in a very good position when it comes to data migration.*
> *Our conversion tools are able to integrate data from the most*
> *important rival products. (Vendor, IV02)*

The underlying resources for this capability are product functionalities, product flexibility and product-related software development assets.

4.3.2.6   Solution adjustment capability

The provider's capacity to adjust a deployed solution according to upcoming requirements during and after the initial implementation. Customers expect the service provider to handle these upcoming requests:

> *Exactly! Developing the best possible solution for the customer actively with the customer. It is important to discuss upcoming (customer) ideas during the implementation process. One cannot expect to deliver a specification and six months after that, the product is developed, all user documentation is written, all business cases are covered and all users are trained. This is not what we expect. (Customer, No. 6)*

According to my interview analysis, this capability includes capacities on the provider side such as (1) providing workarounds for requirements that are not yet implemented into the solution, (2) providing internal training for consultants and developers supporting a customer solution, (3) providing user support, especially when the delivered solution means process changes in the customer organization, and finally (4) storing and tracking customer requests. The underlying resource in this case is the provider's customization management knowledge and experience data.

4.3.2.7   Typology of customization capabilities

According to Day (1994), certain types of capabilities can be recognized in all types of businesses. Corresponding to the core processes of creating economic value, these capability types are outside-in, spanning, and inside-out capabilities. Building upon Day's (1994) introduction, this typology of capabilities has been applied to several contexts, such as market-driven organizations (Day 1994), IS capabilities (Wade and Hulland 2004), open innovation functions (Enkel et al. 2009), and absorptive capacity in IS (Roberts et al. 2012).

First, outside-in capabilities are outward facing. They emphasize anticipating customer requirements, creating durable customer relationships, and understanding competitors (e.g., market responsiveness, managing external relationships). Thus, outside-in capabilities facilitate a firm's knowledge identification capacity (Wade and Hulland 2004). According to the former analysis, business analysis and interpretation capabilities as well as customer integration and expectation management capabilities can be related to this type of capability. In customization projects, both capabilities are responsible for identifying customer knowledge and integrating external resources into the customization process.

Second, inside-out capabilities are inward focused. They are deployed from inside the firm in response to customer requirements and opportunities (e.g., technology or organizational development). Thus, inside-out capabilities increase a firm's knowledge-application capability (Wade and Hulland 2004). The successful (and even unsuccessful) implementation and adjustment of customer-specific software solutions strengthens the knowledge application capacity of a firm. Therefore, solution deployment and adjustment capabilities can be highly related to the inside-out capability type.

Finally, spanning capabilities integrate the firm's inside-out and outside-in capabilities. They involve both internal and external analysis, are needed to gain a better understanding of how new external knowledge relates to knowledge already possessed by organizational members (e.g., managing IS/ business partnerships, IS management and planning) (Wade and Hulland 2004). Requirement management and negotiation and future-proof solution design capabilities involve knowledge integrated from the identified outside-in capabilities and exploited in the inside-out capabilities of software product customization. Thus, requirements management and negotiation and future-proof solution design capabilities can be related to spanning capabilities. Figure 4.9 illustrates the relation of customization capabilities and generic capability types.

4.3.3 Values from software customization

The strategic management literature defines two types of value: use value and exchange value (Lepak et al. 2007). Use value refers to the specific quality of a new task, product, or service as perceived by users in relation to their needs. However, these judgments are to high degree individual specific (Bowman and Ambrosini 2000) and include, for instance, the speed or quality of performance on a new task or the aesthetics or performance features of a new product or service. Exchange value refers to the amount paid by the buyer to the producer or the specific quality of customer knowledge assets, and it is realized when a product or service is sold. The analysis undertaken revealed that in software customization, several types of use and exchange value are important.

4.3.3.1 Use value in software customization

The analysis of interviews revealed that use value in software customization projects can occur in different forms. In particular, I identified four types of customization use value: (1) *customer profitability*, (2) *business development support*, (3) *long-term solution*, and (4) *customer reputation*. Table 4.7 summarizes these use values and corresponding examples.

Customer profitability *Customer profitability* refers to the monetary value that customer firms generate by using or implementing customized software solutions. It is one important issue that drives use value in customization projects. In B2B scenarios, software is not used without a purpose, and generally it has an economic purpose. Customer firms implement software solutions to reduce costs , optimize operationalization, or a combination of both.

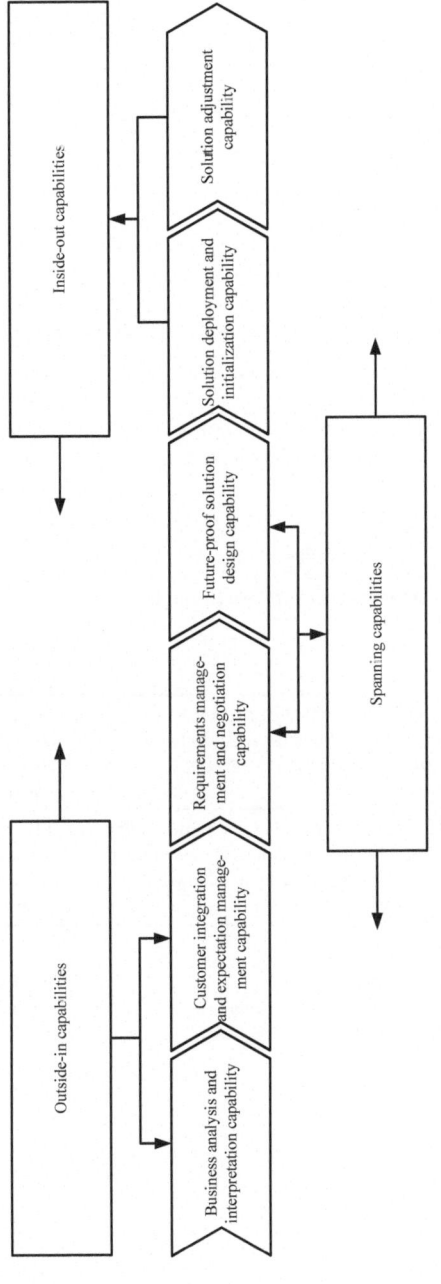

Figure 4.9: Software product customization capabilities related to generic capability types

Table 4.7: Summary of use values, definitions, and examples

Use value	Definition	Example
Business development support	The vendor's support of the customer's business development activities.	Market-oriented "standard" processes, internal solution marketing, reducing resistance to change
Long-term solution	The long-term perspective of customization support through the vendor.	Sequential and appended customization activities, continuous customization support
Customer profitability	The monetary gain produced for customers who use a customized software solution.	Cost reduction, operation enhancement or optimization, or both
Customer reputation	The reputation that a customer firm gains by using a specific customized software solution from a specific vendor.	The myths of SAP software or fulfillment of legal or market requirements

Customer profitability might be reached by reducing costs, for instance, by reducing person hours per task or by optimizing tasks and enabling customers to deploy more services to their customers.

Implementing information systems therefore is seen as an investment, which must pay off over time. In contrast to tailor-made software solutions, customized software is based on a product and a service "standard" that is continuously developed and maintained by the vendor firm. A customized software solution is regarded as being more profitable for a customer firm because it initially includes extensive business logic, which continuously grows based on the vendor's installed base. However, the customization of software products is still a complex and expensive project. It includes tasks that keep the workforce from daily business. With respect to customer profitability, customization therefore must produce real customer value. As the interview participant from the book retailing business explains,

> *Customization is additional work! For me, it is important that the process of customization is finished quickly and that the implemented solution helps me to realize my daily tasks better than before. Else it would not have been worth the effort! For me, successful customization helps me to be more effective and does not mean additional work on my side.* (Customer, IC03)

Vendor firms know about the importance of providing customer value. In the early phases of the customization process, they therefore make an effort to communicate the concrete value from implementing or adapting a specific software or functionality. Of course, those values depend on the customers' specific business and market situation. What they all have in common is that the customer realizes the return on investment. As the interview participant from the email marketing business stated,

> *Customization effectiveness, for us, is defined as the ratio between the effort for implementing a system and the working time saved by the customer through that system.* (Vendor, IV09)

Business development support   *Business development support* refers to the vendor's support of the customer's business development activities. Business development on the customer side has several challenges: business development is not an everyday task, and as such, it reduces the working time of employees in their original line of responsibilities. It is also high risk because of possible user frustration or resistance to change. Furthermore, business development is hard to estimate due to the uncertain number of changes during the implementation process. Thus, instead of building individual solutions, customers prefer to profit from market standards for doing business. The most important step is to identify the need to do something. As the interview participant from the telecommunication business explained,

> *The most important thing is to realize the necessity to do something. In my opinion, we cannot realize that on our own. Informal discussions with software vendors are an important trigger to realize that there is something we can or should do.* (Customer, IC02)

According to the interview participant (IC04) from the aviation industry, business development support might be realized by

- *buying external business knowledge and using it internally,*

- *outsourcing internal tasks to the service provider, or*

- *buying external project management knowledge that is internally used in multiple projects.*

Vendor companies address these challenges in several ways. First, vendor firms have functional knowledge of how to provide business development. For instance, they provide pre-studies for evaluating a business case, training on business process development and other organizational aspects, and support to help the customer to identify the use value for him/herself. Customers do not have to develop that knowledge. Second, in addition to implementation and adaption processes, vendor firms also provide a form of internal marketing for their solutions that helps customer firms to overcome user frustration and resistance. Finally, vendor firms support customer firms with their existing market knowledge and implemented standard functionalities. As the interview participant from the car retailing service business explained,

> *Today, software is only a side product. The much bigger role plays the process of enabling the customers to use the software according to their needs and doing their business better than before. This is the point where we are better than our competitors.* (Vendor, IV07)

Long-term solution As highlighted, business development is expensive and not an everyday task for customer firms. Customer firms therefore search for solutions that provide long-term value for their core business. Thus, a *long-term solution* refers to the long-term value that customized standard software provides for customer firms. Customization projects cannot be seen as individual incidents. They are often an important part of a firm's business development strategy. Therefore, from a customer perspective, long-term standard solutions with the option to adapt to environmental changes offer important value gained through software customization. Long-term solutions also include a set of planned and ad-hoc customization approaches for a specific customer. Those customizations might occur during implementation, adaption or maintenance projects. As the interview participant from the health care business explained,

> *Health care information systems are used for 15 to 20 years. In hospitals, this timespan might be 20 to 25 years. For instance, we are currently replacing a system in Vienna that has not been updated for years.* (Vendor, IV01)

Another important aspect of long-term solutions is that business functions supported or implemented by software are often essential processes. Replacing those processes with a software solution implies that the customer may have some dependence on the vendor. Therefore, the customer firm must be absolutely sure that a software solution is not only functional but also reliable over the long term. This includes aspects such as regular updates, continuous user training and support, bug fixing or change-management support. For instance, the interview participant from the email marketing business explained the importance of a reliable technological and architectural software base:

> Our software product is now 11 years old and I think it will be here for at least 11 more years. That means it is a long-term project and no "fire-and-forget" software. Our software base has to be maintainable and also be able to react to upcoming technological innovations. There is a lot going on behind the curtain: refactoring or technological exchange. Therefore we use Java instead of PHP and build upon a solid basis of reliable software framework for time-zone management, character set support ... our software is an enterprise solution and not a PHP hack. (Vendor, IV09)

Customer reputation Finally, customer companies use software implementations to support their reputation. *Customer reputation* refers to the reputation a customer firm or employee gains by choosing a specific software solution. Strong software product brands such as SAP or Oracle are often used to communicate process maturity and stability, especially when those products and the underlying services are certificated by third-party companies or institutions. Additionally, the maturity and stability of process implementation has a strong effect on the firm's internal and external compliance. As the software vendor from the health care industry explained,

> If we centralized customer data, it is our duty to protect that data. This is important for our customer firms. Therefore, we used sophisticated encryption algorithms in our systems. Actu-

*ally, we certified certain parts of our software through third-party
institutions, such as the T.V.* (Vendor, IV02)

On an individual level, the influence of customization projects on customer reputations is additionally important. Customization projects are
projects managed by project managers from the customer and vendor firm.
Project managers are either "usual" employees promoted to manage customization projects or external project managers hired for their special knowledge in this area. In both cases, the customization result depends on the
project manager's reputation. Is the software product suitable to fulfill the
customer's needs? Does it provide the necessary performance? Has the end-
user been convinced to use the designed solution? Can the project be managed in time? The answers to these and other questions define the individual
project manager's reputation. In addition to the technical and organizational
questions, the internal marketing of a solution plays an important role. Thus,
as the customer from the utilities company explained, integrating key users –
users who are capable of promoting a certain solution in firm – is important
for customization success (Customer, IV01).

4.3.3.2   Exchange value in software customization

Exchange value refers to the amount paid by the buyer to the producer or
the specific quality of the customer knowledge assets and is realized when a
product or service is sold. The analysis of interviews revealed that exchange
value in software customization projects did not only take a monetary form.
In particular, I identified four types of customization use value: (1) vendor
profitability, (2) vendor reputation, (3) customer relationship, and (4) innovation impulses. Table 4.8 summarizes those use values and the corresponding
examples.

Vendor profitability   *Vendor profitability* refers to the amount of money
a customer firm is willing to pay for a specific customization service. From a

Table 4.8: Summary of exchange values, definitions, and examples

Exchange value	Definition	Example
Innovation impulses	Customer-generated requests or expectations that enhance the vendor's capacity to innovate but do not directly lead to commercial success.	Customer requirements that do not go into the standard product but that are put on a roadmap for future implementation
Vendor reputation	The reputation that a vendor company gains during customer interactions.	A positive or negative reputation according to customer expectations
Customer relation	The relationship between vendor and customer firm that originated in interaction activities.	Customer loyalty, trust, or transparency during customization processes
Vendor profitability	The vendor's direct monetary benefit from customization activities.	Software license fees, support, or maintenance revenue

vendor perspective, this amount must be higher than the expenses to make a customization service profitable. Vendor profitability is, therefore, the most important exchange value to keep the vendor company alive. In software customization, vendor companies generate monetary exchange value in many different ways, for instance, (1) licensing fees for software products or additional components, (2) service fees for project management, consulting and customization services, and (3) revenues from maintenance and support contracts that accompany professional business software. Despite these "classical" forms of revenue, vendor companies are always searching for new innovative business and revenue models, such as pay-per-use or rent-based approaches. In sum, vendor profitability must be confirmed for every customization project in one form or another. As the interview participant from the health care industry explained,

> *In the end, a successful customization project depends on revenue generated through services.* (Vendor, IV01)

However, according to his colleague in software customization, it is not always about the direct revenue. There is also revenue generated over time, for instance, through maintenance fees:

> *There are projects with a direct economic success. But you have to see that customer firms pay maintenance and support fees. Therefore, they expect us to further develop the base product and provide additional value to their business. They pay us to innovate the product in their sense.* (Vendor IV02)

The economic perspective on customization is different and depends on the vendor's revenue model. For instance, the interview from the car retailing business explained,

> *Individualization projects are the projects with the most economical success. (Vendor, IV07)*

To the contrary, the interview partner from the information management business explained that revenue generated from customization services is not their primary business:

> *For us, it is essential to keep the customization effort as small as possible. Our revenue model relies on software licenses instead of professional services. Therefore, we try to keep the customization process as efficient as possible.* (Vendor, IV03)

Although it is essential for the survival of a vendor company, interview participants explained that the monetary value of a customization project is not the most important value in every case. In standard customization projects, where no additional value for the vendor is possible, the monetary value drives the customization efforts. In innovative or relationship-building projects, several vendors explained that other types of value (especially with respect to customer satisfaction) are equally important, as they might lead to better relationships and follow-up orders.

> *Sometimes we see standardization potential in customization efforts. In these cases, we charge the customer less than usual. Of course, this is no short-term profit maximization, but therefore it helps us to establish a durable relationship with our customers. We are here for 16 years; that is a long time in our business and our region. (Vendor, IV08)*

Thus, balancing monetary and other types of value is one of the most important business tasks in software customization management.

> *The other aspect is that I do not generate more money with existing customers. The important question is, how can I win new customers with the existing technological base and additional services. (Vendor, IV02)*

Vendor reputation *Vendor reputation* refers to the reputation that vendor companies gain by implementing a software solution in a customer's company. This refers to the internal reputation within a certain customer's firm as well as the vendor's reputation in a market segment of potential customers. Reputation is a very important form of exchange value for vendor companies. To develop a good reputation, it is necessary to earn the customer employee's trust. A vendor might build a reputation by delivering a project in time and on budget or by actively managing a customer's expectations. However, a good vendor reputation is not merely a "soft skill"; it is rather essential for vendor firms' business. For instance, as the interview participant from the aviation industry explained, customer firms maintain ranking lists of potential supplier firms to select partners for future projects:

> *We have contracts with several software service providers. We maintain a list of several indicators for those suppliers, such as revenue, performance, and so on. We evaluate this list every year. When selecting partners for complex projects, we consult that list. Depending on the importance of a certain project, our purchasing department chooses only partners we already have experiences with.* (Customer, IV04)

However, reputation is not important just to keep existing customers; it is especially important for establishing business contracts with new customers. As the interviewee from the monitoring software company explained,

> *We have a customer installment and a project base. This base represents a form of trust for other companies. For instance, when talking to a new potential customer, I can argue from this ground of trust that we are able to handle their kind of project.* (Vendor, IV08)

Vendor companies can build their reputation but can also lose it, for instance, by not achieving expected goals, making false promises during service proposals or not reaching the customers' users and employees. Particularly in markets where only a limited number of potential (big) customers exist, losing reputation might force a vendor out of the market. For instance, in the health care business, with only a limited number of hospitals and therefore of potential customers, a good reputation is essential for the vendor. As the employee from the health care industry explained to me,

> *Trust is important! Our consultants have to - and they do - earn that trust to tell the customer what is possible and what is not. Promising impossible or not economical things is bad! Especially in our industry, with only a limited number of customers. If you screw up only a few projects, other customers will not do business with you.* (Vendor, IV01)

Vendor-customer relation   *Vendor-customer relation* refers to the vendor and customer relationship. A good customer relationship is important to gain acceptance on the customer side and to successfully promote solutions internally. A good vendor-customer relationship is also essential for building a good business relationship. Software vendors that have good relationships with their customers might be included in strategic decisions and thereby strengthen the position of their products and solutions.

From the customers' perspective, a software solution should be able to react to changing requirements in their structures or processes. However, changing complex information systems is difficult. Over time, vendor and customer firms gain experience with each others' business philosophy, and it is possible to establish less formal channels for communication. Customer firms value those channels because they allow them to be more flexible. For instance, as the employee from the aviation industry explained,

> *Now, we have a very good relation established with our IT service provider. So, we can communicate short-term change requests. Of course, we try to keep those short-term requests at a minimum.*

> *We are aware that those requests often imply a lot of work effort on the supplier side. However, changes during an implementation project are the usual case, and we are happy to be able to react quickly.* (Customer, IC06)

In a very similar vein, a project manager from customer IC07 explains how his good relationship with the supplier company helps prevent problems:

> *There are some cases where we face problems that can cause trouble. But, due to my close relation to our suppliers' developers, they call and tell me: "Hey, we have to do something. There is this problem and we have to change this or that somehow!" And then we discuss the matter and find a solution. That works pretty well!* (Customer, IV07)

A good customer-vendor relationship is equally important from a vendor perspective. Vendor firms maintain their customer relationship to stay in close contact with their customers and recognize potential innovation impulses. However, sometimes the relationship is important because it allows them to discuss difficult topics during or prior to a customization project. For instance, the interview participant from the document management business described the importance of a close relationship to key users:

> *Sometimes projects are not started because the customer department does not cooperate. In these cases you have to act very carefully. Even a question such as "How do you mean this?" might lead to a "I have no time for this" reaction. Then, the project is over before it even started! Having key users on your side to overcome such problems then sometimes helps.* (Vendor, IV10)

Vendor firms establish and maintain customer-vendor relationships by implementing "one-face-to-the-customer" structures or by organizing events for their customers. Customer relations are important for maintaining long-term business with a specific customer and for generating recurring revenues. A good relationship helps strengthen the vendor's position and additional business with the customer. However, similar to the customer's habit of evaluating vendor firms, they rank customers according to the value they provide to the vendor. For instance, as the interview participant from the monitoring and workflow system company explained,

> *If a customer is an "alpha customer" our "taking care" is more intensive than for new or smaller customers. This just depends on how much I am willing to invest in a customer. This is a decision based on experience depending on the customer's economic situation, company size, and other factors.* (Vendor, IV08)

Innovation impulses   In software customization, *innovation impulses* refer to customer-induced need for innovation that leads to product, service or strategic enhancements on the vendor side. They may influence the vendor on a different level and lead to incremental or radical innovations. As the name indicates, innovation impulses are not innovations in that sense that they represent a direct commercial success. However, they might be the foundation for innovation potential. In software customization, innovation impulses might be in the context of (1) the product, (2) the service, or (3) the strategy.

First, product innovations might be reporting a bug, experiencing unclear functionalities or receiving customer-specific requirements that are then implemented to enhance the software product functionality or quality. Customer-induced product innovations on this level are essential for the development of the software product. According to the interview with the partner from the car service company, their entire software product results from customer innovation impulses and was developed within customer projects. On this foundation, they are now able to fulfill approximately 98% of customers' business requirements with the standard product and individualize the front-end and back-end graphical user interfaces (Vendor, IV07).

Second, service innovations influence the vendor service proposal and provisioning behavior. An important customization service is the data conversion from one system to another. Conversion occurs during migration projects or in interfaces between different software components. Integrating and providing reliable conversion tools enhances the vendor's service offering and is somewhat expected by the customer (Customer, IV01). Another less technical customization service is the form of the customization service itself. For instance, vendor firms use a specific customization process model for particular customer or problem situations, for instance, a sequential customization process for standard projects and agile or prototype processes for more innovative projects (Vendor, IV10).

Finally, strategic innovations refer to enhancements in the vendor's general business or revenue model. For instance, a vendor might be able to enter a different line of business according to the experiences from a specific customization context or could change their own revenue model from license-based revenues to a per-per-use model.

Customization projects are important for generating innovation impulses through customer input. In a very similar vein, customization projects are a form of benchmarking or evaluation for the vendor's service, product and business offerings. Close cooperation with the customer in customization projects and the perspective gained from several customization projects at different customer firms provide valuable feedback about the vendor's actual position in a market. The following text excerpt summarizes the importance of customer impulses for the vendor's innovation activity:

> *Without customer input we are helpless. Practice changes in practice outside. The requirements become more complex and sophisticated, and we have to adapt to this situation. Perhaps we even have to become a pioneer by claiming this functionality, or this technology helps the customers do their business better or*

faster. Then you have advantages over your competitors (Vendor,
IV02).

4.4   Summary and discussion

The previous study revealed four unique resources necessary for software
customization. In particular, it was shown that customization relies on four
unique firm resources: (1) customer business and market knowledge, (2) customization management knowledge and experience data, (3) product functionality and flexibility, and (4) product related software development assets.
The results suggest that while the first two resources have been identified as
particularly necessary in customization projects, the second two are more
related to development activities. However, in both cases, the resources form
the foundation that defines the prerequisites for a customization project.

Additionally, it was shown that software customization relies on six distinct capabilities. According to Day (1994), certain types of capabilities can
be recognized in all types of businesses. Corresponding to the core processes
of creating economic value, these capability types are outside-in, spanning,
and inside-out capabilities. The results from the interview analysis suggest
that *business analysis and interpretation capabilities* as well as *customer integration and expectation management capabilities* are related to the outside-in
type of capability, while *solution deployment* and *adjustment capabilities* are
highly related to the inside-out capability type, and *requirements management and negotiation* and *future-proof solution design capabilities* are related
to spanning capabilities.

Finally, with respect to value creation, the results of the analysis suggest
that customer firms focus on *use value* in customization projects, while vendor firms must balance *use and exchange values*. Although this implication
sounds trivial at first, it has meaningful implications for the organization of
customization projects. To provide successful software customization, vendor
firms must simultaneously provide use value and generate exchange value.

Use value depends on the customer's goals for the customization projects and might economically take a short-term or long-term perspective. Exchange value on the vendor side might either be monetary or innovative with respect to developing a product or service and strengthening the vendor's position in a market. Thus, while use value is set as a necessary constant, exchange value is a variable for vendor firms. To be successful from a vendor perspective, firms must economically and prudently deploy their resources and employ their capabilities.

Chapter 5

Qualitative investigation II: Elaborating the strategic role of customization for software product development

The study in this chapter builds upon the existing body of knowledge on software customization, the concepts of resources, capabilities and value from the RBV as well as the insights presented from the last investigation. It aims to provide an elaborative understanding of software customization activities and their strategic role for a software vendor's software product management. Building upon the theoretical concept of dynamic capabilities, this study employs a qualitative multiple case study design within two different software vendor firms. Each explores how innovation impulses from software customization projects are managed within each firm's software product development. Thus, the study presented in this chapter can be regarded a elaborative study to address the thesis' main research question:

> **MRQ:** *How do software vendor firms align their software product management and customization activities?*

To answer this question, this study objective is to explain how software development companies can benefit strategically from product software customization or from innovation impulses generated by customization activities. Thus, it specifically addresses the following sub-research question:

SRQ 3: *Which specific dynamic capabilities do software vendor firms develop to manage innovation impulses from software customization in their productization activities?*

Figure 5.1 illustrates the data collection, consolidation, and display steps employed in this study as well as its workshop-based evaluation.

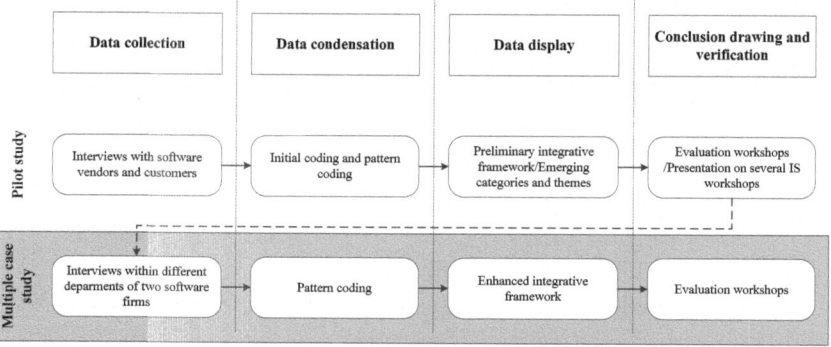

Figure 5.1: The integration of qualitative investigation II in the overall research design

5.1   Empirical setting and data collection

Investigating dynamic capabilities and their micro-foundations as determinants of competitive advantage in turbulent and customer-oriented software development environments is a complex and context-bound organizational issue. Drawing on the results from the previous study, I employed an elaborative, qualitative research approach within two cases from software development companies. While the elaborative approach allowed me to evaluate and reflect the preliminary results from the previous study (Auerbach and Silverstein 2003), the multi case study approach enabled me to employ pattern matching and comparative case analysis (Miles et al. 2013; Yin 2009). Due to this specific research approach, the study is positioned between deductive and inductive qualitative studies, being neither a test of an already developed theory nor the development of a new theory. Rather, it is a contribution to theory building through dialectic interaction between field studies and existing theory (Strauss et al. 1990). Therefore, the study is in line with the postpositivist's research paradigm, which my research in this thesis relies on.

5.1.1 Site description

Using theoretical sampling (Patton 1990), I selected two firms from the hybrid software business with rich experience, both positive and negative, in software development and customization. Expert interviews served as primary data and archival documents as secondary data; these provided me with a rich set of data for analyzing the role of software customization for product development.

The selected cases for the dissertation represent two typical software development and professional services environments in small- and medium-sized firms. The company in the first case can be characterized as a traditional software developer with no explicit professional service department to date. Case two is a traditional software development company with two departments, one for development and one for professional services. They share similarities in *company characteristics* such as year of founding, number of employees, and value chain activities; in *software product characteristics* such as product architecture, programming language, and database as well as in *service characteristics* such as service operations and service channels. Despite these similarities, both companies also differentiate in their business orientation. While the first company's business environment is the telecommunication industry, especially small- and mid-sized telecommunication companies, the second company's business focuses on the management of idea generation processes, which is a more cross-departmental/general market. For reasons of confidentiality, I will refer to the firm from the telecommunication business as Alpha and to the firm from the idea management business as Beta.

5.1.1.1 Company Alpha

Company Alpha is a German small-sized firm providing software solutions for billing-intensive industries and businesses. Today, the company has approximately 25 employees and their software product is used in over 60 installations in Germany, Austria, and Switzerland. The company was founded in 1999 and quickly specialized in billing and rating projects for telecommunication businesses. In this business, the company has developed extensive business and technological knowledge to support billing-relevant business processes. Over time, the company has conducted dozens of implementations and hundreds of interface and adaption projects. According to Alpha's website, their system philosophy is based on three technical pillars: reusability, modularity, and scalability.

Company Alpha has consistently used their project business to develop the software suite. Starting with the billing and rating model, their suite today include modules for customer care, product and tariff management, reporting, online invoicing, and system administration. Customer firms can buy several of those modules or the complete suite. Additional components are partner invoicing and dunning. Based on their product, the company has developed special support for the telecommunication business and provides several business scenarios that can be adapted to specific customer needs. Those scenarios are VoIP/Telephone, Data, Mobile, Interconnection, Value-Added Services, and Hosting.

In the mobile reseller scenario, Alpha's customer is a company that offers mobile contracts to its customers. To do so, the reseller rents mobile infrastructure from a mobile service provider (such as Deutsche Telekom, Vodafona or E-Plus), develops its own tariff and product bundles and offers these to

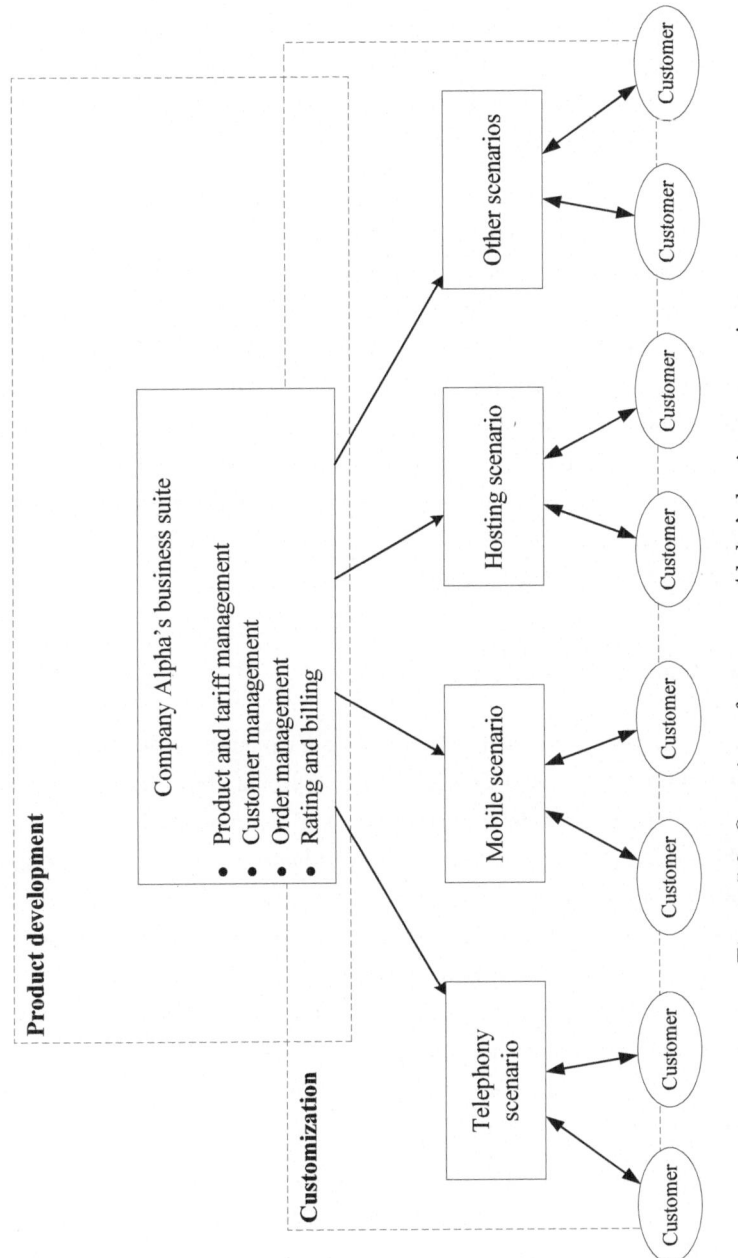

Figure 5.2: Overview of company Alpha's business scenarios

its customers. The revenue model behind this business depends on charging the end customer and sharing the revenue with the mobile service provider. The end customer might be a private consumer or an organization that offers organization-wide mobile contracts for their employees.

Alpha's customer uses their software system to define tariff and product bundles, which are offered to its customers. If an end-customer buys a bundle, the mobile service provider is informed that a new customer wants to use its infrastructure. The mobile service provider informs the reseller that the customer can use the infrastructure. The customer receives the information, at which time he can use the infrastructure. Optionally, the customer receives a mobile device to use the infrastructure. At a given point in time, the mobile reseller sends their CDR data to the reseller, who then generates customer specific call information and invoices. Finally, the share is calculated, which the reseller must pay to the mobile service provider. Additionally, the reseller is responsible for customer support.

5.1.1.2 Company Beta

Company Beta describes itself as a global leader in enterprise social software for idea and innovation management. With approximately 80 employees and 170 installations worldwide, the company is a medium-sized software company. The company was founded in 1999 and has over 13 years of experience in innovation management projects and best practices; this experience has been used to develop software support for innovation management processes. Today, company Beta's software solution supports a full life-cycle innovation management process from idea to market. In particular, their innovation process supports closed innovation management inside the company and more open innovation processes with external communities such as customers, suppliers and partner environments.

Similar to company Alpha, Beta has consistently used their project business to develop a product platform for their innovation management system. Today, Beta offers three different solution packages including a traditional

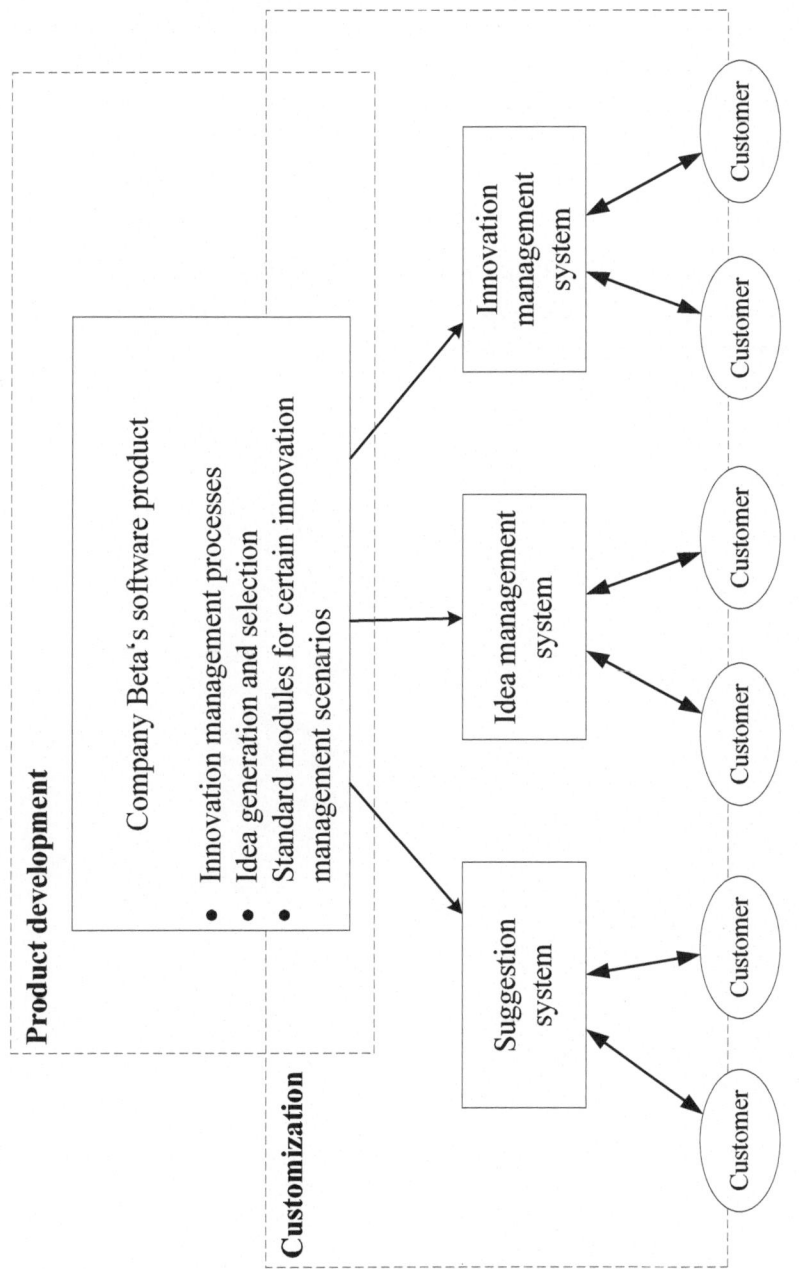

Figure 5.3: Overview of company Beta's business scenarios

employee suggestion system, idea management and innovation management. Customers can purchase those packages as well as additional reporting and interface modules. Beta's customers use the system to manage internal or external suggestions or ideas and identify those with the highest innovation potential. The core of Beta's software system, the idea generation process, can be adapted to the existing firm's prerequisites or to the customer's needs

Table 5.1 summarizes Alpha's and Beta's similarities and differences with respect to *company characteristics*, *software product characteristics*, and *software product and service characteristics*.

Table 5.1: Key characteristics of the case studies

Company characteristics	Alpha	Beta
Company characteristics		
Year of founding	1999	1999
Size	25	80
Value chain activities	Software development, sales, and service and support	
Business environment		
Number of installations	40	110
Customer structure	Small- to medium-sized telecommunication (B2B) companies	Medium-sized to enterprise (B2B) companies
Market structure	Specific market with few target companies	Cross-departmental market structure
Software product characteristics		
Functions/Operations	ERP operations (e.g., customer-care, billing, provisioning, merchandizing, ...)	In-house innovation management operations (e.g., identification, rating, suggestion system, ...)
Architecture	Two/three tier architecture	
Programming language	Delphi/C#	Java
Database	Several SQL Server implementations	
Service characteristics		
Operations	Implementation, adaption of software product; Maintenance and support; Integration in/of third party software	
Service channels	Service management system (including personal, telephone, email, and remote servicing)	

5.1.2   Primary and secondary data

Primary data collection consisted of 19 interviews conducted with firm representatives from both firms between 2011 and August 2013. For the interviews, extensive notes were taken and transcribed immediately after each session. A typical interview lasted approximately 1 hour, although long interviews that lasted up to two hours took place and short follow-up interviews of less than an hour were conducted in later stages of the research. The interviews were conducted in an open-ended and semi-structured manner in accordance with the elaborative nature of this case study. The primary data collection was complemented by observations and informal face-to-face discussions during the field research. Table 5.2 summarizes the interview participants, their roles and the types of interviews conducted per case.

Table 5.2: Primary data consisting of interviews and fieldwork

Code	Participant	Participant's role	Interview types
Company Alpha			
A01	Jennifer	Key Account Manager	Customization interview
			Product development interview
A02	Harald	Senior Software Developer	Customization interview
			Product development interview
A03	Jens	Marketing and Sales Manager	Customization interview
			Product development interview
A04	Sascha	Senior Project Manager	Customization interview
			Product development interview
A05	André	Chief Executive Officer	Customization interview
		Chief Technology Officer	Product development interview
Company Beta			
B01	Marco	Senior Consultant	Customization interview
B02	Klaus	Senior Software Developer	Customization interview
B03	Maren	Team Leader Consulting	Customization interview
B04	Heinz	Chief Marketing Officer	Product development interview
B05	Tom	Software Product Manager	Product development interview
B06	Katherine	Vice President Consulting	Customization interview
			Product development interview
B07	Peter	Vice President Development	Customization interview
			Product development interview

In addition, for triangulation purposes, secondary data were collected and analyzed. These data included presentation slides, web site content and online available statements from the reference customer. Table 5.3 summarizes the secondary data in in this study.

Table 5.3: Secondary data that were collected for comparison with primary data

Type of data	Description
Vendor data and presentation slides	Contained secondary data on the vendor organization. Data were gathered from the vendor's website and from presentation slides provided by the vendor. Data included information on the vendor's organization and structure, whitepapers on specific business cases, and an architectural overview of the product software and service organization.
Reference customer data	Contained information on existing reference customers for each organization. Data were gathered on customer websites and included customer-specific information such as business cases, size, structure, and legal organization.
Project management data	Contained information about certain customization and development projects. The information included the status of each project as well as the steps already taken to reach that status. Data were gathered from issue tracking or project management systems as well as from the Excel spreadsheets used to manage customer projects.

5.1.3   Interview guide

The overall interview processes included two types of interview within each case: (1) interviews about product characteristics and customization processes and (2) interviews on the role of customization in product development activities. The customization interviews within both cases were structured as described in the previous study. However, because I was able to interview different employees for each case, the interviews provided a broader perspective of the company's products and customization activities as in the previous study.

The product development interviews were semi-structured to focus on the participant's experience of customization services and their role in software product development. To structure the interviews, I relied on the structure of the dynamic capability concept. This resulted in three primary interview sections: (1) which sensing capabilities does the company implement to identify strategically relevant opportunities from customization, (2) how does the company seize these opportunities, and (3) how do opportunities influence the strategic decisions in product development. During the interviews, informants were encouraged to talk freely about their real life experiences in customization projects. Again, the implementation of the interviews followed the guidelines introduced by Myers and Newman (2007). Table 5.4 summarizes the interview guide for this study.

In the first part of the interviews, respondents were informed about the topic and aim of the interview. Then, as an "ice-breaking" opening question, they were asked about their position in the company and how long they had been working for that company. This question was initially used as an easy entry question to put the respondents in a relaxed mood for the rest of the interview, and it was not designed to gather relevant data. However, it provided interesting contextual and demographic data about the respondent and their experience in their line of work.

In the second part, I asked the participant to talk about the microfoundations for sensing product development opportunities from software customization activities. The questions concerned who recognizes opportunities in customization projects; what prerequisites (or previous knowledge) that person must have to identify opportunities; how opportunities from several customization projects are integrated; and which types of customization projects provide the most potential for development opportunities. This part aimed at generating examples of micro-foundations for a dynamic sensing capability and a deeper understanding of the importance of customization for product development.

Table 5.4: Interview guide template

I. Introduction and opening question
What is your position in [company name]?
How long have you been working for [company name]?
What is your background [technical/managerial]?

II. Sensing opportunities
Who recognizes relevant knowledge? Customization or development?
What prerequisites must someone have to identify and recognize valuable knowledge?
Which type of customization is more likely to lead to identifying or recognizing valuable knowledge?
Is knowledge identified or recognized from more than one project?

III. Seizing opportunities
How is the identified knowledge integrated into the company?
Who talks to who? What mechanisms exist to foster communication?
Who decides which features will be developed for the next release? What are the underlying decision criteria?
Who decides how these features are developed? Which criteria are used for this decision?

IV. Reconfiguration
How has customization led to strategic innovations? Which type of innovations were these?
Are there feedback mechanisms from software development to customization? Which?
How does this knowledge output affect future release cycles?

VI. Closing
Thank participant & Reassure that transcriptions are entirely confidential.
Ask for permission to contact again in case of unclear recording.

In the third part, I asked participants about their own experience seizing opportunities from customization projects in their company, for instance, how are identified opportunities assimilated and communicated through the organization? How are product development decisions from customization projects made and who is responsible for deciding? Which technical and organizational systems are employed to seize opportunities from customization projects? In this section, I mainly attempted to understand how participants judge the concrete potential of a customization project for product development and which systems are used to seize this development potential.

In the fourth part, I asked participants about how opportunities or threats from customization projects have led to strategic reconfiguration attempts. How has customization led to strategic innovations? Which types of innovations were these? This part also included questions on how development activities find their way into customization projects. For instance, what are the feedback mechanisms between product development and customization? This part aimed at identifying the importance of the opportunities identified in customization projects for the company's (temporary) competitive advantage.

In the closing section of the interview guide, respondents were advised to report on their views of customization-driven product development. I also asked for potential topics that had not yet been addressed in the interview guide but that might also be of interest in the domain of customization.

As during the first study, to avoid the potential pitfalls of interview research such as "active listening" (Myers and Newman 2007; McCracken 1988), I carefully phrased questions to elicit responses in an objective, nondirective manner. I also tried to let the interview participant choose the direction of the interview, only intervening when a topic was too distant from my objectives. My main objective was to facilitate the emergence of key characteristics, capabilities and resources grounded in the manager's own language rather than capturing already specified variables.

5.2 Data analysis and interpretation

5.2.1 Analytical lens and coding approach

For this second study, I employed the elaborative coding approach to further develop my theoretical resource-capability-value framework on the role of customization for product development. Elaborative coding is appropriate for investigations that build on or corroborate previous research or investigations (Saldaña 2009). Thus, this second study elaborates on the findings of the first study. Elaboration, however, not only refers to supporting or strengthening previous evidence but also may include modification or even disconfirmation of previous results.

Technically, elaborative coding is a top-down coding approach in which theoretical constructs from one or more previous studies are used. In contrast to initial coding, in elaborative coding, the qualitative researcher uses the theoretical constructs from previous studies as analytical lenses and selects text keeping those constructs in mind. Thus, a elaborative study at least needs two different but related studies: one completed and one in process (cv. Auerbach and Silverstein 2003).

In this study, I drew the theoretical construct of dynamic capabilities as described in the theoretical chapter of this thesis. Regarding the research question and research objectives of this study, I rely on Teece's (2007) definition of dynamic capabilities for analytical reasons. According to him, dynamic capabilities can be disaggregated into

"the capacity (1) to sense and shape opportunities and threats, (2) to seize opportunities, and (3) to maintain competitiveness through enhancing, combining, protecting, and, when necessary, reconfiguring the business enterprise's intangible and tangible assets." (p. 1319).

By separating these dynamic capabilities from their "organizational and managerial processes, procedures, systems, and structures that undergird each class of capability" (p. 1321), Teece (2007) provided an analytical framework for their identification. This framework is the theoretical foundation for the analytical lens applied in this study. Table 5.5 illustrates the resulting coding structure.

Table 5.5: Dynamic capability codes from the theoretical and analytical lens

Code structure	
Attributes	Firm- and interview-specific attributes and contextual information.
Development	This code includes codings that are related to software development activities that are of a more technical nature and do not directly relate to the software management activities above.
Customization	This code includes codings that are related to software customization activities such as (1) implementation, (2) adaption, and (3) maintenance and support.
Dynamic capabilities	
Sensing	The company's capability to sense (and shape) new opportunities or threats. Sensing and shaping is very much a scanning, creating, learning, and interpreting activity. Investment in research and related activities is usually a necessary complement to this activity.
Seizing	The company's capability to maintain and improve technological competences and complementary assets and, when opportunity is ripe, to invest heavily in the particular technologies and designs most likely to achieve market acceptance.
Reconfiguring	The company's capability to recombine and reconfigure assets and organizational structures as the company grows and as markets and technologies change. Reconfiguration is needed to maintain evolutionary fitness and, if necessary, to try to escape from unfavorable path dependencies.
Micro-foundations	
Sensing	Analytical Systems (and Individual Capacities) to Learn and to Sense, Filter, Shape, and Calibrate Opportunities.
Seizing	Enterprise Structures, Procedures, Designs and Incentives for Seizing Opportunities
Reconfiguring	Continuous Alignment and Realignment of Specific Tangible and Intangible Assets

However, as already argued by (Teece 2007), one should note that

> "the identification of the micro-foundations of dynamic capabil-
> ities must be necessarily incomplete, inchoate, and somewhat
> opaque and/or their implementation must be rather difficult.
> Otherwise sustainable competitive advantage would erode with
> the effective communication and application of dynamic capabil-
> ity concepts." (p. 1321).

The primary interview data were transcribed. Together with the relevant secondary data, this resulted in approximately 450 pages of information. Using this extensive data, I developed a case description for each company aiming to identify the micro-foundations for dynamic capabilities that link customization and product development activities. An assessment of customization activities and product development activities substantiated the micro-foundations. I used several of the display techniques introduced in the methodological chapter to describe, explore and explain customization-driven product development processes and decisions. To ensure reliability, I continuously discussed my ideas with fellow researchers and practitioners from each case and re-evaluated the importance of themes and my interpretation of them.

All data were coded using MAXQDA. Following the elaboration coding approach, I extracted the most relevant themes from primary and secondary data and arranged them in the coding hierarchy. I then documented the precise meaning of the most relevant codings using MAXQDA's memo functionality. For instance, notions such as

> *The customer is the innovation engine for the software. The cus-*
> *tomer needs and requests are crucial for us. From my experience,*
> *over the last years, we have started to increasingly and systemat-*
> *ically gather customer requests.*

> *There is no checklist or catalog. Identifying what is important for*
> *the customer depends on experience and intuition. It is a personal*
> *thing; it is subjective.*

or

> *If the customer has a change or new feature request, we have to*
> *think about its implication for other customers and how we can*
> *build it in a generic way.*

were identified as micro-foundations of the sensing capability. Similar procedures were used for the identification of micro-foundations for the seizing and reconfiguring capabilities.

Following Eisenhardt's (1989) advice, the data analysis started with the within-case analysis so that I could familiarize myself with the specifics of each company. After the reports for each case were written-up and analyzed, I applied Yin's (2009) qualitative pattern matching logic in a cross-case analysis to synthesize the findings.

5.2.2 Descriptive results

Overall, the first coding cycle resulted in 988 coding segments: 368 in the interviews with participants from company Alpha and 620 in those with participants from company Beta. Based on the coding plan on the highest-level general attributes, customization and product development characteristics and dynamic capability related issues were coded.

On the highest level, I analyzed case attributes, customization, product development and dynamic capabilities between customization and product development. The results show that for both cases, the relative importance of each of the codes is similar between Alpha and Beta. Regarding attribute codings, there is a only slight difference between both cases (7% for Alpha and 5% for Beta). With respect to the relative amount of codings, both companies are similar in customization related codings (26% for Alpha and 25% for Beta), product development related codings (13% for Alpha and 10% for Beta) and codings for customization-related dynamic capabilities (54% for Alpha and 60% for Beta). Figure 5.4 illustrates the distribution of codings within both cases.

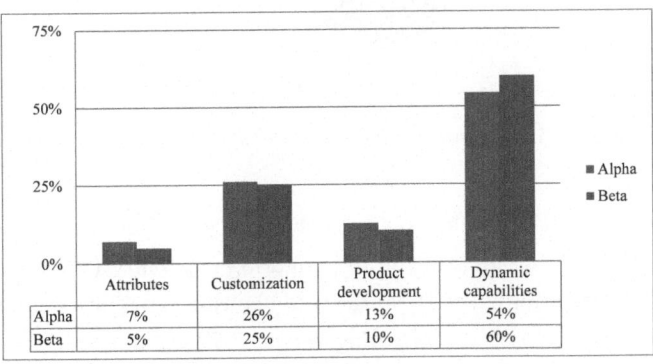

Figure 5.4: Overall codings in Alpha and Beta company

With respect to the dynamic capability concept, the first and second coding cycle resulted in a total of 571 coding segments. Of these, 35% were found in company Alpha and 65% in company Beta. Figure 5.5 illustrates an overall view of the study's codings from the first two cycles and their distribution between Alpha and Beta.

These 571 codings could be further categorized according to the theoretical concepts as follows: 299 (52%) codings were assigned to the sensing capability category, 111 (19%) were assigned to the seizing capability category and 161 (28%) were assigned to the reconfiguration category. Figure 5.6 illustrates an overall view of the study codings in the first cycle and their distribution between the Alpha and Beta cases.

The results suggest that both cases have similar results for the importance of sensing capability and related micro-foundations (56% for Alpha and 50% for Beta). The importance of seizing and reconfiguring capabilities

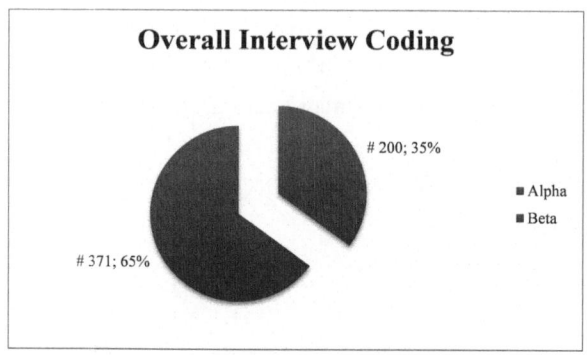

Figure 5.5: Dynamic capability codings in Alpha and Beta

and micro-foundations differs between the two cases. For Alpha, the seizing capability slightly dominates the reconfiguring capability (23% seizing versus 21% reconfiguring). For Beta, the reconfiguring capability dominates the seizing capability (33% reconfiguring versus 17% seizing). Figure 5.6 illustrates the relative distribution of dynamic capability codings for Alpha and Beta.

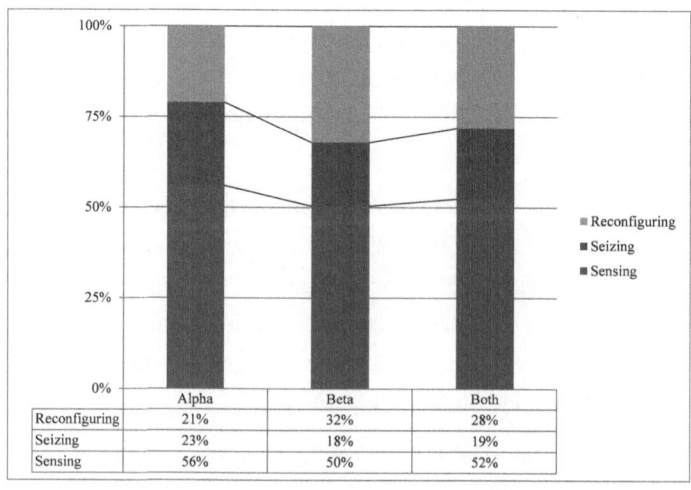

Figure 5.6: Codings in dynamic capability concepts

During the third coding cycle, the codes identified in the sensing, seizing and reconfiguring categories were further analyzed using pattern coding. This coding cycle resulted in four patterns of sensing, four patterns of seizing, and four patterns of reconfiguring.

Within the first category, I was able to discover four patterns that build micro-foundations for the sensing capability: COLLECT, EVALUATE, IN-STALLBASE, and MARKET. As Figure 5.7 shows, the most codings were identified for the COLLECT pattern (Alpha: 54% and Beta: 40%), followed by the EVALUATION (Alpha: 21% and Beta: 29%) and INSTALLBASE (Alpha: 13% and Beta: 19%) patterns and finally the MARKET (Alpha: 13% and Beta: 13%) pattern.

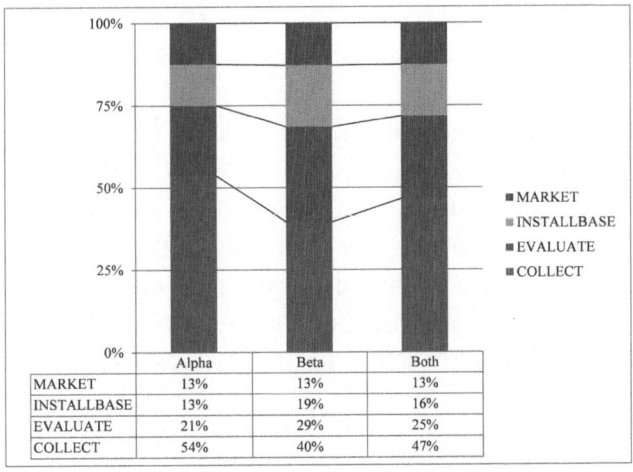

	Alpha	Beta	Both
MARKET	13%	13%	13%
INSTALLBASE	13%	19%	16%
EVALUATE	21%	29%	25%
COLLECT	54%	40%	47%

Figure 5.7: Second coding cycle: Sensing

Within the second category, I was able to discover four patterns that build micro-foundations for the sensing capability: REVENUE, PRODUCT, COMMUNICATION, and RELEASE. As Figure 5.8 shows, the most codings were identified for the REVENUE pattern (Alpha: 46% and Beta: 25%), followed by the COMMUNICATION (Alpha: 28% and Beta: 40%) and PROD-UCT (Alpha: 22% and Beta: 22%) patterns and finally the RELEASE (Alpha: 4% and Beta: 14%) pattern.

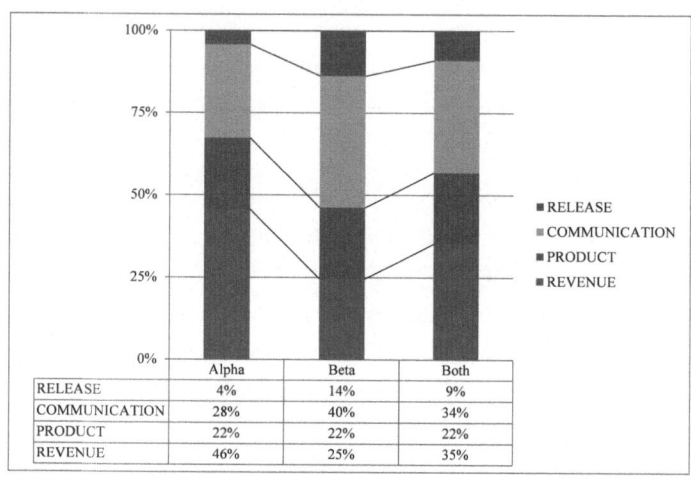

	Alpha	Beta	Both
RELEASE	4%	14%	9%
COMMUNICATION	28%	40%	34%
PRODUCT	22%	22%	22%
REVENUE	46%	25%	35%

Figure 5.8: Second coding cycle: Seizing

Within the third category, I was able to discover four patterns that build
micro-foundations for the sensing capability: MODULARIZATION, STAN-
DARDIZATION, KNOWLEDGEBASE, and REVENUE. As Figure 5.9 shows,
the most codings were identified for the KNOWLEDGEBASE pattern (Alpha: 43% and Beta: 29%), followed by the STANDARDIZATION (Alpha:
19% and Beta: 33%) and MODULARIZATION (Alpha: 17% and Beta: 23%)
patterns and finally the REVENUE (Alpha: 21% and Beta: 15%) pattern.

5.3   Findings and discussion

5.3.1   Cases' product and customization characteristics

5.3.1.1   Company Alpha

Alpha's product characteristics   From a technical perspective, company
Alpha's product was based on a Delphi 7 implementation. In 2008, the company started to successfully transfer their solution to Microsoft's .NET plat-

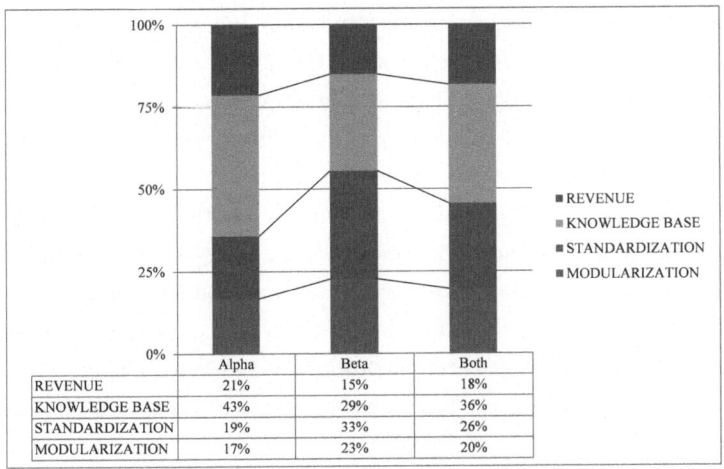

Figure 5.9: Second coding cycle: Reconfiguring

form to provide a future-proof solution for their customers. Over time, the company integrated modules from several third party providers. Today, company Alpha's enterprise suite supports the use of multiple database servers (including Oracle), uses SAP's Crystal Report Engine for several reporting tasks, and connects to AxCMS.NET, a CMS solution for their partner and customer portal solution.

Case Alpha's software product includes several modules for organizing processes in telecommunication rating and billing contexts. These include a software module for managing customer data, product and tariff data, partner commissioning, rating and billing processes, interfaces to input and output systems such as carrier data or print shop formats, and carrier provisioning as well as offering interfaces to web content management systems.

The software modules are native Windows applications that access data stored in a SQL Server database. The Windows applications are implemented through an adapted version of the Model-View-Controller (MVC) Framework. It includes data objects for items and lists, view objects for presenting data and enabling the user to interact with the data and objects that are responsible for business logic and communication between data and view objects. Based on this architecture, the user is able to create, edit, and delete as well as to invoke actions on the data stored in the system. However, because rating and billing applications in particular are performance intensive, certain processes are implemented directly on the database server. Interfaces to peripheral systems are implemented in the form of plug-ins that encapsulate interface descriptions and that can be integrated into the system as needed. These interfaces are, for instance, responsible for reading input call-data records (CDR) that describe customer user data on the carrier side, provisioning data that initializes carrier functions when a customer contract is valid and a specific export format for professional printing solutions.

Alpha's customization characteristics Company Alpha has developed several specific scenario configurations and best practices that describe typical customer needs and that can be relatively easily adapted to specific customer needs. Although these best practice approaches help reduce the initial adaption effort, the customization in case Alpha is complex and takes place on several levels. The system allows configurations in the form of (1) data configuration, (2) orchestration of software modules and configuration of processes, and (3) implementation of customer-specific interfaces and reports. *Data configuration* refers to the configuration of data that is used to produce invoices. In the telecommunication industry, this includes customer data, product and tariff data, and provisioning data. Data configuration is actually the customer's daily business. It includes adding, editing and deleting customer data, configuring new product and tariff descriptions, and so on. *Orchestration of software modules* refers to the configuration of necessary software modules to implement the desired processes. In a simple telecommunication scenario, the process as follows: the CDR data are imported from the carrier systems, the customer is identified along with the specific products and tariffs for this customer and prices are evaluated and integrated into an invoice. To handle this process, the customer needs data from several software modules: customer data, product and tariff data, and CDR

data. Finally, the *implementation of customer-specific interfaces and reports*
refers to the configuration of input and output channels to peripheral socio-
technical systems. *Interfaces*, for instance, are necessary to configure the
systems needed to establish a telephone or mobile connection. Depending on
the end customer's tariff and business needs, this might include multiple independent carrier systems. *Reports*, on the other hand, are usually generated
in human-readable form. This includes tariff contracts, invoices and itemized
bills. Figure 5.10 illustrates the product and customization characteristics in
company Alpha.

Alpha's business characteristics   Company Alpha offers several license
models for their customer solutions: traditional buy or rent licenses, software
leasing, software as a service, and outsourcing/managed services. Traditional
license models focus on selling product licenses and additional maintenance
and support contracts. The customer may buy the licenses or rent them on
a monthly basis. As is typical in professional software business scenarios,
in both cases, maintenance and support contracts establish the company's
service-level agreements (SLA). Software leasing describes a model in which
the customer leases software at a monthly rate and has the opportunity to
buy it after 36 months. This model is equivalent to car leasing examples.
Instead of only leasing products or product modules, the customer also has
the opportunity to lease service offerings. These services may include installation, adaption and maintenance services. The software as a service model
describes a license model in which the company provides not only software
and additional services but also hardware and IT infrastructure. In this case,
customer firms do not need to buy and maintain additional hardware. Instead, they can access the software over remote tools. Finally, with outsourcing and managed services, company Alpha provides outsourcing functionality
for their customer. Customer firms can outsource entire business processes
or only single tasks regularly or in an ad-hoc manner.

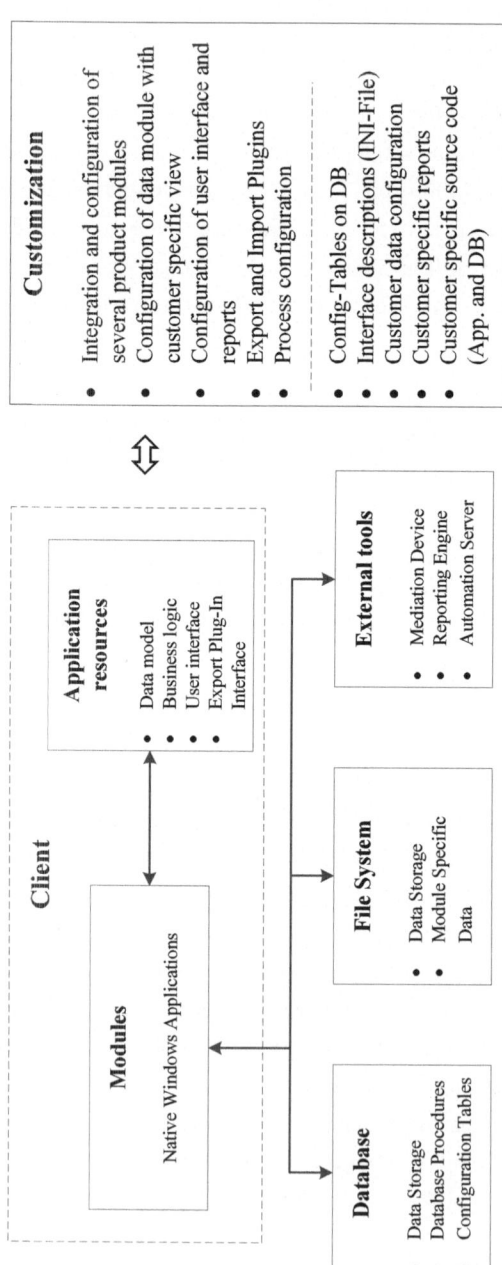

Figure 5.10: Overview of company Alpha's product characteristics

5.3.1.2   Company Beta

Beta's product characteristics   Company Beta offers a highly customizable software product to support enterprise idea and innovation management. Customer firms can use the software to integrate their employees, customer users and external business partners into their innovation process. The product offers the opportunity to share innovation ideas and to discuss them with superiors and colleagues. If an idea is considered to be valuable - in the sense that it has true innovation potential - central management can evaluate it and select it for implementation or utilization. Employees can continuously follow the development and evaluation of their ideas. Therefore, the software not only supports the process of creating and generating ideas or innovation but also increases organization-wide transparency for implemented idea management.

Company Beta offers three different types of innovation management modules that suit different processes for idea and innovation management: traditional suggestion management, idea generation and innovation management. Additionally, Beta offers several support modules for integrating the software into the customer's enterprise as well as additional functionalities for the end user. Modules from the first group include technical infrastructures such as Active Directory/LDAP or external SQL database integration. The second group of modules includes enhanced reporting tools, dynamic key performance indicators, or idea exchange based on the logic of an online stock game. Modules are licensed separately for the customer and can be loaded dynamically as needed.

Beta's customization characteristics   Independent of Beta's modular software architecture, it is possible to adapt the product to customer-specific idea and innovation management needs. The software is designed using a three-tier architecture that separates the data models, business logic and user interface. These components are on the same architectural layer as the standard components and can be configured separately. Thereby, it is possible to generate completely new customer-specific data models, implement the business logic as needed, and design the user interface as desired. The architecture makes sure that customer-specific components are not affected by vendor-released updates on standard components. This is especially necessary for offering product software in the hybrid software business.

Beta's software product offers a dynamic configuration mechanism that enables professional service employees and customers to change the user interface, design and business logic during run-time. The configuration mechanism is implemented in the form of a web-based configurator tool. Usually, the following components are modified in different customer projects:

- The *idea workflow* represents the customer firm's innovation process. This processes is highly individual and builds the foundation for most of Beta's software processes. Thus, the idea workflow must be planned accurately at the beginning of a customer project.

- The *user entry masks* are responsible for gathering and storing all information necessary for the company's idea workflow. Although Beta offers many standard masks, which are equal in all of their customers' implementations depending on the customers' industry and business needs, it is possible to adapt the masks accordingly.

- The *user authorization rules* are necessary for managing user- or group-specific read and write permissions. The planning processes for authorization rules is complex and must be performed thoroughly to ensure that user groups can only see (and change) information necessary for their work.

Figure 5.11 highlights the core product and customization characteristics of Beta's software product.

Beta's business characteristics   In contrast to Company Alpha, Beta offers only the more traditional license models for their customer solutions.

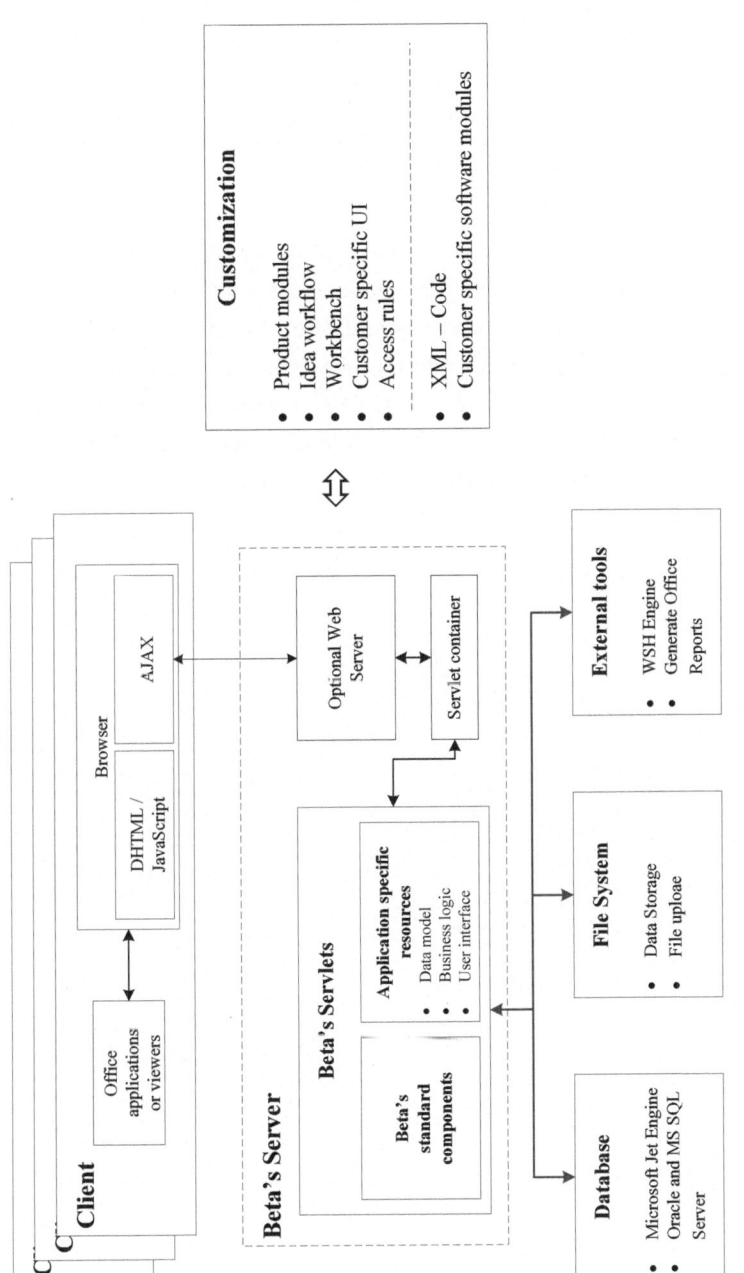

Figure 5.11: Overview of company Beta's product characteristics

The customer pays for software product licenses as well as paying maintenance and support contracts as established in the company's SLA. However,
company Beta more explicitly offers and charges for consulting services for
implementing and adapting their software product to the customer firm's
needs.

The previous sections have shown that both companies use various customization mechanisms to offer customer-specific solutions. Although the
existing literature has categorized customization in terms of parameterization, configuration and source code development, to understand software
customization from a specific vendor's perspective, it is important to understand the firm's path development and underlying software architecture as
well as the existing customer installations. Table 5.6 summarizes the results
of the previous sections.

Table 5.6: Comparison of product and customization characteristics

	Case Alpha	**Case Beta**
Product characteristics	• Native Windows Application • Multi-Tier Architecture • Processes are implemented in Windows Modules and SQL Server procedures • Interfaces are implemented in plug-in technologies and a mediation device • Software supports a multi-client architecture • MVC-Pattern approach as underlying development framework • Supports different business and revenue models	• Web application • Multi-Tier Architecture • MVC pattern separates data models, business logic, and user interface • Product includes a software engine and XML descriptions • Multi device support (desktop and mobile devices) • Supports different business and revenue models
Customization characteristics	• Database configuration • Process configuration • Interface configuration • UI configuration • Connect modules through DB configuration	• Customization and customer specific application development • Configurator tool with XML output • Process and UI configuration

5.3.2   Overall conceptual framework

Following the research design approach as described, the study identified
twelve micro-foundations and strategies that define a software company's
dynamic capability. Figure 5.12 integrates the identified micro-foundations
into an overall research framework.

5.3.3   Sensing capability

In fast-paced, competitive environments such as the B2B software business,
consumer needs, technological opportunities, and competitor activity are constantly changing. While some emerging marketplace trajectories are easily
recognized, others are hard to discern (Teece et al. 1997). To react to market changes or actively form opportunities, a firm needs sensing capability.
Sensing new opportunities refers to a scanning, creating, learning, and interpreting activity that is complemented by research and related activities.
However, sensing not only includes the identification of customer needs and
technological possibilities, it further includes (1) understanding latent demand, (2) the structural evolution of industries and markets, and (3) likely
supplier and competitor responses (Teece 2007). Following Teece's (2007)
argumentation, I thus define the micro-foundations for a firm's sensing capability as *Analytical systems to learn and to sense, filter, shape and calibrate
opportunities.*

With respect to sensing, the analysis revealed that for both companies,
the customer is the most important source of innovation for product management. Additionally, customization projects such as implementation or
adaption projects are an important source for gathering information on customer needs and requirements. However, both cases showed that although
the customer is essential for identifying innovation potential, it is not the
only source. Additional sources such as the market and an internally oriented perspective are important influential factors for deciding if and how
customer requests should lead to standard product features. This is not sur-

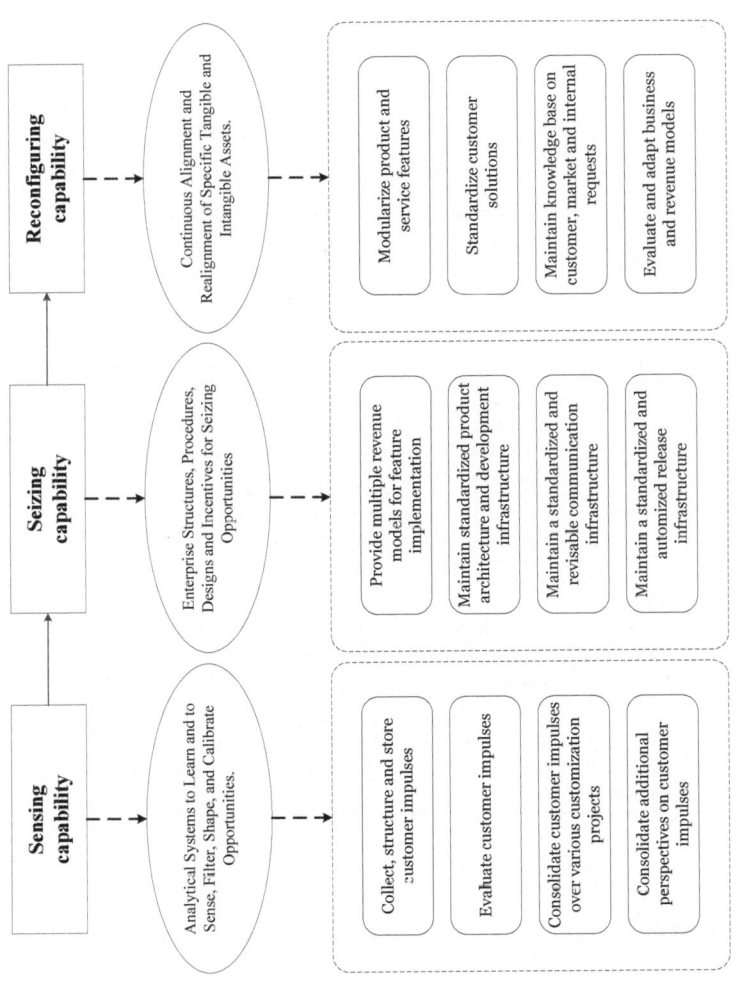

Figure 5.12: Resulting overall framework

prising because existing dynamic capability research has already described the customer, market, and internal perspective as important resources for developing competitive advantage.

Drawing on Teece's (2007) definition of micro-foundations for sensing capability, I was able to identify four distinct micro-foundations that software companies use to implement a sensing capability in the hybrid software business: (1) to collect, structure and store customer requests, (2) to evaluate customer requests, (3) to consolidate customer impulses from the product's installed base, and (4) to consolidate additional perspectives on customer impulses. Table 5.7 summarizes those micro-foundations.

Table 5.7: Sensing capability: Definitions and microfoundations

Micro-foundation	Description
Collect, structure and store customer impulses	Collecting and storing new feature and change requests in a structured and revisable manner helps filter and evaluate requests.
Evaluate customer requests	Separating maintenance from change or new feature requests is a key micro-foundation in the product development business.
Consolidate customer impulses from the product's install-base	New product features usually need to be valuable to multiple customer firms. Thus, sensing opportunities involves consolidating and anticipating multiple customers' needs.
Consolidate additional perspectives on customer impulses	Although the customer is considered to be the most important impulse giver, product development also involves consolidating market and internal needs.

5.3.3.1 Collect, structure and store customer requests

This micro-foundation refers to the vendor's ability to *collect and store customer requests in a structured and revisable manner, which helps filter and evaluate specific requests according to their product potential.* In both companies, the customer is regarded as the most important source for software innovation impulses and as the engine that drives further software development. For instance, as the key account manager from company Alpha stated,

> *The customer is the innovation engine for the software. The customer needs and requests are crucial for us. From my experience, over the last years we have started to increasingly and systematically gather customer requests.*

The importance of customer requests for the product development of both firms can be illustrated by two numbers. According to Alpha's senior product developer, approximately 90% (or more) of the features implemented in one release are customer driven. In Beta's case, the product manager states that approximately 70–80% of the product features planned for one release are customer driven. Those numbers highlight the necessity of actively managing customer requests.

Customer requests might result from the usage of an implemented system, during simple or complex customization activities, within an initial implementation or during the adaption of a customer solution, or from different phases. The sales employee from company Alpha states that they use every opportunity to collect innovation ideas from customers. To systematically manage customer requests, both companies have continuously professionalized their request management processes, as the key account manager from company Alpha stated:

> *From my experience, we have done a lot over the last years to explicitly manage customer requests and include them into our product development. And the customer firms appreciate this. It is a classical win-win situation: the customer profits from our product development, and we profit from offering the customer what he wants.*

Company Alpha has built its entire sensing capability around a project management system and implemented organizational processes and structures that enable it to systematically collect customer requests; distinguish support, change, and new product feature requests; and store them in a centralized database system available to all roles active in the company. A customer can provide input over several communication channels, such as email, telephone, fax, and personal discussion. Written requests such as faxes or emails are (semi-)automatically transformed into projects or tickets and related to specific customer and product modules. Alpha's employees are instructed to generate request tickets from the customer based on personal discussions or meetings where they describe the challenge or problem, the possible solution and an implementation idea.

> *We have an internal project or ticket management system. Project or ticket depending on the level of a customer request. This system is used to collect support requests, feature requests and error messages from internal and external sources. Means, if something comes up, usually a ticket is created.*

In a similar vein, company Beta started to collect customer requests in an unstructured way, using Microsoft Excel and Word documents. In recent years, the company has started to use their own idea management tool to collect, store and structure customer requests. Currently, in particular, service employees active in the customer's environment use the system to collect customer requests. Similar to Alpha's approach, requests are structured in a description of the problem, the possible solution and an idea for implementation. Today, the system includes thousands of customer ideas, which makes the further management of requests difficult. As the product manager from Beta highlights:

> *We have a product that we use, our own product, to record all of this information, it is called the tracker. And it's full, it's got up to a thousand ideas about and it's impossible to manage, but every time a customers says or a prospect says we need this or we need that, it's the job of the person who hears it to put it in the*

system. And then we try to evaluate it and say how long would it take, we have all these fields in it that say what kind of feature is it, how long roughly would it take to build, anybody else interested in it, does in fit on the roadmap in any particular way so we have all these kind of criteria to judge the input.

The last interview excerpt shows that initial customer requests are not generalized with respect to the existing installed base or the anonymous market. Thus, before seizing customer impulses, the vendor companies must evaluate customer impulses against internal technological prerequisites, market and installed base requirements and, finally, must evaluate how specific requests will be addressed in product development. The following sections will elaborate on how customer requests are evaluated in both companies.

5.3.3.2 Evaluate customer requests

This section describes micro-foundations that implement the vendor's ability *to distinguish maintenance and support requests from change or new product feature requests.* Customer requests are usually unstructured, and often things that do not work as expected by the customer are regarded as software errors. From the software vendor's perspective, there are at least three types of customer requests in relation to the software product:

- error and bug fixing requests,

- change requests, and

- new feature requests.

Separating maintenance from change or new feature requests is a key competence for software vendors because depending on the type of request, other processes may be triggered. *Error and bug fixing requests* are usually directed to the development team and fixed within the current or next release.

How soon a fix will be delivered depends on the estimated risk of a software error or bug. *Change requests* are evaluated according to their fit to the existing feature implementation and their usefulness. If a feature is regarded as useful, it is planned for one of the next releases. *New feature requests* are evaluated for their usefulness and their fit into the company's strategy for the product (portfolio). New features are usually more complex, and therefore the evaluation process is also more complex; it might include a more or less detailed design and specification process. Alpha and Beta have established different structures and processes to identify feature requests.

Company Alpha has established a support role that is responsible for pre-evaluating incoming customer requests. The support employee evaluates new requests based on his experience and uses the project management system to align them to specific modules and customers. From this point on, the employee responsible for the particular product module must maintain the customer request and further evaluate whether a request should lead to product development or should be handled in the form of a support task. To do so, this employee evaluates the scope and costs for implementing a specific feature and discusses implementation with general management. The final decision of whether a specific feature is implemented is made by general management. An Alpha senior developer describes the rationale behind this process as follows:

> *If the customer has a request, we evaluate how it can be included into the product. Usually, if the customer needs new data objects or something else, then against the background of new or changed market needs. Thus, potentially, the new functionality can be useful for other customers as well.*

Company Beta has a less tool-supported way of evaluating customer requests. Although customer requests are separated into bug fixes and product feature requests, as in company Alpha, company Beta has implemented a sponsor-oriented organizational process for deciding whether a certain feature is implemented in the product standard. For a new feature to become part of the product, the requesting employee (independent of function: service, marketing or development) must convince one of the vice presidents of the importance and value of that feature. Only if one of the vice presidents agrees and acts as an internal sponsor for a specific feature is it included into further product management.

In both companies, the evaluation produces several additional pieces of information added to the customer's request in the project management system; this information includes

- the estimated cost for implementing a feature

- the resources and time necessary to implement a feature

- the priority for implementing a feature (e.g., bug fixes usually have the highest priority and are scheduled for implementation with less evaluation to avoid the risk of software failure)

In both cases, software product management uses this information to construct the product release plan and road map. Once the parameters for the implementation of a new software feature are clearer and the feature has been determined as potentially useful, the software vendor must evaluate its usefulness against general market requirements, its influence on the existing installed base as well as internal technical prerequisites. Collecting additional perspectives on a new feature from already existing customers is therefore the next important step in sensing product potential.

5.3.3.3 Consolidate customer impulses from the existing installed base

If a customer's change or new feature request is regarded as being potentially valuable for the software product, the software vendor collects more information to evaluate if and how to implement it. While sometimes the decision is made easily due to technical or architectural preliminaries, software vendors must reflect on the request's influence on the existing installed base. To make this decision, they need more information to anticipate its influence on the installed base. To do so, the software provider must be able to review existing requests from other customers or other customization projects. Thus, identifying the value of a certain feature for multiple customer firms is an essential capability for software firms in the hybrid software business. This section describes the micro-foundations implemented to *consolidate and anticipate the needs from multiple customer firms.*

The easiest way to gather information from potential users of new product features is to contact the customer firm and ask if a certain feature is regarded as valuable or not. Company Alpha, for instance, has implemented this through its sales and support functions. The key account manager uses her regular contact with customer firms to evaluate if specific features are needed. This channel is also used to evaluate the customer's willingness to pay for a certain product feature.

> *If a customer tells me something is important, I ask 2–3 other customers as a reference about this topic or feature. If they tell me, yes, we would like this, too, it is a hint for me that the requested feature is important.*

However, it is not always that easy to gather information as described. For instance, although the customer says a specific feature is needed, it is not directly clear how a new feature influences the existing installed base. Thus, for a deeper analysis, company Beta extensively analyzes historical customer contacts and projects. As the vice president of solutions explained,

> *So, we know we need to employ campaigns to collect ideas. We know from our business how this process has to be established. However, evaluating customer projects and thinking about and anticipating implications for these projects is the most important thing.*

Both companies also include the customer's experience with the software product and customization processes into their evaluation activity. As Alpha's senior product developer explained,

> *From a quantitative perspective, new customers or inexperienced customers provide the most requests with product potential. The reason for this is that they are not biased by their experience with a specific IT system. They do not know "the normal way". Those customers have completely different ways of thinking and might provide valuable input for us. Experienced customers provide more detailed feedback with respect to technical specifications. However, since those customers have a years-long experience with our system, they might not think out of the standard.*

Another way to gather more valuable information from the installed base is to identify a key or lead user. Company Beta, for instance, has recently started to establish a process for continuously collecting customer feedback from the installed base. As the product manager from company Beta explained,

> *What we're trying to do the last six months is to identify the lead ones. And trying forming a group of, say, 10 that we meet with every quarter and just ask questions and find out what they think. So that's what we're trying to do.*

The software vendor's installed base is an important source for evaluating potential product features. However, because software firms are naturally interested in opening new market opportunities or segments, the software vendor has to evaluate product implementation from a more general market perspective. The following section will elaborate on how the two investigated cases employ a wider market perspective in their product development.

5.3.3.4   Consolidate additional perspectives on customer impulses

While the customer's perspective on change or new feature requests is essential for software product development, it is not the only source of information for the software vendor. To determine whether changing or implementing a feature will be valuable, the software vendor must also evaluate the market perspectives on this feature. This wider perspective helps evaluate the feature's effect on the market, the product architecture and the vendor's strategic position. The micro-foundations in this section describe different structures and processes established in both cases to use information from these sources to evaluate product features.

Integrating market perspectives from several sources is essential for identifying market potential. Both companies highlight that they use all sources available to gather information on the potential benefits and costs of newly implemented product features. In particular, the sales employee from company Alpha describes how reflecting against market needs is a daily process in the company:

> *Absolutely. It is an almost daily process. We try to use every opportunity to discuss product development or strategic positioning of our software product. So we gather information from three or four different perspectives, and this helps us to evaluate what the market wants and how it evolves.*

One of the most important sources for market information is the service employees, who have contact with existing customer firms and prospects. Usually, interested customer firms contact the sales department first to gather information on whether a certain product functionality is available. For the software hybrid business, the sales function therefore has high strategic influence. By promising functionality to customers, they have great influence on the software vendor's product development department. Therefore, as the product manager from company Beta explained, the alignment between sales and product development is essential:

> *So you have the service folks out there, selling all of the time and trying to sell and they're having to promise things that don't exist. And they're saying "hey, can we make this happen, can we do this, can we do this...". And I guess some of that is just strategic, because you are looking at these promises and saying "well, yes it fits with our general roadmap. So yes, you can promise that." We didn't wanna do it now, but we can if we have to. And there are some things that don't make sense, we never gonna do that. So, 'I'm sorry sales, we just cannot promise that, it's not gonna happen.*

However, the product is not only driven by customer or prospect needs. From a strategic perspective, it is necessary to evaluate the offerings of the market partner or direct competitors. Thus, firms in the hybrid software business use market studies from firms such as Gartner Inc. or Forrester Research. However, firms also use available presentation materials from competitor firms to identify potential changes to their products. As one manager from company Beta explained,

> *For instance, we met this competitor several years ago in Silicon Valley. They had this attack slide against us telling potential customers what we do wrong and where we fail. And what they do better. This is business, but you usually don't do this on slides. However, this competitor also presented an interesting idea for our idea management system. We adapted this idea and integrated it in our existing product portfolio.*

Another important source of market information are the developers in the firm. Developers, in particular, are intrinsically motivated to learn new technologies such as programming languages, new web server technologies, or integrative technological frameworks. Thus, these employees help identify new opportunities to implement and reorganize the existing product portfolio. The senior developer in company Alpha describes the essential function of this market sensing mechanism as follows:

*Which other sources do we have? The developers themselves. I
think, they are a good source. There have been several impulses or
ideas about what is technologically possible. It is a kind of private
market analysis. Since developers are interested in certain topics
and look around how things are done in the market.*

Finally, the product manager from company Beta highlights the necessity
of balancing market perspective and current customer demands. Recently,
company Beta started to institutionalize this balance by hosting a customer
event during which they present portions of their strategic road map for
the next releases. By doing so, they were able to make sure to meet their
customers' needs and not just needs identified from an anonymous market.
The following text excerpt describes the product manager's perspective:

*We had a forum recently, where a lot of customers came for two
days and we all sat down and did discussions, and round table
sessions and people spoke and gave presentations. What was really interesting. I was run two, four round table sessions with
customers and it was all about "here is our roadmap for the next
twelve months, what do you think?" And there was a certain
portion of our roadmap that has to do with integration of all the
systems into us. And the feedback was unanimous. They didn't
care for it. It just didn?t make any sense. And actually what
they wanted was something far more simple. So in terms of integration they were saying "we just care about our daily job." So
if you think about it, most of the things we do are an email. So
why can't you integrate with our email-system? Do stuff in Microsoft outlook to make it easier for us. We never thought about
it, because it's not sexy, it is not interesting, who cares?*

The interview data show a difference in how deeply the idea tracking or
project management systems are integrated in product management operations. Company Alpha, on the one hand, not only uses the system for collection, structuring and storing but also uses it to distinguish support, change

and new product feature requests. Company Beta, on the other hand, uses the idea tracker mostly to collect and store product feature requests.

Table 5.8: Comparison of micro-foundations for sensing capability

	Case Alpha	Case Beta
Collect, structure and store customer requests	• Ticket and project management system • Create a ticket for every customer request • Employees and customers can create tickets • Elaborate tagging system to categorize tickets	• Issue tracker system • Employees create issues based on customer feedback
Evaluate customer impulses	• Bug fixes and maintenance requests • Change requests • New feature requests • Service and support requests	• Bug fixes and maintenance requests • Change requests • New feature requests • Service and support requests
Consolidate customer impulses from various customization projects	• Review feature requests from other customers • Task for the product manager and the module-responsible developer • Elaborate filter mechanisms in ticket system (Project, customer, module-specific filter)	• Review feature requests from other customers • Task for the product manager role
Consolidate additional perspectives on customer impulses	• Marketing, service and support, and management use ticket system	• Marketing, service and support, and management use tracker system

5.3.4   Seizing capability

Dynamic capability theory suggests that once a new (technological or market) opportunity has been recognized, a firm must address it with products, processes, or services. According to Teece (2007), this includes development and technological activities. He states that, from a technological perspective, addressing opportunities involves maintaining and enhancing a firm's technological competences and complementary assets by investing in the particular technologies necessary to most likely achieve market acceptance. However, seizing an opportunity is not just about how much effort to put in development; it also includes selecting or developing business and revenue models that form a valid case for a firm's business success. According to Teece (2007), the firm's seizing capability refers to its potential to capture opportunities.

Table 5.9: Seizing capability: Definitions and microfoundations

Micro-foundation	Description
Provide multiple revenue models for feature implementation	Balancing costs and revenues in product development is essential for software companies. Thus, they need to maintain a set of revenue models for generating revenue from development activities.
Maintain a standardized product architecture and development infrastructure	A standard product architecture and development infrastructure is essential for rapid and yet reliable feature development.
Maintain a standardized and revisable communication infrastructure	Product feature requests change over time. However, sometimes it is important to understand which inputs have led to which decisions. Thus, software companies need to establish a standardized and revisable communication system.
Maintain a standardized and automatized release infrastructure	Software product development is not only about developing features but also about deploying those features to customer firms. Therefore, software companies need a distinct and automatized release strategy and infrastructure.

Once a change or new feature request has been determined to be valuable for the standard product, the development company must integrate it into its product (portfolio). Drawing on Teece's (2007) definition of micro-foundations for seizing capability as *enterprise structures, procedures, designs and incentives for seizing opportunities*, I was able to identify four distinct micro-foundations that software companies use to implement a seizing capability in the hybrid software business: (1) they provide multiple revenue models for feature implementation, (2) they maintain a standardized product architecture and development infrastructure, (3) they maintain a standardized and revisable communication strategy, and (4) they maintain a standardized and automatized release infrastructure. Table 5.9 summarizes those micro-foundations.

5.3.4.1 Provide multiple revenue models for software feature implementation

Product feature development is an expensive task. Design, specification, development, test and documentation are time-consuming, complex tasks usually performed by highly educated experts. Especially for small- to medium-sized enterprises with small or even no research and development budgets, it is essential to generate a foreseeable return on investment through their product development activities.

Thus, balancing costs and revenues in product development is essential for software companies. They need to maintain a set of revenue models for generating revenue from development activities. The case analysis revealed four distinctive types of revenue models applied in the hybrid software business:

- product development is financed by the software vendor firm although there is no direct customer budget due to the strategic importance of a specific feature;

- product development is financed by multiple customer firms with a need for a specific feature; or

- product development is paid for by a customer who has an essential need for a specific feature.

The manager from company Alpha describes the rationale behind those opportunities as follows:

> *If an idea is good and we are convinced that the new feature is useful, there are three options: (1) if we think the feature is strategically important or there is a broad usage potential in our customer base, then we develop this feature for free, (2) if we know that 2–3 other customers would like to have this feature as well, then we ask them if they are willing to bear the development cost, and finally, (3) if we think an idea is important for one customer but not that relevant for others, then this customer must bear all implementation costs.*

Additionally, companies use maintenance and support contracts to manage smaller change requests or product development issues. Those contracts are usually long-term contracts over the time a software product is used by customers. Both companies in this case study use this mechanism to cover small, customer-specific product development. For instance, company Beta offers their customers an additional support package with the first time implementation that is used to handle the new customer requests that come up during initial projects. Thus, a fourth way to finance product development can be described as follows:

- the new feature is a change request for an already existing feature, and development is financed within a customer's maintenance or support contract.

Although this process might raise the impression that maintenance and support contracts have nothing to do with product development, the following comment from Alpha's sales employee illustrates how important change requests are for the product standard:

> *Often complaints from customers have an important influence on product development. Complaints have to be evaluated seriously and the software provider has to be open-minded for critical feedback. In our case, critical feedback through customer complaints has resulted in important product features or functional updates.*

However, the customer cannot only influence whether a feature is going to be implemented into the standard. As the senior developer from company Alpha states, the customer can also influence the priority of product feature implementation by offering payment for certain features. In particular, new customer or prospect firms have an important influence on product development. Due to the royalty fee that accompanies the sale of a new product, it is easier for a new customer to get features into the product standard. The senior project manager from company Alpha describes this as follows:

> *So, I think it is easier for a new customer to get their requirements into the standard. They bring a huge license revenue, which we do not get from existing customers. They have already paid their licenses. And if a new customer says that something is especially important or 'I will take a look at competitor products', then he has a good argument.*

5.3.4.2 Maintain standardized product architecture and development infrastructure

Professionally used software has several requirements that go beyond simple product features. Customer firms using such software also need maintenance and support services. During the analysis, I found two micro-foundations to ensure this requirement: (1) a solid and standardized product architecture and (2) a standardized product development infrastructure.

A solid product architecture helps implement features in an expected process for customer and software vendor firm alike. Furthermore, applying standards to architecture and development activities is essential for establishing reliable and calculable maintenance and support services. With respect to product architecture, the analysis revealed that firms develop framework libraries for encapsulating common product functionalities. For instance, the Model-View-Controller (MVC) Framework helps separate the data model, user interface and business functionality. Figure 5.13 illustrates the components of the MVC pattern and their interaction.

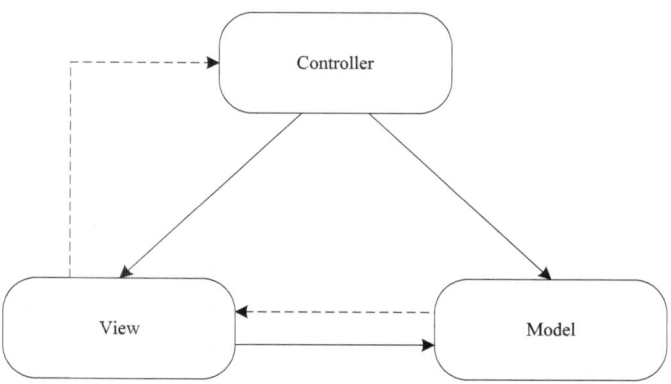

Figure 5.13: Overview model-view-controller

Furthermore, company Beta's product has another architectural component. It not only separates models, views, and controller components but also distinguishes engine and product specific components. The engine is the pure standard of Beta's product. It is responsible for implementing the idea management processes or presenting data to the user. Based on this engine, Beta has developed several XML configurations that represent distinct products based on the engine.

However, using frameworks such as that described above, influences the flexibility with which customer requests can be addressed in product development. The senior project manager from company Alpha explained that the existing architecture influences how he interacts with the customer:

> We, as the software developing firm, know how our system works, which philosophy lies behind it. Therefore, during consulting, I have to lead the customer in a way that he stays within the boundaries of our system. This is the case for changes as well as for new product features.

Similar to the product technological architecture, the development infrastructure has an influence on the quality of product features. Both companies have implemented several mechanisms to standardize their development process. For instance, with respect to the development, infrastructure coding guidelines as well as versioning systems are implemented in each firm's standard processes. Additionally, both companies work with similar project management processes in development and customization.

Furthermore, company Beta has established a "Godfather Principle" that is quite similar to the Pair Programming concept in eXtreme Programming (Beck and Andres 2004). Following the "Godfather Principle", customer-induced product features are always developed by paired consultants and developers. While the developer is responsible for implementing the feature according to the firm's development guidelines and architectural prerequisites, the consultant must make sure that the feature is implemented as expected by the customer. The vice president consulting from company Beta describes the intention of the godfather concept as follows:

> The idea behind the godfather principle is to create private ownership for developer and consultants. The godfathers of a product feature shall defend it, although other consultants from other customers argue for a different functionality. Thus, they have to ensure the business or use case behind a product feature.

5.3.4.3 Maintain a standardized and revisable communication infrastructure

Feature requests are complex. Customer firms have specific requests, and vendor firms must evaluate how those features can be addressed and if they should lead to product development. If they should, the vendor must evaluate the potential benefit of a specific feature for existing and potential customers as well as the potential implementation risk. Therefore, in an extreme case, an initial customer request can evolve over time to a full-grown new feature request. To manage the evolution of customer requests over time, software vendors must maintain the request history as well as the customer or internal input that led to the reevaluation of a specific request. Thus, *tracking and storing the evolution of customer requests is an essential capability for firms active in the hybrid software business.* Companies Alpha and Beta have developed different mechanisms and processes to implement this capability.

Company Alpha uses the ticket system to organize internal and external communication. Thus, communication with other departments in the company as well as with customer firms is centralized and stored in a structured manner. The ticket system provides the opportunity to generate emails from messages. Thus, the communication is stored in one place and not decentralized in multiple email boxes across the firm. Furthermore, the ticket system allows the state of a specific development task to be maintained. Tasks might be New, In Development, Pending, Finished or Closed. Sales and business administration uses the information stored with the task for invoicing.

With respect to communications, the ticket system plays a central role in Alpha's organization: (1) it provides a platform for asynchronous discussions with customer employees or colleagues, (2) it integrates the development process from pre sales, analysis and design, implementation, test, deployment, and invoicing; (3) it provides a platform for aligning and archiving customer messages to product modules or specific features; (4) it helps organize and prioritize customer requests.

Company Beta's communication strategy is less IT dependent. The company has adapted a scrum-like project management process for development and customization activities. Thus, the developer and consultants use equal structures to organize their work. Following scrum, Beta uses its tracker system to maintain sprint and backlog lists and organizes daily stand-up meetings and sprint demos. The rationale behind Beta's organization of communication can be best described as based on the book "Getting Real" by Fried et al. (2009):

They say, you will create a feedback form or blog or something where people can post ideas. The question is then, what do I do with thousands of entries per year? The answer is, read it and delete it. Every approach to prioritize or organize those things, create top-ten lists, ... forget it! The human brain is a great filter, read it and what stays in mind is important. So, for us the tracker is a good tool for communication. However, the final prioritizing takes place in the heads of people.

Recently, Beta established an explicit product management role. The product manager is responsible for organizing releases and planning the strategic road map. He is not involved in operational development activities and concentrates on the strategic perspective of product development.

I have been here for a year now as the product manager. So, in the previous company, I was the main developer and then the lead developer for the team, as a group, and then I was kind of a double role of the head of the product development and head of product management at the time. So it was very difficult doing both things. Here I am not really involved in coding anymore, I am just the product manager.

5.3.4.4 Maintain a standardized and automatized release infrastructure

Software product development is not only about developing features but also about deploying those features to customer firms. Delivering new product modules or feature updates to an existing customer base is an essential and frequent task in the hybrid software business. Deployment activities might be scheduled regularly in the form of minor or major releases or irregularly in the form of bug fixes. Packaging and deploying a software product has multiple steps, is error-prone, and might result in customer dissatisfaction if poorly performed. Thus, professionalizing and automating the packaging and deployment processes is a necessary task to increase the vendor's internal productivity and the customer's perceived product quality. In the hybrid software business, it is necessary to have a reliable and automatized release infrastructure that helps distinguish product and customer solution versions to enable customization services for multiple customer firms. Companies Alpha and Beta have developed different mechanisms and processes to implement this capability. The micro-foundations presented in this section describe those mechanisms and processes.

Company Alpha has established different cycles for different types of releases. A fixed point in Alpha's release strategy is minor releases. To date, Alpha has tested several release cycles to optimize their strategy and is now deploying minor releases every 2–3 months. Major releases are more complex and thus much less frequent. At the time of the interviews, Alpha has not established a fix release cycle for those. Bug fix or maintenance releases are the most frequent types of releases and occur within the minor release cycles depending on the software bugs identified.

However, for company Alpha, releasing the software product to its customers is not just a technical issue. According to Alpha's sales employee, it is also a good mechanism for aligning marketing or sales activity with product development. According to him, sales and marketing start before the product is finalized. Having promised certain features to certain customers within a certain release creates positive pressure and helps organize feature priorities for the development department:

> *Sometimes, sales and marketing have to push product develop-*
> *ment. And I think this is a good thing, a positive pressure, if you*
> *like. So, if some variants or versions of a certain feature are pre-*
> *sented to or sold to customer firms, it creates a certain pressure*
> *on the development department.*

However, although new releases provide new functionality, they also bear the risk of including new bugs or other software errors. Alpha's strategy is therefore to only release a product to a customer if it is necessary from a technical or a business perspective, for instance, if the underlying technology of a module has changed or new business functionalities valuable to the customer have been implemented. Thus, not every customer receives every new version at release time; versions are deployed according to customer needs.

To implement their release strategy and keep the promises made to their customers or prospects, company Alpha has established a standardized and semi-automatized compilation process for their different software modules and an automatized deployment process that allows them to deploy different versions to different customers while automatically keeping track of which versions have been released to whom. Several days before a new version is released, the actual source code in the configuration system is frozen and compiled to executable software modules. Because Alpha's modules are native windows applications consisting of an .exe file and a handful of .dll libraries, Alpha has implemented a form of copy deployment. Necessary changes to the underlying SQL database are deployed in the form of update scripts, which are implemented up front in a module update. Alpha can define which releases are available for each customer, and if an release is available, the customer employee is notified by the software to download and use the new version. The update process automatically replaces the existing software in the customer's environment with the new version.

Company Beta's release strategy is mostly identical with that of company Alpha. Beta provides minor releases every 4 weeks and major releases every quarter. As is the case in Alpha, the fixed release cycle is essential for Beta's release strategy. According to Beta's vice president consulting,

> *We have official minor releases every 4 weeks and a main release every 3 months. The minor releases may be deployed to the customer but are not advertised that much. However, there is not much which is as sacred as the release cycles in our company!*

However, due to Beta's different product architecture and customization strategy, releasing their software requires a different mechanism than that used by Alpha's. Beta has two types of software: customer-specific applications developed for a single customer and the main product engine, which is the foundation of all customer solutions. Customer specific applications must be deployed to a single customer if changes have been made. This requires an extra compilation and deployment step in Beta's release cycle. Changes to the main product are customer independent and thus only compiled once. However, because changes to the main product might require changes to the servlet container, the web server infrastructure or the database system will require manual service or support work.

Another important point is the update safety with respect to already used and productively implemented software functions. In the professional software business, software releases cascade over multiple systems to test the functionality and integrity of a new version before going productive with a customer. Both companies separate between test and productivity systems and use their release mechanisms to allow tests before going productive with new functions.

Overall, both companies have used their project experience to professionalize their release activities. Due to architectural prerequisites and the organization of customization activities, Alpha has established a more automatized process, while Beta's update strategy includes more manual tasks.

Table 5.10: Comparison of micro-foundations for seizing capability

	Case Alpha	Case Beta
Provide multiple revenue models for feature implementation	• Customer finances product feature • Multiple customers pay for product feature development • Vendor pays for feature development • Management decides which features to implement	• Similar to Alpha's revenue models • Sponsorship model; management decides which features to implement
Maintain a standardized product architecture and development infrastructure	• MVC pattern • Separation of application and DB server logic • Programming standards and guidelines • Versioning system	• MVC Pattern • Product- and customer-specific application development • Engine and configuration development • Versioning system
Maintain a standardized and revisable communication infrastructure	• Central support channel/function • Ticket system as a central communication tool • Project-, ticket-, and task-specific message system	• Tracker system, short-term and long-term roadmaps • Sprint demo meetings for internal communication • "Godfather model" - developer and consultants share responsibility
Maintain a standardized and automatized release infrastructure	• Product compilation and deployment are mostly automatized • Release management system keeps track of deployed version for customer • Customer can instantly download new versions • Fixed release cycles	• Deployment not automatized • Customer specific developments need specific release and configuration management • Fixed release cycles

5.3.5 Reconfiguration capability

Dynamic capabilities theory suggests that a key to sustained profitable growth is the ability to recombine and reconfigure a firm's assets as the enterprise grows or as markets and technologies change. Success causes a firm to evolve in a path-dependent manner. Thus, over time, successful firms implement hierarchies, processes and structures that begin to unnecessarily constrain certain interactions and behaviors (Teece 2007). Furthermore, reconfiguration may also involve business model redesign (Capron et al. 1998). Thus, for the following analysis, I rely on Teece's (2007) definition of micro-foundations to reconfigure capability as *a firm's measures to continuously align and realign specific resources and capabilities.*

Table 5.11: Reconfiguring capability: Definitions and micro-foundations

Micro-foundation	Description
Modularize product features	Software product features are the elements for building customer-specific business processes. The modularization of complex product features helps keep product features customizable and maintainable.
Standardize customer solutions	As the markets of software products mature, customer firms expect more standardized solutions from the software provider. Thus, software firms need to continuously standardize and professionalize product features to maintain competitive advantage.
Maintain knowledge base on previous customer, market and internal feature requests	Continuously reflecting product ideas against already existing customers, the market and internal requests helps develop a customer- and market-oriented product. Software companies need to maintain and actively include a knowledge base of such requests in their development activities.
Evaluate and adapt business and revenue models	Product development and support is expensive. Software companies thus need to continuously reconfigure and adapt their business and revenue models to finance development activities.

Drawing on Teece's (2007) definition of micro-foundations for reconfiguring capability, I was able to identify four distinct micro-foundations that software companies use to implement a reconfiguring capability in the hybrid software business: (1) modularizing product features, (2) standardizing customer solutions, (3) maintaining a knowledge based on customer, market and internal innovation impulses, and (4) evaluating and adapting business and revenue models. Table 5.11 summarizes those micro-foundations.

5.3.5.1   Modularize product and service features

Modularity in general refers to the degree to which a system's elements may be separated and recombined. In software design, it refers to the logical partitioning of the software design to make complex software manageable for the purpose of implementation and maintenance. The continuous modularization of product features is an important capability for software product development companies. Product features are the elements for implementing customer-specific business processes. The modularization of complex product features helps keep them customizable and maintainable. From a technological perspective, modularization refers to refactoring activities as described in the software engineering discipline. Particularly in Alpha's case, modularization is an important step for providing their solution to a wider market. As the key account manager from Alpha explained,

> *That is a good question. We would like to have both, standard and flexibility. We have a certain standard. But to be more flexible - our product will never be suitable for a mass market - but to cover as much customer needs as possible, we need a modular product. And this is a theme or a goal we follow in our product development.*

A common business case in the hybrid software business is that specific features are initially implemented for a single customer and over time transformed into a general solution for a more anonymous market. Modularizing the initial feature helps break down the complexity of a single function and facilities the recombination of a feature in multiple contexts. The senior developer explains how this is realized in company Alpha:

> *To serve our very special customer base or market, we need relatively flexible solutions. It is often the case that a feature is implemented for one customer - because they pay for it - and then modularized during the next releases so that other customers can benefit from it, too. If this iterative approach is the best is discussible. But it is the one that is most realistic and achievable with respect to effort and costs.*

An important mechanism for modularizing their product features from a strategic and not an operative "daily-business" perspective for company Alpha are major releases. These releases are more strategically planned and result from a long-term road map. However, because major releases include extensive programming effort on the vendor side, they are usually not free for customers. Particularly because major releases do not always include specific customer-demanded features, it can be difficult to convince customers to switch to those releases. However, despite these difficulties, Alpha's general manager describes the importance of major releases for sustained competitive advantage:

> *For us, development without customizing background is done in major releases. For instance, we are working on a completely new version of our software with a new UI, usability and some technical improvements. Its completion is planned for Q3 and the roll out for Q4. We put a lot of development effort in it which was not driven directly by customer projects. But it was necessary to stay competitive on the long run.*

In general, the interview results within company Beta showed similar results with respect to product feature modularization. According to the product manager, rewriting software code according to the customer base or customization needs is also common at Beta:

> *Yes, for example, you may have a part of software what doesn't*
> *perform. So there's a need for the development to say "hey, we*
> *need to rewrite this piece. That has to go in the roadmap".*

However, interestingly, it is not the modularization that drives that actual development efforts at company Beta. It is the other side of the spectrum - the standardization. Again, as the product manager illustrated,

> *So, typically, this company always wants to make things more*
> *flexible. That's the ideology of this company. So everything we*
> *put into the software, people always saying, "well, how can we*
> *do that in more even abstract way in case it gets used in five*
> *different ways". But if I'm honest, that's changing now. Because*
> *it has to. And that's the thing I was talking about with the market*
> *space. That behavior must change at some point. So now we?re*
> *putting them in the software in a more overdesigned way, so we?re*
> *designing each feature so that it has a clear purpose.*

The next section will more closely describe why standardization in the hybrid software business is as important as modularization.

5.3.5.2 Standardize customer solutions

The standardization of customer solutions is somewhat the opposite of the modularization of product features as described during the interviews. It refers to the process of limiting the customer's degree of freedom in specific functionalities. The usual assumption is that customer firms need flexibility. However, although this is true in innovative business scenarios, it is not necessarily true for existing and elaborate business scenarios. In these cases, the customer expects the vendor to provide expert functionality and the "one best way of doing things". Thus, while on the one hand, vendor firms must modularize product features, they also have to standardize features as markets evolve. Standardization, similar to modularization, is a form of refactoring as described in the software engineering discipline.

As described in the last section, company Alpha focuses on modularization instead of standardization. However, with respect to separating the development from the service and support functions in the company, they try to implement standard features so that they are configurable. By doing so, company Alpha tries to achieve a clearer separation between the two business functions. The general manager illustrates these trends in company Alpha:

> *There is a trend in professionalizing and separating development from service and support. We try to implement things as configurable as necessary and transfer them from the development department to the service and support department. So that whenever standard things are necessary in a configuration, they can be done by service employees.*

Company Beta has already successfully separated service and support from pure development activities. In doing so, modularization became "a huge part of the company's DNA" as the general manager explained. However, according to the interviews, they are still aiming for greater standardization in their software product. Company Beta's general manager described this as follows:

> *We should try to do less additive development of small features here and there and provide one systematic solution, one basic idea. Three bullet points that describe what the software does, and from these we derive everything else. This is where we have to go, this is what was my biggest learning from our firm history.*

However, although the general manager would like to have more standardization, he does not want to completely give up flexibility of modularization. Instead, he claims that the company is actually working on providing a standardized user interface for a flexible business process engine. This, he argues, would combine the best from both worlds. So, at the time of the interviews, Beta was thinking about refactoring the user interface so that it provides the "one best way of doing" and similarly keep the underlying processes as flexible as possible. According to the CEO, this not only separates service and support from development but also would be the first step towards a partner business model:

> *Today we have no partner business model. We can only get there if we can say: "Look, this is our configuration workbench, super easy to operate, this is the manual". Only then we can try to establish a business like this.*

The CEO's arguments and ideas are supported by the product manager, who explains that company Beta has recently started to focus on usability instead of flexibility:

> *The most successful way, so, we changed our philosophy this year dramatically. That now says it's okay everything that goes in the system we want our designer to look at it, we want usability person to look at it and to do the best way of doing it. Just one way.*

5.3.5.3 Maintain knowledge base on customer, market and internal requests

Modularization and standardization require a continuous reflection on the benefit of product features for customers, markets and internal stakeholders. Absorptive capacity theory suggests that a company's absorptive capacity depends on its existing knowledge in the relevant area (Lane et al. 2006). Thus, to be able to do this, the software vendor must have access to previous, ongoing, and potential requests from each of these areas. Alpha and Beta have established different processes and structures to implement this important reconfiguring capability.

In addition to the ticket system, which keeps structured information on customer requests and their current state, Alpha maintains release notes that describe the core functionality implemented in each release. These release notes are the written document of internal presentation meetings; these are scheduled up front for each new release and are used to present the new functionalities from each module to the entire company. Furthermore, Alpha has also implemented and continuously maintains a more static wiki-system, which keeps information on

- current customer firms, a short description of their core business, contact persons, and implemented software modules

- their product portfolio: modules and their key functions, which developers are responsible and contact persons for questions regarding this module

- and their internal employees with experience and skills.

The wiki system is useful for organizational functions, which are not often included in development and support tasks; it allows people to look up certain information to ease their business tasks. It is also a good reference for training new employees.

In a very similar manner, company Beta stores customer requests in its tracker management system and holds sprint meetings after each release cycle. According to the product manager, these meetings are

[...] given to whole company at the end of every sprint. These meetings are at least two or three hours, with drinks and food, and we explain what we did in this period and why we did that. And that's the best that we've got so far. But it's not perfect.

5.3.5.4 Evaluate and adapt internal processes and business models

Continuous improvement is not only important for the software product. Internal processes and business models must be adapted as markets demand or strategic orientation changes. During the interviews, experts from both cases have highlighted how their companies have changed from their founding until today.

With respect to internal processes, company Alpha has continuously improved its project and ticket management system. Although initially, the system was only used to manage IT projects, it has evolved to become a central part of Alpha's organizational structure. Today, it is not only the development or service and support departments that use the system but also marketing, sales, and general management. More recently, Alpha has started to open its system to customer firms, so that they have access to their own request tickets. By doing so, the customer can follow the development and support process and gain greater transparency on how their requests are being addressed. Over the years, the system has also evolved to a central point in product management. The system has become a central database for customer requests to specific software modules from support, maintenance and development perspectives. However, as shown in multiple interview examples, Alpha's reconfigurations are not limited to their project management system but also include adjourned organizational structures and processes. For instance, they include the continuous definition and delineation of organizational functions that are not directly development or customer related, such as marketing or sales. Last but not least, because the Alpha project management system was built upon their own architectural software framework, Alpha had direct feedback on how the work with their product influences customer firms.

In a similar vein, company Beta has integrated their tracker software into their own organization to store customer requests and structure communications. However, the interview revealed that Beta's tracker system has not yet been integrated into the company's structure and processes, unlike Alpha's ticket system. For instance, particularly with respect to product management, it serves as a database with customer requests but does not integrate business functions such as marketing or sales, as is done in Beta company. Nevertheless, Beta has changed and reinvented itself over the years as well but on a more purely organizational level. For instance, as the vice president development explained,

> *And the other things are internal processes, which we are trying to optimize. For instance, for two years now, we do not get direct customer feedback but channel them through consulting teams that write down customer requests in a more structured manner.*

Additionally, and in contrast to Alpha, Beta has realized the separation of development and service and support in two distinct departments. Why Beta took this step is still open to interpretation, but the different and more general market structure might be one explanation. Beta started with three types of software adaption: (1) configuration of XML code, (2) customer-specific application development, and (3) product development. At the time of the interviews, Beta was already thinking about standardizing this structure and leaving out customer-specific application development.

As technologies evolve, new business and revenue models arise for software firms. Over recent decades, those models have evolved from traditional license royalties and maintenance and support fees to leasing contracts and pay per use models. With the ongoing change from a product to a service software business, new opportunities for generating revenue in the hybrid software business might arise. Thus, to keep up with potential opportunities, development software firms must continuously evaluate and realign their underlying business and revenue models.

Company Alpha has built multiple business and revenue models over time. These include traditional license fees, rent or leasing offerings as well as manager services and application server platforms or cloud computing. More recently, Alpha has started to enter the new market of utilities and

energy data management. In discussion with potential customers, they have
discovered that many of the processes from the telecommunication and hosting business can be transferred to optimize energy data management as well.

> *We are trying to enter new market, to offer our system in other*
> *industries. Not just telecommunication. More recently, we had*
> *contact with the utilities industry, which seems to be very promis-*
> *ing. Another market would be IT system houses. They have to*
> *invoice their services as well. These are the directions we are*
> *moving today.*

Company Beta has also evolved with respect to its business and revenue
model. They have provided multiple best practice modules, which are the
foundation for each of their customization projects, or have released mobile
applications so that their idea management system can be accessed anywhere.
The next step is opening their business model for partner companies. As the
vice president consulting explained,

> *Consultants configure our system, experienced customers can do*
> *so as well. As a next step, we would like to work with partner*
> *firms. However, to do so, our system has to become more simple.*

The examples show that both companies have passed multiple phases of
procedural and structural changes. Both companies have been open minded
over the years and have changed according to actual market situations or an-
ticipation of how markets may evolve. One important micro-foundation used
by both companies to establish their reconfiguring capability was to build
their own IT support for organizational processes. The interviews revealed
that both companies have continuously adapted organizational processes and
IT support, which was — in this form — only possible through their in-depth
knowledge. This section did not provide many of the mechanisms that both
cases have used to reconfigure their resource base. However, it provides a
glimpse of the importance of continuous change and adaption in the hybrid
software business.

Table 5.12: Comparison of micro-foundations for reconfiguring capability

	Case Alpha	Case Beta
Modularize product features	• Separate business logic, data model, and UI logic • Separate module specific, DB server logic and interface logic	• Separate business logic, data model, and UI logic • Separate engine and product specific logic • Separate core functionalities from additional modules
Standardize customer solutions	• Provide similar UI functions in all modules	• Corporate design of web UI • Standardize lists
Maintain knowledge base on customer, market and internal innovation impulses	• Marketing, service and support, development and management use ticket system to store product ideas • Product ideas are structured (Problem, Solution, Implementation idea) • Product ideas evolve over time (Cost estimation, ...)	• Marketing, service and support, development and management use tracker system to store product ideas • Product manager responsible for releases and road map
Evaluate and adapt business and revenue models	• Software as a service and application service providers • Pay per use models (Number of produced invoices, ...) • Support and service business models (Managed services, ...)	• Mobile application for IT system • Pay per use models

5.4   Project typology in the hybrid software business

The presented studies investigated the nature of customization and software product development in the hybrid software business. The first study analyzed vendor and customer perspectives on software customization and revealed unique resources, distinctive capabilities and sources of value. This second study investigated the nature of software product development in two cases with independent software vendors. It elaborates on the results from the first study and introduces micro-foundations for a software firm's dynamic capability. Figure 5.14 illustrates an extended framework that integrates the conceptual insights from each of the two studies.

Building upon the results from the previous studies, first a new classification of software projects within the context of hybrid software offerings is developed. For this, it is argued that a firm's existing resources characterize the project type. Then, how the resulting project types influence the degree of customization is discussed, as well as the product development capabilities needed to generate a specific type of value from a specific type of project.

The proposed classification of software contains two dimensions and thus results in four types of software project. The first dimension refers to whether the vendor has the necessary customization resources to perform a specific project. This dimension is built upon *customer business and market knowledge* as well as *customization management knowledge and experience data* resources. The second dimension refers to whether a software vendor firm has the necessary productization resources to perform a specific project. Therefore, this dimension builds upon the *product functionality and flexibility* and *product related software development assets* resources.

Depending on the vendor's resources, software projects can be categorized into four different types: (1) projects where the vendor has high customization and productization resources, (2) projects where the vendor has high customization and low productization resources, (3) projects where the ven-

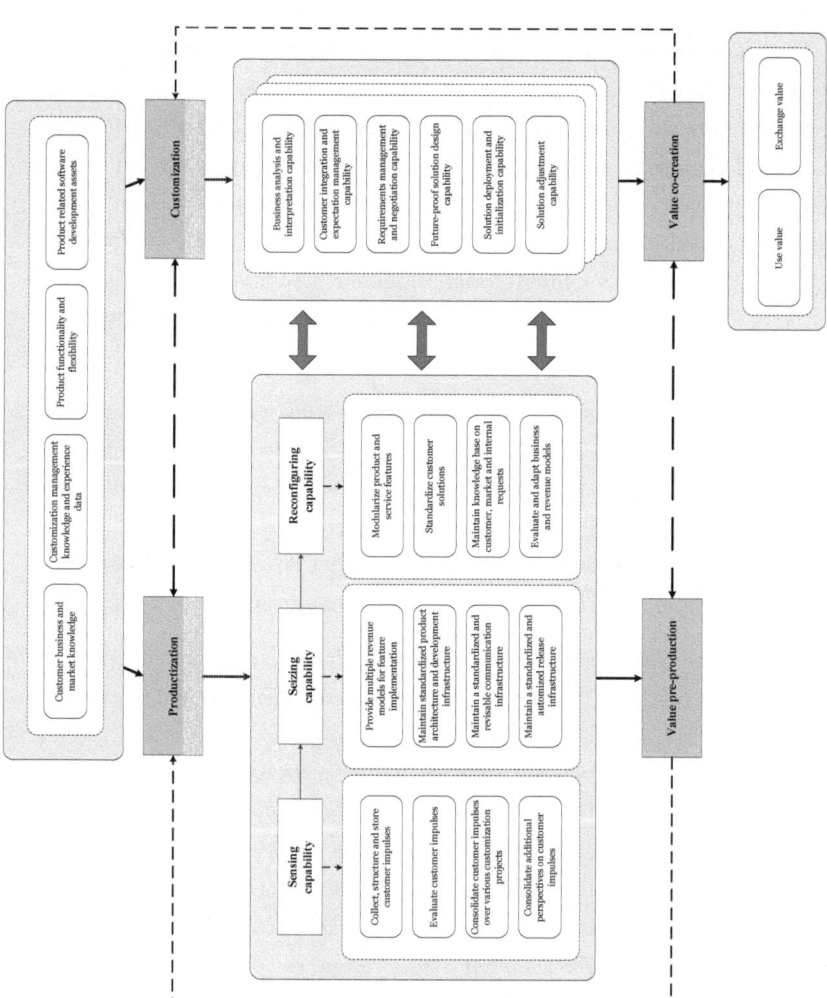

Figure 5.14: Final overall research framework

dor has low customization and high productization resources and finally, (4) projects where the vendor has low customization and low productization resources. Depending on this initial stock of resources, the vendor's role can be described as an overall *solution expert*, an *industry or business expert*, a *technology expert* or as a *layman*. Figure 5.15 summarizes the previously discussed project types and their characteristics.

5.4.1 Solution delivery projects (SDP)

The software vendors from the two investigations described customization projects in which they already have a high degree of customer-related business knowledge as well as a high degree of technological assets to implement the desired customer solution. For example, software company Alpha explained that they adapt best practices and software solutions from one customer to another within the mobile or telephony business. These type of customization projects can be defined as *software projects that implement existing business-specific software solutions into the customer firm.* In particular, the vendor can be regarded as a solution expert who already has experience with a specific customer scenario and the internal customer firm structure and processes and who has implemented his products in equal or similar business scenarios.

Due to the high degree of customer-related business knowledge and product-related technological knowledge, the degree to which customization and productization capabilities must be employed can be considered to be "low" in comparison to other project types. Thus, none of these capabilities are primarily needed to compensate for missing resources during the project.

Regarding the output, the software vendors stated that these provide the most use value of all project types because they deploy the vendor's existing business knowledge and because product features are already implemented and integrated in an existing maintenance and support system. Additionally, the preexisting knowledge from previous customization projects ensures that

		Type/ Vendor role	Technology driven project (TDP) / Technology expert	Type/ Vendor role	Solution delivery project (SDP) / Solution expert
Productization resources	**high**	Definition	Software projects to implement existing software products in new business scenarios.	Definition	Software projects to implement existing business-specific software solutions into the customer firm.
		Examples	Implement network monitoing software to automize and optimze health care processes in hospitals.	Examples	Implement billing soulution for mobile business at different mobile reseller firms.
		Primary capabilities	Outside-in customization capabilities; Reconfiguring productization capabilities	Primary capabilities	No primary capability requirements
		Potential exchange value	Vendor reputation; Innovation impulses; Vendor profitability	Potential exchange value	Vendor reputation; Customer relation; Vendor profitability
		Potential use value	Long term solution; Customer profitability	Potential use value	Business development support; Long term solution; Customer profitability; Customer reputation
	low	Type/ Vendor role	Undefiend project (UP) / Layman	Type/ Vendor role	Business support project (BSP) / Business expert
		Definition	Software projects that do not build upon preexisting vendor technologies or existing business scenarios.	Definition	Software projects to implement existing business-specific logics in new customer specific software solutions.
		Examples	Demanding highly specialized vendor firms to implement CMS or webshop solutions.	Examples	Implement a new innovation process based upon an existing software configuration.
		Primary capabilities	Potentially high degree of customization and productization capabilities required	Primary capabilities	Spanning and Inside-out customization capability; Sensing producatization capability
		Potential exchange value	Undefiend	Potential exchange value	Vendor reputation; Innovation impulses; Vendor profitability
		Potential use value	Undefiend	Potential use value	Business development support; Customer profitability
		low		**high**	
		Customization resources			

Figure 5.15: Types of customization projects

the customer's profitability is a given. Finally, the reputational risk for the responsible customer employee is low. From an exchange value perspective, such projects provide mostly vendor profitability and help firms to strengthen their reputation in their line of business as well as with existing customers. However, because these projects focus on areas that the vendor is already an expert in, they can only be considered a source for minor and incremental innovation impulses.

5.4.2 Business support projects (BSP)

This type refers to customization projects where the vendor has a high degree of customer-related business knowledge and a low degree of product-related technological knowledge, for instance, as stated by employees from company Beta, the implementation of a new innovation process based upon an existing software configuration. Therefore, these projects can be defined as *software projects that implement existing business-specific logics in new customer-specific software solutions.* In these projects, the vendor can be regarded as an industry or business expert who already has experience with a specific customer scenario but never implemented it with his products in equivalent or similar business scenarios.

Projects where the vendor is regarded as an industry expert have specific prerequisites for vendor capabilities. In these projects, the vendor already has a very good understanding of the business processes and the customer needs. Thus, the necessity for an outside-in capability on the customization side is relatively low and comparable to solution delivery projects. However, because the technical customer solution does not exist, it can be assumed that during customization, the spanning and especially inside-out customization capabilities are more important for building and deploying the final solution. For the same reason, the vendor must put more effort in the productization of the technical product or module. In particular, an understanding of the technical requirements for a solution requires a high sensing capability. Seizing and reconfiguring can be assumed to be slightly less important.

In customization projects where the vendor acts as a business or industry expert, he provides extensive business development support for his customer. However, because the vendor cannot provide a standard product for the customer's solution, the long-term support and customer profitability cannot be expected to be as high as they are in solution delivery projects. Furthermore, due to the vendor's business expert status, the customer can be sure not to risk his reputation if the project fails. From a vendor perspective, the innovation impulses from such a project are not as high as in a solution delivery project and are more limited to technical innovations or rather small industry-related innovations. However, vendor reputation and customer relationships are both valuable outcomes from such projects. Finally, vendor profitability can be considered to be medium to high, depending on the vendor's strategic investment in a technical product solution.

5.4.3   Technology support projects (TSP)

As introduced, technology support projects are characterized by a low degree of customer-related business knowledge but a high degree of product-related technological knowledge by the software vending company. As the employee from the network and monitoring business explained, this might be the implementation of network monitoring software to automatize and optimize health care business processes in hospitals. In those projects, the vendor can be regarded as a technological expert who already has experience with and the necessary assets for a specific technology but who has never implemented it in the specific customer's business scenario. From a customization perspective, in these projects, the vendor must invest extensive effort in the outside-in customization capabilities to understand the customer's business needs and to gather product requirements. However, because the vendor has already invested in a technological platform and customization infrastructure, the investments in spanning and inside-out capabilities are less high.

With respect to use value, such projects provide only a low value with regard to business development support for the customer firm. However, with respect to a long-term solution and, for instance, business automation, the value can be regarded as being high. Additionally, these projects provide a considerable amount of customer profitability because, for instance, automation might result in more profitable customer business processes and productivity. However, because the investment on the customer side is rather high, this profitability is costly. However, because the vendor has already been regarded as an expert in technological issues, the customer can profit from his reputation in other business scenarios.

Similar to solution support projects, these types of projects provide a medium to high level of innovation impulses from the customer side. However, in contrast, they provide innovation impulses with respect to business scenarios rather than technological developments. With respect to vendor reputation, these projects can be regarded as highly valuable because they allow the vendor to implement an existing technology in a new market or customer segment. If successful, a technology support project provides a relatively high customer reputation value because they help enhance the customer's profitability and productivity. However, vendor profitability can be regarded as lower than, for instance, solution delivery projects because a project like this produces extensive implementation effort that the customer might pay for. However, if the vendor is able to sell his existing solution to other customers in the same market segment, these projects can be considered to be extremely valuable.

5.4.4   Undefined projects (UP)

Undefined projects refer to customization projects in which the vendor has only a low degree of customer-related business knowledge as well as a low degree of product-related technological knowledge. Multiple participants from both studies gave the example of implementing a CMS or webshop technology for new customers. Because the vendors from the interview study were all highly specialized in their business and technological environment, this did not fall into any of their lines of business. The vendor's role in such projects can be regarded as one of a technological and business layman, who has no experience with a specific technology and has never implemented it in a specific customer business scenario.

Regarding customization and productization, these projects can be assumed to require a high investment in all capabilities. On the one hand, the vendor must build up the product and its development and release infrastructure. On the other hand, he does not have any experience with the customer's business or market requirements. However, it was stated that it is not foreseeable whether and to what extent an undefined project will contribute to customer- and vendor-related value. Thus, they can be regarded as a high risk for the vendor company that does not provide use or exchange value and that might even destroy them (vendor reputation).

5.5   Research quality and evaluation

Due to the large amount of interview transcripts and pages, a *computer-assisted qualitative data analysis software* (CAQDAS) was used to support the data analysis. In particular, MAXQDA was used to manage interview transcripts, identify recurrent themes and as a means to use a coding scheme in each qualitative investigation. As advised by Yin (2009), the MAXQDA files included all data material for the analysis and thus represented the dissertations' research database.

To ensure reliability as well as internal and external validity, as described in chapter 4 of the thesis, the resulting frameworks and definitions from each study were presented to CEOs/CTOs in two evaluation workshops and in multiple informal meetings. Additionally, the systematic literature review as well as the framework results were presented in scientific workshops. The managers individually reviewed the framework and its definitions and provided feedback on how well it reflected actual practices. They agreed on the overall structure of the framework and provided only minor suggestions regarding the wording of resources, capabilities, and value and of their definitions.

During the scientific workshops, the studies and the preliminary results were presented to an audience of international information systems and service researchers. The feedback from these presentations was addressed to the content and the resulting framework as well as to the applied methodological approach. Both helped to further develop the final results and the rigorousness of the research approach.

5.6   Summary and discussion

The previous studies investigated the nature of customization and software product development in the hybrid software business. The first study analyzed vendor and customer perspectives on software customization and revealed unique resources, distinctive capabilities and values. This second study investigated the nature of software product development in two cases with independent software vendors. It elaborated on the results from the first study and introduced micro-foundations for a software firm's dynamic capability. Finally, the results from both studies were integrated into an extended framework that elaborates on the interaction between customization and product development activities in the hybrid software business and the different roles of software vendors within these interactions.

Chapter 6

Conclusion: Summary, contributions and implications, limitations and outlook

6.1 Summary of research and contributions

6.1.1 Research motivation and approach

Over the past decade, the software industry has developed three types of business logic: (1) *the software product business*, (2) *the software service business* and (3) *the hybrid business*. Firms following a software product business logic develop highly standardized and productized software products that are sold to a mass of customers or consumers in the market with limited or even without additional service. Firms that follow a software service logic develop software in the form of projects for one specific customer that is implemented for that customer's IT landscape. However, the distinction between the software product and service businesses is not exclusive. Between those two poles of the spectrum lies a hybrid software business logic.

Today, most of the companies that develop professional software products for the business-to-business market usually apply a hybrid business logic. They develop a core product that encapsulates common functionalities for their customers' businesses and also offer additional customization services to adapt their product to the customers' needs. These software companies are challenged with specific issues from the software product and software project business logic.

Existing research has shown that there are several streams of research that address those challenges. For instance, as shown in Chapter 1, the software engineering discipline has identified different types of software products and provided multiple frameworks and best practices that help firms to manage the challenges arising during the development of software products. Additionally, as shown in Chapter 2, the information systems literature has provided streams of research that are concerned with customization as (1) a form of product delivery and customization and (2) a form of co-creation of value. While the first specifically addresses the implementation aspects of the software business, the second stream of research regards customization not only as a form of delivery but also as an innovation source for software development companies. Although essential contributions have been made from both disciplines, the literature still lacks an integrated perspective on the hybrid software business. Thus, the dissertation at hand started by asking the primary research question:

MRQ: *How do software vendor firms align their software product management and customization activities?*

The main research question was separated into three sub-questions, which were addressed in two qualitative investigations. Figure 6.1 illustrates the research questions related to each investigation.

The first investigation aimed at identifying specific resources and capabilities that software vendor firms need to provide successful software customization services. Therefore, it addressed the sub-question:

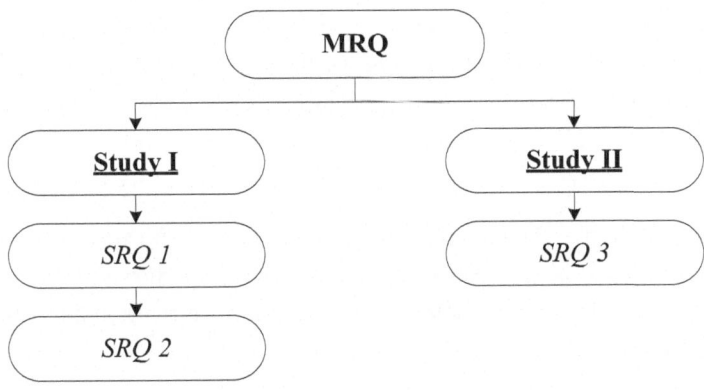

Figure 6.1: Thesis research questions

SRQ 1: *Which resources and capabilities do firms from the hybrid software business need to offer valuable software systems for their customers?*

However, to answer this specific question, it was necessary to investigate the nature of success in software customization and the meaning of value from the perspective of customer firms and vendor firms. Thus, the following additional research question was asked:

SRQ 2: *What value does software customization provide for vendor and customer companies?*

As described in chapter 5, both questions were answered by employing a qualitative research design based on textual data collected from 22 interviews with experts from software vendor and customer firms. Informants on both sides were people with several years of experience in customization projects, such as CEOs, CTOs, Senior Developers/Consultants and Department Heads. Respondents from the vendor side represent industrial companies operating in various product markets including health care, mechanical engineering, social platform applications, software as a service firms, monitoring and work-flow systems, email marketing and document management as well as consultancies and business intelligence firms. From the customer side, respondents represent industrial companies operating in various service or product markets including utilities, financial services, telecommunication services, IT services in the aviation industry and consulting services.

The second investigation aimed at analyzing how software customization activities influence software development activities, and how software vendor firms strategically manage those influences. This investigation addresses the research question:

> **SRQ 3:** *Which specific dynamic capabilities do software vendor firms develop to manage innovation impulses from software customization in their productization activities?*

This question was answered by investigating two cases of software vendors: Companies Alpha and Beta. The selected cases for the dissertation represent two typical software development and professional service environments in small- and medium-sized firms.

Company Alpha is a German small-sized firm providing software solutions for billing and rating intensive industries and businesses. Currently, the company has approximately 25 employees, and their software product is used in over 60 installations in Germany, Austria, and Switzerland. In general, Alpha can be characterized as a traditional software developer that, to date, includes no explicit professional services department.

Company Beta describes itself as a global leader in enterprise social software for idea and innovation management. With approximately 80 employees and 170 installations worldwide, the company is a medium-sized software company. Thus, this company can be regarded as a traditional software development company with two departments, one for development and one for professional services. In both companies, the customization activities as well as their influence on software product development were investigated.

As is the case for any research project, the study choices in this dissertation create some *(1) methodological as well as (2) conceptual limitations and design limitations*. While *methodological limitations* can only be addressed to a limited degree, *conceptual and design limitations* might offer fruitful avenues for further research.

A qualitative research methodology has numerous strengths when properly conducted, such as issues can be examined in detail and in depth, interviews are not restricted to specific questions and can be guided/redirected by the researcher in real time, and the research framework and direction can be quickly revised as new information emerges. However, from a methodological perspective, qualitative research has been criticized for overusing interviews or focus groups. Data are usually collected from a few cases or individuals, so findings cannot be generalized to a larger population. Although the results from the interview analysis were crosschecked with secondary data such as archival records, the investigation in this thesis is also affected by these limitations. Thus, for this qualitative study, the natural nexot step would be a quantitative or experimental validation of the proposed theoretical framework.

From a conceptual perspective, this study included the customization and productization perspective on the hybrid software business and resulted in a theoretical value-oriented framework of resources, capabilities, dynamic capabilities and values to integrate both perspectives. Such a framework seems to make logical sense. It has face validity as established through feedback with selected interviewees, and no data contradict this framework. However, more research is needed to validate the provisional findings regarding such a framework in different contexts. The following list includes some areas of research that can help validate these research findings through replication:

1. the investigations in this study did not explicitly investigate SaaS or open source software and, thus, do not regard the specific characteristics of customization and productization for those types of software products;

2. most of the firms were small- or medium-sized enterprises, thus, it is not evaluated if the resulting framework can be replicated in larger enterprise settings;

3. although all firms could be located in the hybrid software business, they have different levels of product or service intensity, thus, a finer categorization of software firms might help strengthen the framework within different contexts;

4. and finally, this work did not focus on the technological or architectural aspects of software products or customization services; future investigations can help identify or develop technologies or methods that help further integrate both fields.

Although these limitations must be kept in mind when considering the thesis' results and implications, I hope that my findings provide new insights into the phenomenon of software customization for academics and practitioners alike.

6.1.2 Contributions

Prior research provides only limited perspectives on the underlying capabilities and resources needed to generate value in the hybrid software business. This dissertation's findings thus contribute to three main areas by providing a better understanding of how software firms in the hybrid software business can successfully manage and align their customization and productization activities. Figure 6.2 illustrates the final extended research framework described in chapter 6 and integrates the key contributions of each of the two studies.

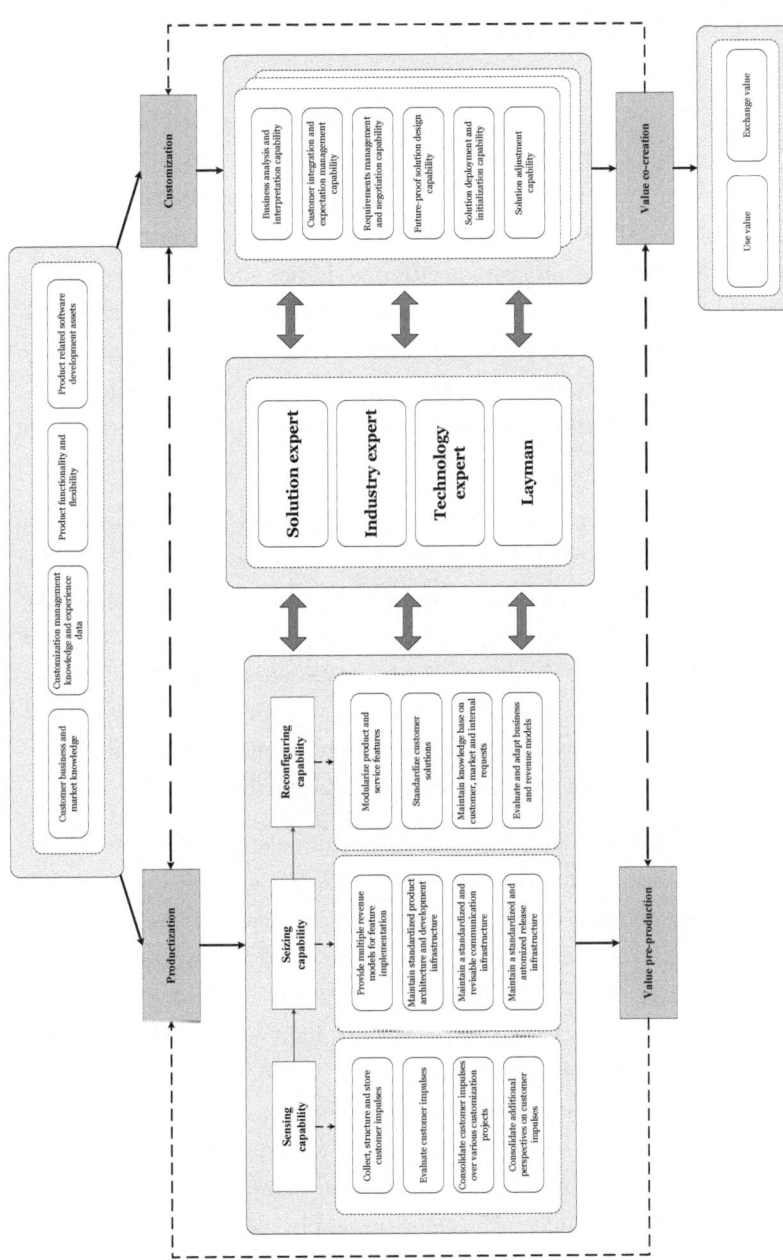

Figure 6.2: Integrated framework and project types

6.1.2.1 Customization framework

In the qualitative study, I analyzed what software providing firms must do to successfully deploy customer-specific software systems and what influence this has on innovation activities in those firms. Thus, I particularly addressed research questions **SRQ 1** and **SRQ 2**. In this study, the concept of value was used to define success in customization activities. In particular, success was defined based on the concepts of use and exchange value, which represent customer- or vendor-specific value generation. The findings from this study contribute to three main areas and help better understand how such firms can organize customization activities professionally and benefit from them in their innovation activities.

The first contribution was to identify six distinctive capabilities that a software deploying firm must develop to deploy customer solutions. The focus was not on generating an exhaustive list of capabilities per se; rather, the goal was to develop a list of distinctive capabilities that reflect the technical specificities and the reciprocal nature of customization deployment. Drawing on a RBV involving knowledge as the most important resource (Eisenhardt and Santos 2000), the investigation additionally identified four unique resources that help software firms to leverage these capabilities.

The second contribution was to identify eight distinctive values generated through software customization capabilities. Those values were further categorized using the conceptual distinction of customer-oriented *use value* and vendor-oriented *exchange value*. It was shown that economic profit is an important driver of customization, but it is not the only one for custom or for vendor firms. Furthermore, the results imply that while customer firms focus strongly on their own value system, vendor firms must consider both types of value to meet the customer's expectations and be successful in customization. Adapting Ulaga and Reinartz's (2011) approach, a comprehensive framework was developed that integrates capabilities, resources and values in a consistent manner to explain success in software customization activities.

Finally, by applying Day's (1994) typology of innovation capabilities, the identified customization capabilities were categorized in terms of their effect on innovation activities in the vendor firm. Based on the empirical results from the qualitative investigation, it was shown how the particular customization capabilities foster outside-in, spanning, and inside-out transfer along the deployment value creation chain.

6.1.2.2   Productization framework

The second investigation addressed research question **SRQ 3** by analyzing which micro-foundations software development companies need to develop to implement the dynamic capability framework in their software product development. In this investigation scenario, the concept of dynamic capabilities has been employed in the context of software customization as a strategic innovation source for software vendors. The existing literature separates dynamic capabilities into sensing, seizing and reconfiguring capabilities. Sensing capability refers *to sensing and shaping opportunities and threats*; seizing capability refers *to seizing opportunities*; and reconfiguring capability refers *to maintaining competitiveness through enhancing, combining, protecting, and when necessary, reconfiguring the business enterprise's intangible and tangible assets* (Teece 2007). In particular, based on these general definitions, I identified micro-foundations in the empirical data for a dynamic capability that integrates customization activities in the software development function of a software vendor.

The key contribution is the identification of four distinctive micro-foundations for each capability within the dynamic capability framework. First, micro-foundations for sensing capability refers *to analytical systems and individual capabilities to learn and to sense, filter, shape, and calibrate opportunities*. Here, the results from the analysis confirm the existing literature in that micro-foundations concentrate on changes in the customer environment, internal R&D processes, processes to tap supplier and partner innovation, and processes to tap exogenous science and technology. However, sensing not only includes the identification of customer needs and technological possibilities, it further includes an understanding of (1) latent demand, (2) the structural evolution of industries and markets, and (3) likely supplier and competitor responses. According to the case study, the sensing capability in the hybrid software business is built upon the following four micro-foundations: (1) collect, structure and store customer impulses, (2) evaluate customer requests, (3) consolidate customer impulses from the product's installed base, and (4) consolidate additional perspectives on customer impulses.

Second, micro-foundations for seizing capability refer *to enterprise structures, procedures, designs, and incentives for seizing opportunities.* The existing literature describes delineating customer solutions and business models, selecting decision-making protocols, selecting enterprise boundaries to manage complements and "control platforms", and building loyalty and commitment. In line with existing findings, the analysis of empirical data revealed that seizing opportunities involves maintaining and enhancing a firm's technological competences and complementary assets by investing in the particular technologies necessary to most likely achieve market acceptance. However, seizing an opportunity is more than determining how much effort to put into development. It also includes selecting or developing business and revenue models that form a valid case for a firm's business success. Thus, in the hybrid software business, the seizing capability relies on the micro-foundations (1) provide multiple revenue models for feature implementation, (2) maintain a standardized product architecture and development infrastructure, (3) maintain a standardized and revisable communication infrastructure, and (4) maintain a standardized and automatized release infrastructure.

Third, micro-foundations for reconfiguring capability refer *to the continuous alignment and reconfiguration of specific tangible and intangible assets.* The existing literature describes decentralization and near decomposability, governance, cospecialization, and knowledge management. Dynamic capabilities theory suggests that a key to sustained profitable growth is the ability to recombine and to reconfigure a firm's assets as the enterprise grows or markets and technologies change. Success causes a firm to evolve in a path-dependent manner. According to Teece (2007), over time successful firms implement hierarchies, processes and structures that begin to unnecessarily constrain certain interactions and behaviors. In the hybrid software business, the following micro-foundations are used to overcome those constraints: (1) modularize product features, (2) standardize customer solutions, (3) maintain knowledge base on previous customer, market and internal feature requests, and (4) evaluate and adapt business and revenue models.

6.1.2.3   Integrated framework and project types

Finally, by integrating the results from studies I and II, the main research question **MRQ** was addressed. The interpretation of both results suggest that depending on the initial stock of resources, the vendor's role can be described as an overall *solution expert*, an *industry or business expert*, a *technical expert* or a *layman*. Furthermore, it was discussed how the vendor's role in a specific software project influences the employment of capabilities as well as the use and exchange value expected from the project. Figure 6.3 illustrates the four types of customization projects.

In particular, it was argued that projects (*solution delivery projects*) in which the vendor is considered to be a solution expert provide the most value for customer firms and provide mostly economic value for the vendor firm. The rationale here is that because the vendor already has the necessary resources to provide a customization project, only minor innovation impulses can be expected for the vendor firm. In projects (*business support projects*) where the vendor is considered to be an industry expert, the firm has a very good understanding of the business processes and the customer needs. Thus, the vendor provides a lot of business development value for the customer. However, because a technological solution does not exist, the vendor also has to focus on standardization and flexibilization issues independent of the specific customer. However, projects (technology support projects) in which the software vendor is regarded as a technical expert provide use value with respect to business automation on the customer side. However, this value

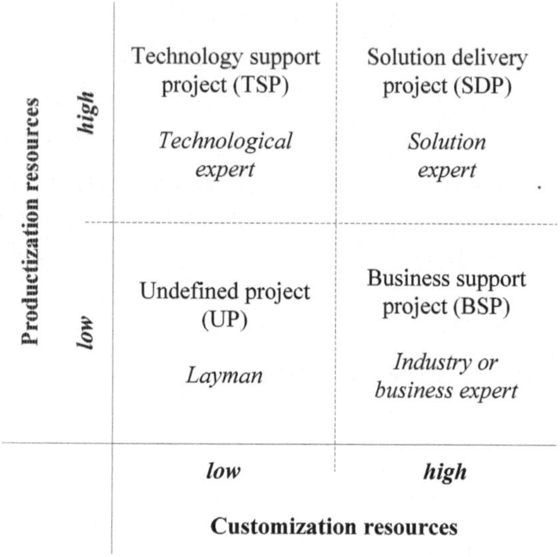

		Technology support project (TSP) *Technological expert*	Solution delivery project (SDP) *Solution expert*
Productization resources	*high*		
	low	Undefined project (UP) *Layman*	Business support project (BSP) *Industry or business expert*
		low	*high*

Customization resources

Figure 6.3: The vendor role in hybrid software business projects

requires a close integration of the customer into the project. Thus, the vendor firm must employ outside-in customization capabilities and must sense productization capabilities. Finally, a fourth project type was identified (*undefined projects*) in which the vendor does not have any customization or productization assets. These projects are identified as extremely risky with respect to the degree of capability employment and project outcome.

6.2   Implications for management and theory

6.2.1   Theoretical implications

The most evident theoretical contribution of this thesis is the integrated framework on software customization and productization presented in chapter 6. As motivation for the thesis research aim, it was stated that the extant literature focuses either on the customization perspective or the productization perspective of the software industry. For this thesis, this was regarded as a gap in existing theory where a broader theoretical understanding of both perspectives and their interaction should be developed.

The customization perspective of the integrated framework was largely built upon the arguments of the RBV (Wernerfelt 1984; Barney 1991) and the concepts of value, value generation and value capture (Bowman and Ambrosini 2000; Lepak et al. 2007). Building upon the work of Ulaga and Reinartz (2011), it was found that resources and capabilities are the most important factors for describing customization activities from a vendor perspective. However, in contrast to a pure competitive advantage perspective regarding capabilities output, the concept of value provided a broader understanding of successful customization activities. Thus, by integrating vendor and customer perspectives on value, the framework provides not only explanations from either side but also helps understand balancing mechanisms among sources of value.

In this area, the study offers at least two new important implications for academic inquiries in service-oriented information systems research. First, most previous studies have taken a limited view of customization from the perspective of customer firms by trying to answer the question of how software systems can be implemented in customer firms. In contrast, the first study investigated customization activities from the software vendor's perspective. In this area, the results contribute by introducing six distinctive capabilities for customization actives and identifying unique properties and dimensions for each. Furthermore, those capabilities were connected to four underlying unique customization resources. Second, customization projects provide continuous interfaces for knowledge exchange between customers and solution providers. To date, IS research has focused on the outside-in perspective on this knowledge exchange and left the inside-out perspective mostly to disciplines such as general management or software development. To consider software customization from an integrated service perspective, however, requires including both views to respect the reciprocal nature of the knowledge exchange in customization projects. The overall framework of (knowledge) resources and capabilities is a starting point for further investigations in that area.

From the productization perspective, the study's key elements from the dynamic capabilities framework were used to investigate software development within the software business. The dynamic capability framework describes organizational and strategic management competences that help firms to achieve and sustain competitive advantage. In particular, it describes sensing, seizing and reconfiguring as the core capabilities that must be maintained in successful organizations. The findings from this second study contribute to existing literature and help develop a better understanding of how firms within the software business can organize and manage their product development processes and systematically include innovation impulses from customization activities.

In this area, the study offers a thick description of concrete micro-foundations that reveals several tensions and interrelations in the dynamic capability framework within the software business. In line with Teece's (2007) argumentation, these tensions can be found between sensing, seizing and reconfiguring capabilities. For instance, managerial skills to sense opportunities differ from those to seize or reconfigure. Additionally, the analysis revealed that similar effects occur not only between but also within particular capabilities, for instance, the described tension between the standardization and modularization micro-foundations within the reconfiguring capability. Highlighting these tensions and interrelations helps develop a better understanding of value pre-production within the software business and to explain decisions in software product development.

Third, previous studies have focused on customization either as a way to deliver a product or as a form of co-creation of value. In this study, a first attempt was made to combine those perspectives and to provide a deeper understanding of the reciprocal nature of customization and productization activities. Depending on the vendor's existing customization and productization resources, four different types of software projects were identified.

By connecting pre-existing vendor resources with the necessary capabilities and potential value outcome, an empirically based conceptual model was developed that helps explain customization project outcomes.

In this area, the study offers a contribution to the growing body of literature on software product management by investigating the topic of software productization. So far, only a few studies have started to explore software product management as a distinct discipline rather than as a sub-discipline of software engineering or information systems research. The thesis at hand contributes to this body of work by focusing on the customization perspective of software development. It emphasizes that although software engineering is important for building reliable software systems and although customization services are essential for implementing these systems in customer environments, it is the reciprocal interaction between both functions that defines success – with respect to customer and vendor value – in the software business. However, more research is needed in this line of research. As Slaughter et al. (2006) suggest, "given the many choices for software development and the notion of that 'one size may not fit all' projects, it is important to examine alignment decisions at a more micro or operational level" (p.1436).

6.2.2   Managerial implications

For software firms operating in the hybrid software business, the most important contribution of this thesis is that it provides a deeper view of the operational firm with respect to customization and productization resources and capabilities. The integrated theoretical framework summarizes the findings from this thesis. Thus, the framework can be regarded as a foundation for multiple managerial implications, such as,

1. it helps managers to identify a firm's portfolio of central resources and capabilities for customization and productization activities;

2. it provides managers with a thorough description of the dimensions and properties as well as the relationship between resources, capabilities and values in customization and productization;

3. managers can use the integrated framework to evaluate and further develop customization and productization capabilities and resources on an organizational level;

4. finally, managers can use this framework as guideline for changing their existing customization practices and as a starting point for defining customization service benchmarks.

More particularly, the managerial implications derived from this thesis embrace three different areas: (1) the customization area, (2) the productization area and (3) the value area.

First, software customization is a complex and difficult business. Due to the complexity included in implementation or adaption projects, existing literature has stated that the customer is not always able to manage this complexity and, therefore, strongly depends upon the vendor's support. As the results of study I show, customer firms struggle with several issues of software customization: (1) they have specific needs that must be transformed into requirements, (2) needs – and therefore requirements – change over time, (3) they have more or less realistic expectations of what customized solutions can do, and (4) they do not always know how their own business will develop over the years. To address these issues in a supportive manner, the vendor company must develop several capabilities to facilitate the interaction between customer firm and vendor firm.

Second, from a productization perspective, firms operating in the software business must develop software products that, on the one hand, provide extensive standardization with respect to standard business features, UI and usability or support services. On the other hand, these products must be flexible enough to be adapted to specific customer needs through customization activities. Additionally, although productization does not generate direct value, it is an important pre-production step to generate value through customization. On the one hand, it produces substantial monetary costs but does not directly contribute to benefit value generation. The dynamic capability framework provides theoretical concepts that help overcome those contradictions, such as the sensing capability, the seizing capability and the reconfiguration capability. However, although the dynamic capability framework works fine as a theoretical construct, the academic literature identifies difficulties regarding its practical implications in business management. By identifying concrete micro-foundations to implement each of these capabilities, the thesis addresses an essential managerial challenge in the software business.

Finally, firms that intend to operate in the software business must be aware of the role of customization and productization for their customers' as well as their own value generation. Although the literature has identified value as a multi-dimensional construct, it is often referred to with respect to economic value. Given the complexity of today's organizational ecologies within customer or vendor firms as well as the complex net of relationships between these two, a sole focus on ecological value creates blinders for managers and researchers alike. Thus, a narrow value perspective might lead to an incomplete understanding of behavioral patterns and decision-making processes. Furthermore, a discussion on value in interactive processes not only involves the understanding of value for one party but also an understanding for the other party as well.

Thus, by identifying multiple dimensions of value and separating customer-oriented use value and vendor-oriented exchange value, this thesis contributes to a more elaborate understanding of value in the software business. Although the results from study I have shown that economic value is important for customer and vendor firms as well, other types of value are equally important to understand the business. With respect to software customization, for example, a successful project is defined by the customers' "customization experience" rather than by an objective result. Thus, for the software vendor, a deep understanding of customer value is essential to employ successful software customization. Additionally, there is always a business perspective on customization. Thus, producing value for the customer is important, but it is not the only goal. For the software vendor, it is also important to generate adequate exchange value. Therefore, a deeper understanding of potential exchange values helps evaluate and estimate project costs and benefits.

Bibliography

Åhlström, P. and Westbrook, R. (1999). Implications of mass customization for operations management: An exploratory survey, *International Journal of Operations and Production Management* 19(3): 262–275.

Alvarez, S. A. and Busenitz, L. W. (2001). The entrepreneurship of resource-based theory, *Journal of Management* 27(6): 755–775.

Alves, V., Niu, N., Alves, C. and Valença, G. (2010). Requirements engineering for software product lines: A systematic literature review, *Information and Software Technology* 52(8): 806–820.

Amit, R. and Schoemaker, P. J. H. (1993). Strategic assets and organizational rent, *Strategic Management Journal* 14(1): 33–46.

Anderson, C. R. and Zeithaml, C. P. (1984). Stage of the product life cycle, business strategy, and business performance, *Academy of Management Journal* 27(1): 5–24.

Armstrong, C. E. and Shimizu, K. (2007). A review of approaches to empirical research on the resource-based view of the firm, *Journal of Management* 33(6): 959–986.

Artz, P., van de Weerd, I., Brinkkemper, S. and Fieggen, J. (2010). Productization: transforming from developing customer-specific software to product software, *Software Business*, Springer, pp. 90–102.

Auerbach, C. F. and Silverstein, L. B. (2003). *Qualitative Data: An Introduction to Coding and Analysis*, New York University Press.

Ballintijn, G. (2005). A case study of the release management of a health-care information system, *International Conference on Software Maintenance (Industrial and Tool Volume)*, pp. 34–43.

Barney, J. (1991). Firm resources and sustained competitive advantage, *Journal of Management* 17(1): 99–120.

Barney, J. B. (1986). Strategic factor markets: Expectations, luck, and business strategy, *Management Science* 32(10): 1231–1241.

Barney, J. B. (2001). Is the resource-based "view" a useful perspective for strategic management research? Yes., *Academy of Management Review* 26(1): 41–56.

Barney, J. B., Ketchen, D. J. and Wright, M. (2011). The future of resource-based theory revitalization or decline?, *Journal of Management* 37(5): 1299–1315.

Barney, J., Wright, M. and Ketchen Jr, D. J. (2001). The resource-based view of the firm: Ten years after 1991, *Journal of Management* 27(6): 625–641.

Barreto, I. (2010). Dynamic capabilities: A review of past research and an agenda for the future, *Journal of Management* 36(1): 256–280.

Bazeley, P. (2003). Computerized data analysis for mixed methods research, *Handbook of Mixed Methods in Social and Behavioral Research*, Sage Thousand Oaks, CA, pp. 385–422.

Beck, K. and Andres, C. (2004). *Extreme Programming Explained: Embrace Change*, Addison-Wesley Professional.

Bekkers, W., van de Weerd, I., Spruit, M. and Brinkkemper, S. (2010). A framework for process improvement in software product management, *Systems, Software and Services Process Improvement*, Springer, pp. 1–12.

Bendapudi, N. and Leone, R. P. (2003). Psychological implications of customer participation in co-production, *Journal of Marketing* 67(1): 14–28.

Berander, P. and Andrews, A. (2005). Requirements prioritization, *Engineering and Managing Software Requirements*, Springer, pp. 69–94.

Bertram, M., Schaarschmidt, M. and von Kortzfleisch, H. (2012). Customization of product software: Insights from an extensive is literature review, *in* B. A. and F. B. (eds), *Future of ICT Research*, IFIP AICT 389, IFIP International Federation for Information Processing 8.2, Tampa, FL, pp. 222–236.

Bertram, M., Schaarschmidt, M. and Von Kortzfleisch, H. (2013). Resources and capabilities of software customization services and their influence in innovation activities: Evidence from an exploratory interview study, *Proceedings of the SIG SVC Pre-ICIS Workshop*, Milano, Italy.

Boehm, B. and Abts, C. (1999). COTS integration: Plug and pray?, *Computer* 32(1): 135–138.

Bosch, J. (2009). From software product lines to software ecosystems, *Proceedings of the 13th International Software Product Line Conference*, Carnegie Mellon University, pp. 111–119.

Bowman, C. and Ambrosini, V. (2000). Value creation versus value capture: towards a coherent definition of value in strategy, *British Journal of Management* 11(1): 1–15.

Brocke, H., Ubernickel, F. and Brenner, W. (2010). Mass customizing it service agreements: Towards individualized on-demand services, *Proceedings of the European Conference on Information Systems 2010*.

Bruton, N. (2002). *How to Manage the IT Helpdesk: A Guide for User Support and Call Centre Managers*, Routledge.

Buttle, F. (2008). *Customer Relationship Management: Concepts and Tools*, Taylor and Francis.

Calvin, R. J. (2004). *Sales Management*, McGraw-Hill Professional.

Capron, L., Dussauge, P. and Mitchell, W. (1998). Resource redeployment following horizontal acquisitions in europe and north america, 1988–1992, *Strategic Management Journal* 19(7): 631–661.

Carlshamre, P., Sandahl, K., Lindvall, M., Regnell, B. and Natt och Dag, J. (2001). An industrial survey of requirements interdependencies in software product release planning, *Proceedings. Fifth IEEE International Symposium on Requirements Engineering, 2001.*, IEEE, pp. 84–91.

Carmel, E. and Becker, S. (1995). A process model for packaged software development, *IEEE Transactions on Engineering Management* 42(1): 50–61.

Castanias, R. P. and Helfat, C. E. (1991). Managerial resources and rents, *Journal of Management* 17(1): 155–171.

Castro, J., Kolp, M. and Mylopoulos, J. (2002). Towards requirements-driven information systems engineering: the tropos project, *Information systems* 27(6): 365–389.

Chiasson, M. and Green, L. (2007). Questioning the it artefact: user practices that can, could, and cannot be supported in packaged-software designs, *European Journal of Information Systems* 16(5): 542–554.

Chrissis, M. B., Konrad, M. and Shrum, S. (2011). *CMMI for Development: Guidelines for Process Integration and Product Improvement*, Pearson Education.

Clements, P. and Northrop, L. (2001). *Software Product Lines: Patterns and Practices*, Addison Wesleyc, MA.

Coase, R. H. (1937). The nature of the firm, *Economica* 4(16): 386–405.

Coff, R. W. (1999). When competitive advantage doesn't lead to performance: The resource-based view and stakeholder bargaining power, *Organization Science* 10(2): 119–133.

Cohn, M. (2004). *User Stories Applied: For Agile Software Development*, Addison-Wesley Professional.

Combs, J. G. and Ketchen, D. J. (1999). Explaining interfirm cooperation and performance: toward a reconciliation of predictions from the resource-based view and organizational economics, *Strategic Management Journal* 20(9): 867–888.

Conner, K. R. (1991). A historical comparison of resource-based theory and five schools of thought within industrial organization economics: do we have a new theory of the firm?, *Journal of Management* 17(1): 121–154.

Conner, K. R. and Prahalad, C. K. (1996). A resource-based theory of the firm: Knowledge versus opportunism, *Organization Science* 7(5): 477–501.

Connor, T. (2002). The resource-based view of strategy and its value to practising managers, *Strategic Change* 11(6): 307–316.

Cooper, R. G. (2001). *Winning at New Products: Accelerating the Process from Idea to Launch*, Basic Books.

Creswell, J. (2009). *Research Design: Qualitative, Quantitative, and Mixed Methods Approaches*, Sage Publications.

Crook, T. R., Ketchen, D. J., Combs, J. G. and Todd, S. Y. (2008). Strategic resources and performance: a meta-analysis, *Strategic Management Journal* 29(11): 1141–1154.

Cusumano, M. A. (2004). *The Business of Software: What every Manager, Programmer, and Entrepreneur Must Know to Thrive and Survive in Good Times and Bad*, The Free Press, New York.

Cusumano, M. A. (2008). The changing software business: Moving from products to services, *Computer* 41(1): 20–27.

Czarnecki, K., Antkiewicz, M. and Kim, P. C. H. (2006). Multi-level customization in application engineering, *Communications of the ACM* 49(12): 60–65.

Czepiel, J. A. (1990). Service encounters and service relationships: implications for research, *Journal of Business Research* 20(1): 13–21.

Da Silveira, G., Borenstein, D. and Fogliatto, F. S. (2001). Mass customization: Literature review and research directions, *International Journal of Production Economics* 72(1): 1–13.

Daneva, M. (2004). Erp requirements engineering practice: lessons learned, *Software, IEEE* 21(2): 26–33.

D'Aveni, R. A. (1994). *Hypercompetition: Managing the Dynamics of Strategic Maneuvering*, The Free Press, New York and Toronto.

Davis, A. (2005). *Just Enough Requirements Management: Where Software Development Meets Marketing*, Addison-Wesley.

Davis, S. (1996). *Future Perfect*, Addison-Wesley Publishing.

Davis, S. M. (1989). From "future perfect": Mass customizing, *Planning Review* 17(2): 16–21.

Day, G. S. (1994). The capabilities of market-driven organizations, *Journal of Marketing* pp. 37–52.

De Luca, L. M. and Atuahene-Gima, K. (2007). Market knowledge dimensions and cross-functional collaboration: examining the different routes to product innovation performance, *Journal of Marketing* pp. 95–112.

De Man, J. and Ebert, C. (2003). A common product life cycle in global software development, *Eleventh Annual International Workshop on Software Technology and Engineering Practice, 2003*, IEEE, pp. 16–21.

Denne, M. and Cleland-Huang, J. (2003). *Software by Numbers: Low-Risk, High-Return Development*, Prentice Hall Professional.

Denzin, N. (2009). *The Research Act: A Theoretical Introduction to Sociological Methods*, Aldine De Gruyter.

Denzin, N. K. and Lincoln, Y. S. (1994). *Handbook of Qualitative Research*, Sage Publications.

Dewan, R., Jing, B. and Seidmann, A. (2003). Product customization and price competition on the internet, *Management Science* 49(8): 1055–1070.

Dewar, R. D. and Dutton, J. E. (1986). The adoption of radical and incremental innovations: an empirical analysis, *Management Science* 32(11): 1422–1433.

Dey, I. (1993). *Qualitative Data Analysis: A User Friendly Guide for Social Scientists*, Routledge.

Dierickx, I. and Cool, K. (1989). Asset stock accumulation and sustainability of competitive advantage, *Management Science* 35(12): 1504–1511.

Eastwood, M. A. (1996). Implementing mass customization, *Computers in Industry* 30(3): 171–174.

Ebert, C. (2007). The impacts of software product management, *Journal of Systems and Software* 80(6): 850–861.

Ebert, C. (2009). Software product management, *The Journal of Defense Software Engineering* 2009: 15–19.

Ebert, C. and Dumke, R. (2007). *Software Measurement*, Springer.

Eisenhardt, K. (1989). Building theories from case study research, *Academy of Management Review* 21(10–11): 532–550.

Eisenhardt, K. M. and Martin, J. A. (2000). Dynamic capabilities: What are they?, *Strategic Management Journal* 21(10/11): 1105–1121.

Eisenhardt, K. M. and Santos, F. M. (2000). Knowledge-based view: A new theory of strategy, *Handbook of Strategy and Management*, Sage Publications, pp. 139–164.

Enkel, E., Gassmann, O. and Chesbrough, H. (2009). Open R&D and open innovation: Exploring the phenomenon, *R&D Management* 39(4): 311–316.

Etgar, M. (2008). A descriptive model of the consumer co-production process, *Journal of the Academy of Marketing Science* 36(1): 97–108.

Feagin, J., Orum, A. and Sjoberg, G. (1991). *A Case for the Case Study*, The University of North Carolina Press.

Feitzinger, E. and Lee, H. L. (1997). Mass customization at hewlett-packard: The power of postponement, *Harvard Business Review* 75(1): 116–121.

Fiol, C. M. (1991). Managing culture as a competitive resource: An identity-based view of sustainable competitive advantage, *Journal of Management* 17(1): 191–211.

Firat, A., Dholakia, N. and Venkatesh, A. (1995). Marketing in a postmodern world, *European Journal of Marketing* 29(1): 40–56.

Fisher, J., Shanks, G. and Lamp, J. (2007). A ranking list for information systems journals, *Australasian Journal of Information Systems* 14(2): 5–18.

Fitzgerald, B., Hartnett, G. and Conboy, K. (2006). Customising agile methods to software practices at intel Shannon, *European Journal of Information Systems* 15(2): 200–213.

Fogliatto, F. S., da Silveira, G. J. and Borenstein, D. (2012). The mass customization decade: An updated review of the literature, *International Journal of Production Economics* 138(1): 14–25.

Fornell, C., Johnson, M. D., Anderson, E. W., Cha, J. and Bryant, B. E. (1996). The american customer satisfaction index: nature, purpose, and findings, *The Journal of Marketing* pp. 7–18.

Foss, K. and Foss, N. J. (2005). Resources and transaction costs: how property rights economics furthers the resource-based view, *Strategic Management Journal* 26(6): 541–553.

Foss, N. J. (1996a). Knowledge-based approaches to the theory of the firm: Some critical comments, *Organization Science* 7(5): 470–476.

Foss, N. J. (1996b). More critical comments on knowledge-based theories of the firm, *Organization Science* 7(5): 519–523.

Frank, U. (2006). Towards a pluralistic conception of research methods in information systems research, *Icb research report*, University of Duisburg-Essen.

Franke, N., Keinz, P. and Steger, C. (2009). Testing the value of customization: When do customers really prefer products tailored to their preferences?, *Journal of Marketing* 73(5): 103–121.

Franke, N. and Schreier, M. (2007). Product uniqueness as a driver of customer utility in mass customization, *Marketing Letters* 19(2): 93–107.

Fricker, S. A. (2012). Software product management, *Software for People*, Springer, pp. 53–81.

Fricker, S., Gorschek, T., Byman, C. and Schmidle, A. (2010). Handshaking with implementation proposals: Negotiating requirements understanding, *IEEE Software* 27(2): 72–80.

Fricker, S. and Schumacher, S. (2012). Release planning with feature trees: Industrial case, *Requirements Engineering: Foundation for Software Quality*, Springer, pp. 288–305.

Fried, J., Hansson, D. H. and Linderman, M. (2009). Getting real: The smarter, faster, easier way to build a successful web application, 37signals.

Gartner (2013). Market share: All software markets, worldwide, Internet.

Garvin, D. A. (1998). *Managing Quality: The Strategic and Competitive Edge*, The Free Press, New York.

Gavetti, G. (2005). Cognition and hierarchy: Rethinking the microfoundations of capabilities' development, *Organization Science* 16(6): 599–617.

Ghosh, M., Dutta, S. and Stremersch, S. (2006). Customizing complex products: when should the vendor take control?, *Journal of Marketing Research* pp. 664–679.

Gibbert, M. (2006a). Generalizing about uniqueness an essay on an apparent paradox in the resource-based view, *Journal of Management Inquiry* 15(2): 124–134.

Gibbert, M. (2006b). Munchausen, black swans, and the rbv response to levitas and ndofor, *Journal of Management Inquiry* 15(2): 145–151.

Gilmore, J. H. and Pine II, B. (1997). The four faces of mass customization., *Harvard Business Review* 75(1): 91–101.

Gorchels, L. (2006). *The Product Manager's Handbook*, McGraw Hill Professional, New York.

Gorschek, T. and Wohlin, C. (2006). Requirements abstraction model, *Requirements Engineering* 11(1): 79–101.

Grant, R. M. (1996a). Prospering in dynamically-competitive environments: organizational capability as knowledge integration, *Organization Science* 7(4): 375–387.

Grant, R. M. (1996b). Toward a knowledge-based theory of the firm, *Strategic Management Journal* 17: 109–122.

Grönroos, C. and Ravald, A. (2011). Service as business logic: implications for value creation and marketing, *Journal of Service Management* 22(1): 5–22.

Haines, S. (2009). *The Product Manager's Desk Reference*, McGraw-Hill New York.

Hansen, M. T. (1999). The search-transfer problem: The role of weak ties in sharing knowledge across organization subunits, *Administrative Science Quarterly* 44(1): 82–111.

Hargadon, A. B. (2002). Brokering knowledge: Linking learning and innovation, *Research in Organizational Behavior* 24: 41–85.

Harrison, J. S., Hitt, M. A., Hoskisson, R. E. and Ireland, R. D. (1991). Synergies and post-acquisition performance: Differences versus similarities in resource allocations, *Journal of Management* 17(1): 173–190.

Hart, C. W. (1995a). Mass customization: conceptual underpinnings, opportunities and limits, *International Journal of Service Industry Management* 6(2): 36–45.

Hart, C. W. (1996). Made to order, *Marketing Management* 5(2): 10–23.

Hart, S. L. (1995b). A natural-resource-based view of the firm, *Academy of Management Review* pp. 986–1014.

Hauser, J. R. and Clausing, D. (1988). The house of quality.

Helfat, C. E., Finkelstein, S., Mitchell, W., Peteraf, M., Singh, H., Teece, D. and Winter, S. G. (2009). *Dynamic Capabilities: Understanding Strategic Change in Organizations*, John Wiley & Sons.

Hoch, D. J., Lindner, S. K., Roeding, C. R. and Purkert, G. (1999). Secrets of software success: Management insights from 100 software firms around the world.

Huff, A. S. (2009). *Designing Research for Publication*, Sage Publications, Thousand Oaks and Calif.

Humble, J. and Farley, D. (2010). *Continuous Delivery: Reliable Software Releases through Build, Test, and Deployment Automation*, Pearson Education.

International Software Product Management Association (2014). Software product management body of knowledge (spmbok), http://ispma.org/spmbok/. Last access: August 2014.

Ireland, R. D., Hitt, M. A. and Sirmon, D. G. (2003). A model of strategic entrepreneurship: The construct and its dimensions, *Journal of Management* 29(6): 963–989.

Jiao, J., Tseng, M. M., Duffy, V. G. and Lin, F. (1998). Product family modeling for mass customization, *Computers and Industrial Engineering* 35(3): 495–498.

Joneja, A. and Lee, N. K. (1998). Automated configuration of parametric feeding tools for mass customization, *Computers and Industrial Engineering* 35(3): 463–466.

Jones, C. (2008). *Applied Software Measurement: Global Analysis of Productivity and Qquality*, Vol. 3, McGraw-Hill New York.

Jourdan, Z., Rainer, R. K. and Marshall, T. E. (2008). Business intelligence: An analysis of the literature 1, *Information Systems Management* 25(2): 121–131.

Kay, M. J. (1993). Making mass customization happen: lessons for implementation, *Strategy and Leadership* 21(4): 14–18.

Kelley, S. W., Donnelly, J. H. and Skinner, S. J. (1990). Customer participation in service production and delivery., *Journal of Retailing* .

Keßler, S. and Alpar, P. (2008). Do best practice frameworks fit open source software customization?, *Proceedings of the European Conference on Information Systems 2008* .

Kirk, R. (2002). Routledge encyclopedia of philosophy, *Mind* 111(442): 386–388.

Kitchenham, B. and Pfleeger, S. L. (1996). Software quality: The elusive target, *IEEE Software* 13(1): 12–21.

Kittlaus, H.-B. and Clough, P. (2009). *Software Product Management and Pricing*, Springer, Berlin Heidelberg.

Ko, D.-G., Kirsch, L. J. and King, W. R. (2005). Antecedents of knowledge transfer from consultants to clients in enterprise system implementations, *MIS Quarterly* pp. 59–85.

Kogut, B. and Zander, U. (1992). Knowledge of the firm, combinative capabilities, and the replication of technology, *Organization Science* 3(3): 383–397.

Kotha, S. (1995). Mass customization: implementing the emerging paradigm for competitive advantage, *Strategic Management Journal* 16(S1): 21–42.

Kotha, S. (1996). From mass production to mass customization: the case of the national industrial bicycle company of japan, *European Management Journal* 14(5): 442–450.

Kotler, P. (1989). From mass marketing to mass customization, *Strategy and Leadership* 17(5): 10–47.

Kotler, P. and Armstrong, G. (2011). *Principles of Marketing 15th Global Edition*, Pearson Prentice Hall, Upper Saddle River, NJ.

Kraaijenbrink, J., Spender, J.-C. and Groen, A. J. (2010). The resource-based view: a review and assessment of its critiques, *Journal of Management* 36(1): 349–372.

Lado, A. A., Boyd, N. G., Wright, P. and Kroll, M. (2006). Paradox and theorizing within the resource-based view, *Academy of Management Review* 31(1): 115–131.

Lampel, J. and Mintzberg, H. (1996). Customizing customization, *Sloan Management Review* 38(1): 21–30.

Lane, P. J., Koka, B. R. and Pathak, S. (2006). The reification of absorptive capacity: a critical review and rejuvenation of the construct, *Academy of Management Review* 31(4): 833–863.

Lau, R. S. (1995). Mass customization: the next industrial revolution, *Industrial Management* 37(5): 18–19.

Lehman, M. M. (1980). Programs, life cycles, and laws of software evolution, *Proceedings of the IEEE* 68(9): 1060–1076.

Lepak, D. P., Smith, K. G. and Taylor, M. S. (2007). Value creation and value capture: a multilevel perspective, *Academy of Management Review* 32(1): 180–194.

Lichtenthaler, U. (2009). Absorptive capacity, environmental turbulence, and the complementarity of organizational learning processes, *The Academy of Management Journal* 52(4): 822–846.

Light, B. (2001). The maintenance implications of the customization of erp software, *Journal of Software Maintenance and Evolution: Research and Practice* 13(6): 415–429.

Light, B. (2005). Potential pitfalls in packaged software adoption, *Communications of the ACM* 48(5): 119–121.

Light, B. and Papazafeiropoulou, A. (2004). Reasons behind erp package adoption: A diffusion of innovations perspective, *Proceedings of the 12th European Conference on Information Systems*, Turku, Finnland.

Lippman, S. A. and Rumelt, R. P. (1982). Uncertain imitability: An analysis of interfirm differences in efficiency under competition, *The Bell Journal of Economics* pp. 418–438.

Lippman, S. A. and Rumelt, R. P. (2003). The payments perspective: micro-foundations of resource analysis, *Strategic Management Journal* 24(10): 903–927.

Madhok, A. (2002). Reassessing the fundamentals and beyond: Ronald coase, the transaction cost and resource-based theories of the firm and the institutional structure of production, *Strategic Management Journal* 23(6): 535–550.

Mahoney, J. T. and Pandian, J. R. (1992). The resource-based view within the conversation of strategic management, *Strategic Management Journal* 13(5): 363–380.

Makadok, R. (2001). Toward a synthesis of the resource-based and dynamic-capability views of rent creation, *Strategic Management Journal* 22(5): 387–401.

Makadok, R. and Barney, J. B. (2001). Strategic factor market intelligence: An application of information economics to strategy formulation and competitor intelligence, *Management Science* 47(12): 1621–1638.

Marris, R. L. (1961). Review of the theory of the growth of the firm, *Economic Journal* 71: 144–148.

Martin, R. C. and Melnik, G. (2008). Tests and requirements, requirements and tests: A möbius strip, *Software, IEEE* 25(1): 54–59.

McCracken, G. (1988). *The Long Interview*, Vol. 13, Sage.

McGuinness, T. and Morgan, R. E. (2000). Strategy, dynamic capabilities and complex science: management rhetoric vs. reality, *Strategic Change* 9(4): 209–220.

Miles, M. B. and Huberman, A. M. (1994). *Qualitative Data Analysis: An Expanded Sourcebook*, SAGE Publications, Incorporated.

Miles, M. B., Huberman, A. M. and Saldaña, J. (2013). *Qualitative Data Analysis: A Methods Sourcebook*, SAGE Publications, Incorporated.

Miller, D. (2003). An asymmetry-based view of advantage: towards an attainable sustainability, *Strategic Management Journal* 24(10): 961–976.

Miller, D. and Shamsie, J. (1996). The resource-based view of the firm in two environments: The hollywood film studios from 1936 to 1965, *Academy of management journal* 39(3): 519–543.

Morse, J. (1994). Emerging from the data: the cognitive processes of analysis in qualitative inquiry'in jm morse (ed.) critical issues in qualitative research methods.

Mowery, D. C., Oxley, J. E. and Silverman, B. S. (1996). Strategic alliances and interfirm knowledge transfer, *Strategic Management Journal* 17: 77–91.

Mustafee, N. (2011). Evolution of is research based on literature published in two leading is journals-ejis and misq., *Proceedings of the European Conference on Information Systems 2011*.

Myers, M. D. and Newman, M. (2007). The qualitative interview in is research: Examining the craft, *Information and Organization* 17(1): 2–26.

Nambisan, S. (2002). Designing virtual customer environments for new product development: Toward a theory, *Academy of Management Review* 27(3): 392–413.

Newbert, S. L. (2007). Empirical research on the resource-based view of the firm: an assessment and suggestions for future research, *Strategic Management Journal* 28(2): 121–146.

Nonaka, I. and Takeuchi, H. (1995). *The Knowledge-Creating Company*, Oxford University, New York.

Oliver, C. (1997). Sustainable competitive advantage: Combining institutional and resource-based views, *Strategic Management Journal* 18(9): 697–713.

Österle, H., Becker, J., Frank, U., Hess, T., Karagiannis, D., Krcmar, H., Loos, P., Mertens, P., Oberweis, A. and Sinz, E. J. (2011). Memorandum on design-oriented information systems research, *European Journal of Information Systems* 20(1): 7–10.

Patton, M. Q. (1990). *Qualitative Evaluation and Research Methods*, SAGE Publications, inc.

Penrose, E. (1985). The theory of the growth of the firm twenty-five years later, *Technical Report 20*, Acta Universitatis Upsaliensis: Studia Oeconomicae Negotiorum (Uppsala Lectures in Business).

Penrose, E. T. (1959). *The Theory of the Growth of the Firm*, Wiley, New York.

Penrose, E. T. (1995). *The Theory of the Growth of the Firm*, Oxford University Press.

Perdue, B. C. and Summers, J. O. (1991). Purchasing agents' use of negotiation strategies, *Journal of Marketing Research* pp. 175–189.

Perks, H., Gruber, T. and Edvardsson, B. (2012). Co-creation in radical service innovation: a systematic analysis of microlevel processes, *Journal of Product Innovation Management* 29(6): 935–951.

Peteraf, M. A. (1993). The cornerstones of competitive advantage: A resource-based view, *Strategic Management Journal* 14(3): 179–191.

Peteraf, M. A. and Barney, J. B. (2003). Unraveling the resource-based tangle, *Managerial and decision economics* 24(4): 309–323.

Phaal, R., Farrukh, C. and Probert, D. (2007). Strategic roadmapping: a workshop based approach for identifying and exploring innovation issues and opportunities, *Engineering Management Journal* 19(1): 3–12.

Pichler, R. (2010). *Agile Product Management with Scrum: Creating Products that Customers Love*, Addison-Wesley Professional.

Piller, F., Schubert, P., Koch, M. and Möslein, K. (2004). From mass customization to collaborative customer codesign, *Proceedings of the European Conference on Information Systems 2004* .

Pine II, B. J. (1993). Mass customizing products and services, *Strategy and Leadership* 21(4): 6–55.

Pitelis, C. (2009). Edith penrose's 'the theory of the growth of the firm' fifty years later, *MPRA Paper 23180*, Munich Personal RePEc Archive.

Polanyi, M. (1962). *Personal Knowledge: Towards a Post-critical Philosophy*, Psychology Press.

Porter, M. (1979). *How Competitive Forces Shape Strategy*, Abril.

Potts, C., Takahashi, K. and Antón, A. I. (1994). Inquiry-based requirements analysis, *IEEE software* 11(2): 21–32.

Prahalad, C. K. and Hamel, G. (1990). The core competence of the corporation, *Boston (MA)* .

Prahalad, C. and Ramaswamy, V. (2000). Co-opting customer experience, *Harvard Business Review* 78(1): 79–88.

Priem, R. L. (2007). A consumer perspective on value creation, *The Academy of Management Review* 32(1): pp.219–235.

Priem, R. L. and Butler, J. E. (2001a). Is the resource-based "view" a useful perspective for strategic management research?, *Academy of Management Review* pp. 22–40.

Priem, R. L. and Butler, J. E. (2001b). Tautology in the resource-based view and the implications of externally determined resource value: Further comments, *Academy of management Review* 26(1): 57–66.

Raijlich, V. T. and Bennett, K. H. (2000). A staged model for the software life cycle, *Computer* 33(7): 66–71.

Rao, P. and Klein, J. A. (1994). Growing importance of marketing strategies for the software industry, *Industrial Marketing Management* 23(1): 29–37.

Regnell, B. and Brinkkemper, S. (2005). Market-driven requirements engineering for software products, *Engineering and Managing Software Requirements*, Springer, pp. 287–308.

Regnell, B., Svensson, R. B. and Olsson, T. (2008). Supporting roadmapping of quality requirements, *Software, IEEE* 25(2): 42–47.

Reichwald, R. and Piller, F. T. (2003). Von massenproduktion zu coproduktion kunden als wertschöpfungspartner, *WIRTSCHAFTSINFORMATIK* 45(5): 515–519.

Reifer, D. J. (2002). *Making the Software Business Case: Improvement by the Numbers*, Pearson Education.

Rhoton, J. (2010). *Cloud Computing Explained: Implementation Handbook For Enterprises*, Recursive Press, Kent: United Kingdom.

Roberts, N., Galluch, P. S., Dinger, M. and Grover, V. (2012). Absorptive capacity and information systems research: Review, synthesis, and directions for future research, *Information Systems* 6(1): 25–40.

Ross, A. (1996). Selling uniqueness, *Manufacturing Engineer* 75(6): 260–263.

Royce, W. (2010). *Software Project Management: A Unified Framework*, 1st edn, Addison-Wesley Professional.

Rus, I. and Lindvall, M. (2002). Knowledge management in software engineering, *IEEE software* 19(3): 26–38.

Safadi, H. and Faraj, S. (2010). The role of workarounds during an open-source electronic medical record system implementation, *Proceedings of the International Conference on Information Systems 2010* .

Saiedian, H. and Dale, R. (2000). Requirements engineering: making the connection between the software developer and customer, *Information and Software Technology* 42(6): 419–428.

Saldaña, J. (2009). *The Coding Manual for Qualitative Researchers*, Sage Publications.

Sawyer, S. (2001). A market-based perspective on information systems development, *Communications of the ACM* 44(11): 97–102.

Schmidt, M. (2002). *The Business Case Guide*, Solution Matrix, Boston.

Shelanski, H. A. and Klein, P. G. (1995). Empirical research in transaction cost economics: a review and assessment, *Journal of Law, Economics, & Organization* pp. 335–361.

Sia, S. and Soh, C. (2007). An assessment of package–organisation misalignment: institutional and ontological structures, *European Journal of Information Systems* 16(5): 568–583.

Simonin, B. L. (1999). Ambiguity and the process of knowledge transfer in strategic alliances, *Strategic Management Journal* 20(7): 595–623.

Singh, H. and Zollo, M. (1999). *Post-Acquisition Strategies, Integration Capability, and the Economic Performance of Corporate Acquisitions*, Working paper - INSEAD99/42/SM.

Sirmon, D. G., Hitt, M. A. and Ireland, R. D. (2007). Managing firm resources in dynamic environments to create value: Looking inside the black box, *Academy of Management Review* 32(1): 273–292.

Slaughter, S. A., Levine, L., Ramesh, B., Pries-Heje, J. and Baskerville, R. (2006). Aligning software processes with strategy, *MIS quarterly* pp. 891–918.

Song, J. H. and Adams, C. R. (1993). Differentiation through customer involvement in production or delivery, *Journal of Consumer Marketing* 10(2): 4–12.

Spalding, G. (2007). Continual service improvement: Office of government commerce (itil), *The Stationary Office Ltd* .

Spira, J. S. (1993). Mass customization through training at lutron electronics, *Planning Review* 21(4): 23–24.

Spohrer, J. and Maglio, P. P. (2008). The emergence of service science: Toward systematic service innovations to accelerate co-creation of value, *Production and Operations Management* 17(3): 238–246.

Stake, R. (1995). *The Art of Case Study Research*, Sage Publications, Inc.

Steinmueller, W. E. (1995). *The US software industry: an analysis and interpretive history*, MERIT.

Strauss, A. L., Corbin, J. et al. (1990). *Basics of Qualitative Research*, Vol. 15, Sage Newbury Park, CA.

Swaminathan, J. M. and Tayur, S. R. (2003). Models for supply chains in e-business, *Management Science* 49(10): 1387–1406.

Szulanski, G. (1996). Exploring internal stickiness: Impediments to the transfer of best practice within the firm, *Strategic Management Journal* 17(WINTER): 27–43.

Teece, D. J. (2000). Strategies for managing knowledge assets: the role of firm structure and industrial context, *Long range planning* 33(1): 35–54.

Teece, D. J. (2007). Explicating dynamic capabilities: the nature and micro-foundations of (sustainable) enterprise performance, *Strategic Management Journal* 28(13): 1319–1350.

Teece, D. J., Pisano, G. and Shuen, A. (1997). Dynamic capabilities and strategic management, *Strategic Management Journal* 18(7): 509–533.

Teece, D. and Pisano, G. (1994). The dynamic capabilities of firms: an introduction, *Industrial and Corporate Change* 3(3): 537–556.

Trott, P. (2011). *Innovation Management and New Product Development*, Prentice Hall, London.

Tseng, M. and Jiao, J. (2001). Mass customization, *Handbook of Industrial Engineering, Technology and Operation Management*, Wiley, New York, pp. 684–709.

Tuli, K. R., Kohli, A. K. and Bharadwaj, S. G. (2007). Rethinking customer solutions: from product bundles to relational processes, *Journal of Marketing* 71(3): 1–17.

Tyrväinen, P., Warsta, J. and Seppänen, V. (2008). Evolution of secondary software businesses: understanding industry dynamics, *Open IT-Based Innovation: Moving Towards Cooperative IT Transfer and Knowledge Diffusion*, Springer, pp. 381–401.

Ulaga, W. and Reinartz, W. J. (2011). Hybrid offerings: how manufacturing firms combine goods and services successfully, *Journal of Marketing* 75(6): 5–23.

van de Weerd, B. S., Nieuwenhuis, R., Versendaal, J. and Bijlsma, L. (2006). Towards a reference framework for software product management, *14th IEEE International Requirements Engineering Conference* .

van Fenema, P., Koppius, O. and van Baalen, P. (2007). Implementing packaged enterprise software in multi-site firms: intensification of organizing and learning, *European Journal of Information Systems* 16(5): 584–598.

Vlaanderen, K., Van De Weerd, I. and Brinkkemper, S. (2010). *Improving software product management processes: a detailed view of the Product Software Knowledge Infrastructure*, PhD thesis, Ph. D. thesis, Utrecht University.

Von Hippel, E. (2005). *Democratizing Innovation*, MIT Press, Cambridge, MA.

Väyrynen, K. (2010). Software business in industrial companies: Identifying capabilities for three types of software business, *Proceedings of the international Conference on Information Systems*.

Wade, M. and Hulland, J. (2004). Review: The resource-based view and information systems research: Review, extension, and suggestions for future research, *MIS quarterly* 28(1): 107–142.

Wallin, C., Ekdahl, F. and Larsson, S. (2002). Integrating business and software development models, *Software, IEEE* 19(6): 28–33.

Ward, J., Griffiths, P. M. and Whitmore, P. (2002). *Strategic Planning for Information Systems*, Vol. 3, Wiley New York.

Webster, J. and Watson, R. T. (2002). Guest editorial: Analyzing the past to prepare for the future: Writing a literature review, *MIS quarterly* 26(2).

Weinmann, M., Robra-Bissantz, S., Witt, M. and Schmidt, E. (2011). Einflussfaktoren auf die präferenz bei produktkonfiguratoren: Eine empirische studie am beispiel der automobilindustrie, *Proceedings of Wirtschaftinformatik 2011* .

Wernerfelt, B. (1984). A resource-based view of the firm, *Strategic Management Journal* 5(2): 171–180.

Williamson, O. E. (1975). *Markets and Hierarchies : Analysis and Antitrust Implications*, Free Press, New York.

Williamson, O. E. (1985). *The Economic Institutions of Capitalism*, Free Press, New York.

Winkler, J., Dibbern, J. and Heinzl, A. (2009). The impact of software product and service characteristics on international distribution arrangement for software solutions, *ICIS 2009 Proceedings*.

Winter, S. G. (2003). Understanding dynamic capabilities, *Strategic Management Journal* 24(10): 991–995.

Wright, P. M., Dunford, B. B. and Snell, S. A. (2001). Human resources and the resource based view of the firm, *Journal of Management* 27(6): 701–721.

Xin, M. and Levina, N. (2008). Software-as-a service model: Elaborating client-side adoption factors, *Proceedings of the International Conference on Information Systems 2008* .

Xu, L. and Brinkkemper, S. (2007). Concepts of product software, *European Journal of Information Systems* 16(5): 531–541.

Yin, R. (2009). *Case study research: Design and methods*, Sage Publications, London.

Zahra, S. A., Sapienza, H. J. and Davidsson, P. (2006). Entrepreneurship and dynamic capabilities: a review, model and research agenda, *Journal of Management Studies* 43(4): 917–955.

Zander, U. and Kogut, B. (1995). Knowledge and the speed of the transfer and imitation of organizational capabilities: An empirical test, *Organization Science* 6(1): 76–92.

Zollo, M. and Winter, S. G. (2002). Deliberate learning and the evolution of dynamic capabilities, *Organization Science* 13(3): 339–351.

Appendix A

Introduction: The neglected role of customization for software product management

Table A.1: Software product management and strategic management (International Software Product Management Association 2014)

Activity	Description
Portfolio management	Portfolio management is responsible for making choices about resource investments and allocations in specific markets, products and technologies. By focusing resources only to a few important activities it ensures balancing risks versus returns, maintenance versus growth, and short term versus long term.
Innovation management	In a product context innovation management refers to the continuous renewal of technologies and product offerings (Trott 2011). Innovations might either be radical or incremental (Dewar and Dutton 1986). The product manager participates in both. He is the driver of radical innovations and the manager of incremental innovations.
Resource management	Resource management is closely related to corporate strategy and portfolio management. It is concerned with the company's production factors (i.e. unskilled labor and capital), firm-specific assets that are difficult to trade (i.e. business knowledge and engineering experience) and organizational resources and competences (Barney 1991; Teece et al. 1997).
Market analysis	Market analysis delivers key inputs to position the company and its products in the industry. It is the foundation for identifying threats and opportunities, for instance analyzing political, economic, social or societal, and technological factors (PEST) (Ward et al. 2002).
Product analysis	Product analysis delivers information about the current product situation and performance. In contrast to market analysis it does not deal with external opportunities or threat, but with the company's internal strength and weaknesses. Data for product analysis is acquired by finance controllers by analyzing product revenues, development and operation costs, profit, sales or support requests (Kittlaus and Clough 2009).

Table A.2: Software product management and product strategy (International Software Product Management Association 2014)

Activity	Description
Product positioning and product definition	The activities product positioning and product definition refer to the product vision and the characterization of target markets, product scope and use (Kittlaus and Clough 2009). In particular it describes (1) the intended differentiation with competitive products and the planned support of the company strategy; (2) the intended product use, characterized by user personas, use cases and value and (3) the intended product scope characterized by a catalog of features. It furthermore describes the process for developing, evolving, marketing, delivering, and supporting the software product. An understood and accepted product vision is important for success. However, although it is only a short and concise statement with product key ideas, it is surprisingly hard to (Fricker 2012).
Delivery model	The delivery model refers to the approach of delivering a software product and additional services (Kittlaus and Clough 2009). It affects the licensing and pricing model and the distribution of activities between the company and the customers. Pricing refers to the process of setting prices to market offerings. A good pricing strategy captures "[...] the value offered by the product, adapts the price structure to the customer segments, ensures that price and value can be communicated, manages customer and employee expectations with an accepted pricing policy, and sets price levels to maximize profitability" (Fricker 2012).
Sourcing	Sourcing refers to the decision of making or buying parts of the software product (Kittlaus and Clough 2009). Both options have advantages and disadvantages. For instance, while the decision to buy parts of the software product might lead to a faster time to market or to reduced development costs it can also lead to a reduced ability to adapt the software or generate integration problems (Boehm and Abts 1999).

Table A.3: Software product management and product strategy (International Software Product Management Association 2014) (continue)

Activity	Description
Product strategy	Another core activity in product strategy is the development of the business case. A business case further describes the product vision and refines it based on economic information such as cost, price or market estimates (Gorchels 2006). Typical software business cases discuss investment based on contributions to business objectives (i.e. sales or financial performance), productivity increases and quality improvements, and avoidance of non-compliance problems (Schmidt 2002; Reifer 2002).
Ecosystem management	Ecosystem management refers to the activity of actively building or integrating into the product's industry. This defines the company's position in the value chain of that industry and affects its business model. In the software industry typical players are: vendors, distributors, resellers, OEMs, integrators, and technical alliances (Kittlaus and Clough 2009).
Legal and IP management	Legal and intellectual property rights management refers to the practices and artifacts for performing business transactions and protecting business (Fricker 2012). In the software business licenses and service level agreements are established methods to resolve customer and vendor conflicts about product functionality or quality, permitted product use and handling if unused but paid product instances (Kittlaus and Clough 2009).
Performance and risk management	Performance and risk management refers to the measurement of the success of a software product and reacting to problems or risks. Monitoring usually depends on the products stage in the product life-cycle (Anderson and Zeithaml 1984). Both factors are important for evaluating business achievements.

Table A.4: Software product management and product planning (International Software Product Management Association 2014)

Activity	Description
Product life-cycle management	Product life-cycle management refers to the planning of a software product life-cycle. A software product initial release explicitly requires different expertise, architectural decisions and economics than its subsequent evolution, servicing, phase-out and close-down (Raijlich and Bennett 2000). During the initial phases a developing company needs to learn about the products application domain and its technological foundation. Following this, it has to retain expertise in the interfaces and operation of the software. During a software products life-cycle the initial architecture is continuously adapted and finally becomes too hard to change (Lehman 1980).
Road-mapping	The activity of road-mapping refers to planning the evolution of a product and its features. A road-map is used to translate the product strategy into a long term plan for research, development, marketing, sales and distribution, and service and support. It captures on the best knowledge and obtains the commitment of the corresponding company functions to the product plan (Phaal et al. 2007).
Release planning	Release planning refers to the selection and assignment of requirements the implementation sequence of product releases. Release decisions aim at usefulness and competitiveness or a product release (Regnell et al. 2008), satisfying stakeholder needs (Cohn 2004), and accounting requirements inter-dependencies (Carlshamre et al. 2001). Research shows that the implementation of a product in incremental steps, rather than implementing the full product scope at once, allows reaching earlier break-even and higher return of investment (Denne and Cleland-Huang 2003). However, incremental development needs explicit prioritization of functionality and quality level (Berander and Andrews 2005).
Product requirements engineering	Product requirements engineering refers to the process of collecting the needs of external and internal stakeholders, their expectations and ideas for technical implementation (Regnell and Brinkkemper 2005). The product manager is responsible for reducing the large amounts of input, ensuring the inputs' relevance (Davis 2005; Gorschek and Wohlin 2006) and feasibility and translation into product features with option for evolution (Fricker and Schumacher 2012).

Table A.5: Software product management and development (International
Software Product Management Association 2014)

Activity	Description
Engineering management	A software company has to actively manage the collaboration and sharing of knowledge between employees to be able to exist even when important employees leave. Establishing a sharing culture and reward systems are common means to organize a software company accordingly (Rus and Lindvall 2002; Bosch 2009). The activity engineering management refers to managing knowledge and staff and structure development to achieve development efficiency at an acceptable level of quality.
Project management	Project management refers to the process steps for developing a software release (Carmel and Becker 1995). To structure and control a development project software companies may employ stages-gates, a software-development life-cycle model and project management practices (Cooper 2001; Wallin et al. 2002). More recently, companies have started to adapt agile project management approaches (i.e. Scrum) (Pichler 2010).
Project requirements engineering	Project requirements engineering refers to the project team's process of gathering and eliciting requirements, design and specifying the desired software system, and validating requirements together with multiple stakeholders (Potts et al. 1994). Product management is important for communicating requirements and developing acceptance on the developed solution (Fricker et al. 2010; Martin and Melnik 2008).
Quality management	Finally, quality management refers to the activities necessary to meet critical success factors and to mitigate business-critical challenges (Kitchenham and Pfleeger 1996). It is responsible for measuring software quality and establishing quality management practices (Ebert and Dumke 2007; Jones 2008). Quality management might include improvement of the software product management process (Bekkers et al. 2010), the software development (Chrissis et al. 2011), or the IT-based service provisioning (Spalding 2007).

Table A.6: Software product management and marketing (International Software Product Management Association 2014)

Activity	Description
Marketing planning	Marketing planning refines the product positioning and definition with respect to marketing goals. It defines these marketing goals, the marketing mix and the measures necessary for reaching and controlling the marketing goals (Kotler and Armstrong 2011). Marketing planning derives target sales, market share, and profits by analyzing strength, weaknesses, opportunities and threats. It also describes the means to achieve defined goals (i.e. action programs, budget planning, or control functions).
Customer analysis	Customer analysis refers to the activities for determining and prioritizing market segments, understanding customer needs, and matching these needs with unique selling points. Software products have to be designed to fit to different levels of market segments: offered for one market, specific customers in that market, or even tailored to individual customers' needs (Kotler and Armstrong 2011). Analyzing the customer needs of those segments and their attractiveness for business are the foundation for identifying actions to serve them (Gorchels 2006).
Opportunity management	Opportunity management refers to refining the product positioning by narrowing the market (Haines 2009). Opportunities are identified based on different criteria, such as resource availability, strategic significance, financial viability, or potential customer satisfaction.
Marketing mix optimization	Marketing mix optimization refers to the definition and improvement of product, price, place, and promotion to influence demand (Kotler and Armstrong 2011). The interplay of the different areas of the marketing mix affects the marketing (or campaign) success (Haines 2009). Product launch refers to the process of preparing the public release of a software product (Gorchels 2006; Haines 2009).
Product launch	The product launch offers a product to a market and initiates its interaction with customers, partners and competitor.
Operational marketing	Finally, operational marketing refers to marketing communication and analyzing the effectiveness of that communication (Gorchels 2006).

Table A.7: Software product management and sales and distribution (International Software Product Management Association 2014)

Activity	Description
Sales planning and channel preparation	Sales planning and channel preparation refer to the definition of the market and the product profiles, preparing sales channels and training sales in how to sell the product (Haines 2009). In case of software product sales channels may include direct sales, tele- and internet sales and sales through partners (i.e. consultants or integrators) (Kittlaus and Clough 2009). Sales materials describe customers and their rational and emotional reasons for buying a product, the role of influencers and customer decision and purchase processes.
Customer relationship management and operational sales	The activities customer relationship management and operational sales refer to the management of interactions with customer and prospects along the customer life-cycle (Buttle 2008) and set adequate incentives for salespeople, forecast customer interactions and monitor the sales progress (Calvin 2004).
Operational distribution	Operational product distribution refers to production, shipment, and deployment activities in case of a packaged software (Humble and Farley 2010) or to server and service operation in case of software-as-a-service (Rhoton 2010). It also includes the management of the update and patch processes (Ballintijn 2005).

Table A.8: Software product management and support and service (International Software Product Management Association 2014)

Activity	Description
Service planning and preparation and service provisioning	Service planning and preparation and service provisioning refers to the facilitation of the product's deployment and use. Those activities are performed to customize, enhance, install, and integrate the software product in customer projects (Kittlaus and Clough 2009). In case of large enterprise software those services are often performed by third party consultants or system integrators.
Technical support	Technical support is a service targeted at users and provides different levels of support for a software product (Bruton 2002).
Marketing support	Marketing support and sales support provide service trainings for customers or sales, prepare promotion events, and produce additional material of publicity and sales (i.e. brochures) (Gorchels 2006).

Appendix B

Qualitative investigation I: Exploring software customization from a vendors' and customers' perspective

Table B.1: Overview: First coding cycle (Vendor)

ID	# Codes	% Codes
IV01	101	7,79%
IV02	144	11,11%
IV03	79	6,10%
IV04	85	6,56%
IV05	45	3,47%
IV06	146	11,27%
IV07	75	5,79%
IV08	151	11,65%
IV09	110	8,49%
IV10	138	10,65%
IV11	98	7,56%
IV12	124	9,57%
Total	1296	100,00%
$\bar{x}_{arithm}$	108	
s^2	33,5	

Table B.2: Overview: First coding cycle (Customer)

ID	# Codes	% Codes
IC01	76	14,21%
IC02	67	12,52%
IC03	43	8,04%
IC04	83	15,51%
IC05	61	11,40%
IC06	35	6,54%
IC07	39	7,29%
IC08	54	10,09%
IC09	28	5,23%
IC10	49	9,16%
Total	535	100,00%
$\bar{x}_{arithm}$	53,5	
s^2	18,1	

Table B.3: Overview: Second coding cycle (Vendor)

ID	Value		Resource		Capability		Total
	#	%	#	%	#	%	
IV01	25	9,80%	41	8,61%	35	6,19%	101
IV02	52	20,39%	57	11,97%	35	6,19%	144
IV03	20	7,84%	36	7,56%	23	4,07%	79
IV04	17	6,67%	39	8,19%	29	5,13%	85
IV05	9	3,53%	15	3,15%	21	3,72%	45
IV06	23	9,02%	50	10,50%	73	12,92%	146
IV07	15	5,88%	30	6,30%	30	5,31%	75
IV08	33	12,94%	47	9,87%	71	12,57%	151
IV09	24	9,41%	40	8,40%	46	8,14%	110
IV10	23	9,02%	37	7,77%	78	13,81%	138
IV11	9	3,53%	42	8,82%	47	8,32%	98
IV12	5	1,96%	42	8,82%	77	13,63%	124
Total	255	100,00%	476	100,00%	565	100,00%	1296
$\bar{x}_{arithm}$	21,25		39,67		47,08		
s^2	12,6		10,43		21,88		

Table B.4: Overview: Second coding cycle (Customer)

ID	Value		Resource		Capability		Total
	#	%	#	%	#	%	
IC01	15	15,15%	23	12,43%	38	15,14%	76
IC02	14	14,14%	22	11,89%	31	12,35%	67
IC03	7	7,07%	17	9,19%	19	7,57%	43
IC04	14	14,14%	29	15,68%	40	15,94%	83
IC05	13	13,13%	19	10,27%	29	11,55%	61
IC06	11	11,11%	11	5,95%	13	5,18%	35
IC07	7	7,07%	13	7,03%	19	7,57%	39
IC08	8	8,08%	20	10,81%	26	10,36%	54
IC09	6	6,06%	9	4,86%	13	5,18%	28
IC10	4	4,04%	22	11,89%	23	9,16%	49
Total	99	100,00%	185	100,00%	251	100,00%	535
$\bar{x}_{arithm}$	9,9		18,5		25,1		
s^2	4,0		6,1		9,5		

Table B.5: Value: Second coding cycle (Vendor)

ID	Use Value		Exchange Value		Total	
	#	%	#	%	#	%
IV01	13	8,97%	12	10,91%	25	9,80%
IV02	32	22,07%	20	18,18%	52	20,39%
IV03	7	4,83%	13	11,82%	20	7,84%
IV04	10	6,90%	7	6,36%	17	6,67%
IV05	6	4,14%	3	2,73%	9	3,53%
IV06	12	8,28%	11	10,00%	23	9,02%
IV07	8	5,52%	7	6,36%	15	5,88%
IV08	18	12,41%	15	13,64%	33	12,94%
IV09	12	8,28%	12	10,91%	24	9,41%
IV10	17	11,72%	6	5,45%	23	9,02%
IV11	6	4,14%	3	2,73%	9	3,53%
IV12	4	2,76%	1	0,91%	5	1,96%
Total	145	100,00%	110	100,00%	255	100,00%
$\bar{x}_{arithm}$	12,08		9,17			
s^2	7,65		5,62			

Table B.6: Value: Second coding cycle (Customer)

ID	Use Value		Exchange Value		Total	
	#	%	#	%	#	%
IC01	15	16,30%	0	0,00%	15	15,15%
IC02	11	11,96%	3	42,86%	14	14,14%
IC03	5	5,43%	2	28,57%	7	7,07%
IC04	13	14,13%	1	14,29%	14	14,14%
IC05	13	14,13%	0	0,00%	13	13,13%
IC06	10	10,87%	1	14,29%	11	11,11%
IC07	7	7,61%	0	0,00%	7	7,07%
IC08	8	8,70%	0	0,00%	8	8,08%
IC09	6	6,52%	0	0,00%	6	6,06%
IC10	4	4,35%	0	0,00%	4	4,04%
Total	92	100,00%	7	100,00%	99	100,00%
$\bar{x}_{arithm}$	9,2		0,7			
s^2	3,8		1,1			

Table B.7: Resources: Second coding cycle (Vendor)

ID	Resource (R1)		Resource (R2)		Resource (R3)		Resource (R4)		Total	
	#	%	#	%	#	%	#	%	#	%
IV01	13	12,04%	13	7,18%	9	9,28%	6	6,67%	41	8,61%
IV02	28	25,93%	5	2,76%	19	19,59%	5	5,56%	57	11,97%
IV03	5	4,63%	15	8,29%	7	7,22%	9	10,00%	36	7,56%
IV04	8	7,41%	14	7,73%	9	9,28%	8	8,89%	39	8,19%
IV05	2	1,85%	8	4,42%	3	3,09%	2	2,22%	15	3,15%
IV06	14	12,96%	15	8,29%	11	11,34%	10	11,11%	50	10,50%
IV07	5	4,63%	12	6,63%	7	7,22%	6	6,67%	30	6,30%
IV08	7	6,48%	25	13,81%	7	7,22%	8	8,89%	47	9,87%
IV09	5	4,63%	16	8,84%	8	8,25%	11	12,22%	40	8,40%
IV10	9	8,33%	17	9,39%	6	6,19%	5	5,56%	37	7,77%
IV11	10	9,26%	21	11,60%	6	6,19%	5	5,56%	42	8,82%
IV12	2	1,85%	20	11,05%	5	5,15%	15	16,67%	42	8,82%
Total	108	100,00%	181	100,00%	97	100,00%	90	100,00%	476	100,00%
$\bar{x}_{arithm}$	9,00		15,08		8,08		7,50			
s^2	7,10		5,47		4,01		3,45			

R1: Customer business and market knowledge; R2: Customization management and experience assets;
R3: Product related software development assets; R4: Product functionality and flexibility;

Table B.8: Resources: Second coding cycle (Customer)

ID	Resource (R1)		Resource (R2)		Resource (R3)		Resource (R4)		Total	
	#	%	#	%	#	%	#	%	#	%
IC01	7	12,07%	12	12,12%	4	22,22%	0	0,00%	23	12,43%
IC02	5	8,62%	8	8,08%	6	33,33%	3	30,00%	22	11,89%
IC03	6	10,34%	8	8,08%	2	11,11%	1	10,00%	17	9,19%
IC04	10	17,24%	13	13,13%	4	22,22%	2	20,00%	29	15,68%
IC05	8	13,79%	8	8,08%	2	11,11%	1	10,00%	19	10,27%
IC06	7	12,07%	4	4,04%	0	0,00%	0	0,00%	11	5,95%
IC07	5	8,62%	8	8,08%	0	0,00%	0	0,00%	13	7,03%
IC08	6	10,34%	12	12,12%	0	0,00%	2	20,00%	20	10,81%
IC09	1	1,72%	8	8,08%	0	0,00%	0	0,00%	9	4,86%
IC10	3	5,17%	18	18,18%	0	0,00%	1	10,00%	22	11,89%
Total	58	100,00%	99	100,00%	18	100,00%	10	100,00%	185	100,00%
$\bar{x}_{arithm}$	5,8		9,9		1,8		1			
s^2	2,5		3,9		2,2		1,1			

R1: Customer business and market knowledge; R2: Customization management and experience assets;
R3: Product functionality and flexibility; R4: Product related software development assets

Table B.9: Capabilities: Second coding cycle (Vendor)

ID	Capability (C1)		Capability (C2)		Capability (C3)		Capability (C4)		Capability (C5)		Capability (C6)		Total	
	#	%	#	%	#	%	#	%	#	%	#	%	#	%
IV01	9	8,04%	11	8,87%	5	5,38%	4	4,88%	2	3,08%	4	4,49%	35	6,19%
IV02	8	7,14%	9	7,26%	4	4,30%	2	2,44%	2	3,08%	10	11,24%	35	6,19%
IV03	6	5,36%	5	4,03%	5	5,38%	4	4,88%	1	1,54%	2	2,25%	23	4,07%
IV04	8	7,14%	5	4,03%	5	5,38%	4	4,88%	3	4,62%	4	4,49%	29	5,13%
IV05	3	2,68%	5	4,03%	2	2,15%	3	3,66%	4	6,15%	4	4,49%	21	3,72%
IV06	18	16,07%	14	11,29%	11	11,83%	11	13,41%	8	12,31%	11	12,36%	73	12,92%
IV07	6	5,36%	8	6,45%	6	6,45%	4	4,88%	3	4,62%	3	3,37%	30	5,31%
IV08	14	12,50%	17	13,71%	12	12,90%	9	10,98%	9	13,85%	10	11,24%	71	12,57%
IV09	8	7,14%	6	4,84%	7	7,53%	9	10,98%	7	10,77%	9	10,11%	46	8,14%
IV10	13	11,61%	19	15,32%	14	15,05%	11	13,41%	10	15,38%	11	12,36%	78	13,81%
IV11	7	6,25%	10	8,06%	8	8,60%	9	10,98%	4	6,15%	9	10,11%	47	8,32%
IV12	12	10,71%	15	12,10%	14	15,05%	12	14,63%	12	18,46%	12	13,48%	77	13,63%
Total	112	100,00%	124	100,00%	93	100,00%	82	100,00%	65	100,00%	89	100,00%	565	100,00%
$\bar{x}_{arithm}$	9,33		10,33		7,75		6,83		5,42		7,42			
s^2	4,16		4,92		4,05		3,64		3,63		3,68			

C1: Business analysis and interpretation capability; C2: Customer integration and expectation management capability;
C3: Requirements management and negotiation capability C4: Future-proof solution design capability
C5: Solution deployment and initialization capability; C6: Solutions adjustment capability

Table B.10: Capabilities: Second coding cycle (Customer)

ID	Capability (C1)		Capability (C2)		Capability (C3)		Capability (C4)		Capability (C5)		Capability (C6)		Total	
	#	%	#	%	#	%	#	%	#	%	#	%	#	%
IC01	5	10,20%	12	15,58%	8	13,56%	1	3,70%	6	46,15%	6	23,08%	38	15,14%
IC02	5	10,20%	9	11,69%	8	13,56%	4	14,81%	2	15,38%	3	11,54%	31	12,35%
IC03	4	8,16%	6	7,79%	2	3,39%	5	18,52%	0	0,00%	2	7,69%	19	7,57%
IC04	11	22,45%	12	15,58%	7	11,86%	4	14,81%	3	23,08%	3	11,54%	40	15,94%
IC05	6	12,24%	9	11,69%	10	16,95%	1	3,70%	0	0,00%	3	11,54%	29	11,55%
IC06	3	6,12%	5	6,49%	4	6,78%	1	3,70%	0	0,00%	0	0,00%	13	5,18%
IC07	4	8,16%	7	9,09%	6	10,17%	1	3,70%	0	0,00%	1	3,85%	19	7,57%
IC08	4	8,16%	6	7,79%	5	8,47%	6	22,22%	1	7,69%	4	15,38%	26	10,36%
IC09	5	10,20%	3	3,90%	3	5,08%	1	3,70%	0	0,00%	1	3,85%	13	5,18%
IC10	2	4,08%	8	10,39%	6	10,17%	3	11,11%	1	7,69%	3	11,54%	23	9,16%
Total	49	100,00%	77	100,00%	59	100,00%	27	100,00%	13	100,00%	26	100,00%	251	100,00%
$\bar{x}_{arithm}$	4,9		7,7		5,9		2,7		1,3		2,6			
s^2	2,4		2,9		2,5		1,9		1,9		1,7			

C1: Business analysis and interpretation capability; C2: Customer integration and expectation management capability;
C3: Requirements management and negotiation capability C4: Future-proof solution design capability
C5: Solution deployment and initialization capability; C6: Solutions adjustment capability

Appendix C

Qualitative investigation II: Elaborating the strategic role of customization for software product development

Table C.1: Overall coding: Cases Alpha and Beta

	Alpha		Beta		Total	
	#	%	#	%	#	%
Attributes	26	46,43%	30	53,57%	56	100,00%
Customization	69	30,80%	155	69,20%	224	100,00%
Product Development	46	42,20%	63	57,80%	109	100,00%
Dynamic Capabilities	200	35,03%	371	64,97%	571	100,00%
Total	341	35,52%	619	64,48%	960	100,00%

Table C.2: Overall coding: Dynamic Capabilities

Case	Sensing Capability		Seizing Capability		Reconfiguring Capability		Total	
	#	%	#	%	#	%	#	%
Alpha	112	56,00%	46	23,00%	42	21,00%	200	35,00%
Beta	187	50,00%	65	18,00%	119	32,00%	371	65,00%
Total	299	52,00%	111	19,00%	161	28,00%	571	100,00%

Table C.3: Overall coding: Dynamic capabilities (Case Alpha)

ID	Sensing Capability		Seizing Capability		Reconfiguring Capability		Total	
	# Codes	% Codes	# Codes	% Codes	# Codes	% Codes	# Codes	% Codes
A01	15	13%	3	7%	3	7%	21	11%
A02	27	24%	11	24%	5	12%	43	22%
A03	25	22%	10	22%	12	29%	47	24%
A04	41	37%	15	33%	15	36%	71	36%
A05	4	4%	7	15%	7	17%	18	9%
Total	112	100%	46	100%	42	100%	200	100%
$\bar{x}_{arithm}$	22,4		9,2		8,4		40	
s^2	13,85		4,49		4,98		21,59	

Table C.4: Overall coding: Dynamic capabilities (Case Beta)

ID	Sensing Capability		Seizing Capability		Reconfiguring Capability		Total	
	# Codes	% Codes	# Codes	% Codes	# Codes	% Codes	# Codes	% Codes
B01	14	8%	9	14%	3	3%	26	7%
B02	13	7%	8	12%	5	4%	26	7%
B03	5	3%	4	6%	9	8%	18	5%
B04	15	8%	12	18%	32	27%	59	16%
B05	29	16%	6	9%	23	19%	58	16%
B06	36	19%	9	14%	27	23%	72	20%
B07	73	39%	17	26%	20	17%	110	30%
Total	185	100%	65	100%	119	100%	369	100%
$\bar{x}_{arithm}$	26,43		9,29		17		52,71	
s^2	23,06		4,23		11,36		32,54	

Table C.5: Case Alpha: Micro-foundations sensing

ID	COLLECT # Codes	% Codes	EVALUATE # Codes	% Codes	INSTALLBASE # Codes	% Codes	MARKET # Codes	% Codes	Total # Codes	% Codes
A01	10	16%	2	10%	0	0%	3	20%	15	13%
A02	18	29%	5	24%	2	14%	2	13%	27	24%
A03	14	23%	4	19%	4	29%	3	20%	25	22%
A04	17	27%	10	48%	8	57%	6	40%	41	37%
A05	3	5%	0	0%	0	0%	1	7%	4	4%
Total	62	100%	21	100%	14	100%	15	100%	112	100%
$\bar{x}_{arithm}$	12,4		4,2		2,8		3			
s^2	6,11		3,77		3,35		1,87			

Table C.6: Case Alpha: Micro-foundations seizing

ID.	REVENUE		PRODUCT		COMMUNICATION		RELEASE		Total	
	# Codes	% Codes	# Codes	% Codes	# Codes	% Codes	# Codes	% Codes	# Codes	% Codes
A01	2	11%	0	0%	1	8%	0	0%	3	7%
A02	9	47%	0	0%	2	15%	1	25%	12	26%
A03	6	32%	2	20%	2	15%	1	25%	11	24%
A04	2	11%	6	60%	7	54%	0	0%	15	33%
A05	0	0%	2	20%	1	8%	2	50%	5	11%
Total	19	100%	10	100%	13	100%	4	100%	46	100%
$\bar{x}_{arithm}$	3,8		2		2,6		0,8			
s^2	3,63		2,45		2,51		0,84			

Table C.7: Case Alpha: Micro-foundations reconfiguring

ID	MODULARIZATION		STANDARDIZATION		KNOWLEDGEBASE		REVENUE		Total	
	# Codes	% Codes	# Codes	% Codes	# Codes	% Codes	# Codes	% Codes	# Codes	% Codes
A01	0	0%	1	13%	2	11%	0	0%	3	7%
A02	0	0%	0	0%	4	22%	1	11%	5	12%
A03	3	43%	2	25%	4	22%	3	33%	12	29%
A04	4	57%	3	38%	5	28%	3	33%	15	36%
A05	0	0%	2	25%	3	17%	2	22%	7	17%
Total	7	100%	8	100%	18	100%	9	100%	42	100%
$\bar{x}_{arithm}$	1,4		1,6		3,6		1,8			
s^2	1,95		1,14		1,14		1,3			

Table C.8: Case Beta: Micro-foundations sensing

ID	COLLECT		EVALUATE		INSTALLBASE		MARKET		Total	
	# Codes	% Codes	# Codes	% Codes	# Codes	% Codes	# Codes	% Codes	# Codes	% Codes
B01	8	11%	7	13%	0	0%	0	0%	15	8%
B02	10	14%	5	9%	1	3%	0	0%	16	9%
B03	2	3%	4	7%	0	0%	0	0%	6	3%
B04	4	5%	4	7%	7	20%	3	13%	18	10%
B05	9	12%	10	19%	3	9%	3	13%	25	13%
B06	14	19%	12	22%	3	9%	6	25%	35	19%
B07	27	36%	12	22%	21	60%	12	50%	72	39%
Total	74	100%	54	100%	35	100%	24	100%	187	100%
$\bar{x}_{arith}$	10,57		7,71		5		3,43			
s^2	8,24		3,59		7,46		4,39			

Table C.9: Case Beta: Micro-foundations seizing

ID	REVENUE		PRODUCT		COMMUNICATION		RELEASE		Total	
	# Codes	% Codes	# Codes	% Codes	# Codes	% Codes	# Codes	% Codes	# Codes	% Codes
B01	4	25%	0	0%	7	27%	0	0%	11	17%
B02	2	13%	3	21%	2	8%	0	0%	7	11%
B03	3	19%	0	0%	1	4%	0	0%	4	6%
B04	1	6%	1	7%	8	31%	3	33%	13	20%
B05	2	13%	2	14%	2	8%	0	0%	6	9%
B06	3	19%	2	14%	3	12%	1	11%	9	14%
B07	1	6%	6	43%	3	12%	5	56%	15	23%
Total	16	100%	14	100%	26	100%	9	100%	65	100%
$\bar{x}_{arithm}$	2,29		2		3,71		1,29			
s^2	1,11		2,08		2,69		1,98			

Table C.10: Case Beta: Micro-foundations reconfiguring

ID	MODULARIZATION # Codes	% Codes	STANDARDIZATION # Codes	% Codes	KNOWLEDGEBASE # Codes	% Codes	REVENUE # Codes	% Codes	Total # Codes	% Codes
B01	3	11%	1	3%	0	0%	0	0%	4	3%
B02	2	7%	2	5%	2	6%	0	0%	6	5%
B03	3	11%	4	10%	2	6%	0	0%	9	8%
B04	2	7%	12	31%	6	17%	7	39%	27	23%
B05	6	22%	7	18%	4	11%	6	33%	23	19%
B06	4	15%	7	18%	15	43%	1	6%	27	23%
B07	7	26%	6	15%	6	17%	4	22%	23	19%
Total	27	100%	39	100%	35	100%	18	100%	119	100%
$\bar{x}_{arithm}$	3,86		5,57		5		2,57			
s^2	1,95		3,69		4,93		3,05